The Blakesley Miniature Railway
and the Bartholomew family

The Blakesley Miniature Railway
and the Bartholomew family

Celebrating the centenary in 2009 of
BLACOLVESLEY, the world's oldest
surviving working internal-combustion
locomotive

Dr Bob Tebb

Silver Link Publishing Ltd

This book is dedicated to all those who created,
and have protected and cared for, *BLACOLVESLEY*
over the past century.

My special thanks go to my wife Kath,
and to our sons Pete and Matthew for their support and help,
with this locomotive and in so many other ways.

May those who care for *BLACOLVESLEY*
in the century to come treat it as gently.

© Dr Bob Tebb 2009

All rights reserved. No part of this publication may be reproduced, stored in a retrieval system or transmitted, in any form or by any means, electronic, mechanical, photocopying, recording or otherwise, without prior permission in writing from Silver Link Publishing Ltd.

First published in 2009

British Library Cataloguing in Publication Data

A catalogue record for this book is available from the British Library.

ISBN 978 1 85794 324 5 (Subscribers' hardback edition)
ISBN 978 1 85794 339 9 (paperback edition)

Silver Link Publishing Ltd
The Trundle
Ringstead Road
Great Addington
Kettering
Northants NN14 4BW

Tel/Fax: 01536 330588
email: sales@nostalgiacollection.com
Website: www.nostalgiacollection.com

Printed and bound in the Czech Republic

Half title A wooden panel in Blakesley Hall, showing the Bartholomew Arms. *Author*

Title page The Railway Club visit of 17 August 1912 uniquely featuring their special train being 'topped and tailed' by the Cagney and *BLACOLVESLEY*, seen here on the 1910 extension between the farm manager's bungalow and the farm buildings; the latter loco unusually faces east in this view looking north. *John Alsop collection*

Left A selection of E&WJR, S&MJR, LMS and BR tickets from the Blakesley area. *Author's collection*

Contents

Foreword by Doreen Birks 7
Introduction 9

1 Blakesley and its Hall 11
2 The Bartholomew family – engineers 14
3 Charles William Bartholomew 26
4 Railways, large and small 44
5 The miniature railway arrives 59
6 Locomotives and carriages 76
7 Blakesley sows a miniature seed 89
8 Delivering the goods 93
9 Enter internal combustion 103
10 The world's first 'steam outline'
   loco emerges 117
11 An Indian summer 125
12 Closure and dispersal 140
13 The 'Two Trees' saga 152
14 A nomadic period for
   BLACOLVESLEY 157
15 Preservation at last 167
16 Full circle Blakesley? 175

References 177
Acknowledgements 180
Index 183

The Blakesley Hall Miniature Railway

The only photograph showing Charles William Bartholomew ('CW') on (more or less!) one of his locomotives, taken during the trials of *BLACOLVESLEY* on 11 September 1909. The other people include W. J. Bassett-Lowke, Fred Green, Alec Wyatt and Henry Greenly. *Northamptonshire County Records Office*

Foreword by
Doreen A. Birks MB FRCS FRCS(Ed) FRC(Ophth)
elder daughter of Ivy Bartholomew

I am one of the ageing granddaughters of C. W. Bartholomew, and the author of this publication has graciously invited me to contribute this brief foreword to his worthy and extensively researched volume.

I, myself, have little knowledge of railways beyond collecting the 'Railway Engines' series from my parents' cigarette packets, although when I was a medical student I was placed in 'digs' with the Whitbread family in Letchworth. Mr Whitbread was a signalman and on one occasion he invited me to visit him in his signal box at Arlesey and allowed me to pull a large signal lever and to ring the telegraph bell to indicate the passing of 'The Flying Scotsman' that evening.

My grandfather, a diabetic, died well before I was born, but my grandmother survived him by many years and continued to live at Blakesley. My sister Heather and I spent most of the Easter holiday and half of our summer school holidays with our grandmother. Here we were joined during the summer visit by our two older first cousins (Hermione and Charles) for part of the time.

The house with its extensive gardens, park and farm provided endless sources for exploration, exercise, occupation and interest, not to mention stimulating the wild imagination of youth through its age and historical importance.

The miniature railway in the grounds gave us an alternative focus, which was of course reinforced when the engine *BLACOLVESLEY* and carriages were exhibited on certain occasions.

I have welcomed this opportunity presented to me to recall such glowing memories of this happy period in my childhood.

CW's children operate the line! Ivy, Doreen Birks's mother (in 'BMR' hatband), is driving the Cagney, with James ('Engine Driver' hatband) seated on the tender. Percy Wyatt, son of Alec, stands by the chimney, with a bewhiskered Mark Groom (who ran a garage in Towcester) acting as Superintendent of the Line. *Charles Simpson collection, courtesy of Sir William McAlpine*

Above BLACOLVESLEY is seen on the occasion of The Railway Club special on 20 June 1914; it is on the 1910 extension, with the farm manager's bungalow in the background. Alec Wyatt maintains his statuesque pose on the now-deserted train. The loco has a home-made 'jaw' coupling for working the tip wagons. The small pipe from the silencer box ahead of the driving wheels provided exhaust gas 'power' for the whistle. *Charles Simpson collection, courtesy of Sir William McAlpine*

Below One Bassett-Lowke 15-inch locomotive worked on each of the first four such miniature estate lines in Britain, and the three survivors came together at Ravenglass in November 2008 – Sand Hutton's SYNOLDA (1912) is framed by BLACOLVESLEY (Blakesley, 1909) and COUNT LOUIS (Higham Railway, 1923). *Author*

Introduction

Apart from a locally written booklet of about 1980, most histories dealing with 15-inch-gauge railway development merely sandwich the Blakesley (Hall) Miniature Railway – and its mentor – as something of a 'backwater' curiosity between the 'minimum gauge' period of Sir Arthur Heywood and the 'scale model' era of Bassett-Lowke.

It is equally clear that such references contain little research to establish the true role of this line. Work on this book, with extensive primary research, started late in 2003, following my re-publication of that original booklet to mark the centenary of the line's opening.

With much of the rest of 15-inch recorded history, far too many books similarly rely on the redrafting of other authors' earlier interpretations of events. For this reason, much emphasis is placed here on recording what is actually known – and what is necessarily interpretation.

Blakesley's significance in the evolution of such railways proved to be totally disproportionate to its own size – and was probably far more influential than the much-recorded and reported work of Heywood, as well as setting out the foundations of not just Bassett-Lowke's, but most other people's, future 15-inch ideas too!

It pioneered American steam locos and carriages on estate lines in Britain. Its own staff built among the earliest of all internal-combustion locos (to haul German wagons) around this estate; it regularly carried public passengers (charging fares on one day each year); and even apparently endured a period as a pseudo-military line!

The research also revealed that, far from being simply the toy railway of a rural Northamptonshire Squire, the moving spirit was a member of a family, almost unknown today, that was on a contemporary par with the Stephensons and had a colossal strategic influence on waterway and railway engineering and development in the old West Riding of Yorkshire for a century, in the creation of the inland port of Goole, and in the exploitation of coal reserves in the Dearne Valley. The family's own history is itself so closely interwoven, and interacts so extensively, with the story of Blakesley, its Hall and its railway, that they need treating together.

The Blakesley railway expired long ago, having changed its detailed layout many times in its life, and those people who do still remember it only saw it in its latter days. Memories play tricks after such a long time, and I have frequently had to make the best I can of often conflicting recollections, including ones 'handed down' from previous generations.

Railways are created, and their development influenced, by people, and many others too are relevant to this story – there is a strong possibility that a major stage character was, at least in part, based on the Squire's long-term partner, while a (previously!) very close family friend and business colleague became the centrepiece of a celebrated major fraud case during the Second World War, badly affecting their own finances – but in the process helping to secure the long-term future of some of the line's historically important equipment.

From this research, it became clear that most contemporary historical events are capable of quite different interpretations from those usually quoted. This book therefore looks beyond Blakesley, its railway and its people in an attempt to reassess much of the early story of 15-inch-gauge railways. Readers may disagree with some of my interpretations, but I submit that they are just as valid, if not more valid, than some of the more commonplace stances.

Nevertheless, I accept full responsibility for any errors or misinterpretations that may have

The Blakesley Hall Miniature Railway

In June 2006 Anne Frost (née Hempson), niece of James Bartholomew and great-niece of CW, has a short ride and drive on BLACOLVESLEY, which her Uncle Jim had driven during its first trials in September 1909. *Robert Frost*

occurred. Much has had to be developed from strong circumstantial evidence – but, while very strong, is it such or is it coincidence? Readers must choose for themselves. Information and photographs that develop, or perhaps even dispute, what is written herein would be welcomed.

The subsequent histories of the railway's locomotives, carriages, track and other components after Blakesley are just as interesting and tangled (and equally important for progressing 15-inch railway evolution), and their stories to date have needed to be recorded for completeness.

The interest and content of pictures has come before the quality of the originals in making the selection, and those in the collection of the Bartholomew family and friends have come before those in other collections. The author is truly grateful to all those individuals who have freely made available information and illustrations.

Finally, it is archaeologically important that a few (fortuitously perhaps the most significant) of the truly historic items from this line have survived into today's conservation era. I consider myself privileged to be the current custodian of some of those artefacts – particularly *BLACOLVESLEY* – and feel equally privileged when on occasions I drive it, the first internal-combustion railway loco in the world to reach its centenary – in 2009.

Dr Bob Tebb
Ravenglass
2009

Note regarding bridges, turnouts (points) and gates

In certain parts of the text and in some picture captions, the various bridges, turnouts (points) and gates on the Blakesley estate and railway are referred to by letters and numbers: bridges as, for example, 'B1', turnouts as 'T2', gates as 'G3', and so on. These identifiers are solely of the author's own invention and are used purely to identify and help sort out the confusion of such items on this little railway's elaborate layouts. They have no 'official' or colloquial standing or other significance.

1 Blakesley and its Hall

The villages of Blakesley and Woodend

The neighbouring villages of Blakesley and Woodend, though separate civil parishes, lie in the single ecclesiastical parish of Blakesley cum Woodend in the heart of the Northamptonshire countryside. Much of that county has experienced the upheaval arising from extensive ironstone mining during the last 100 years or so (and which is now extinct).

Other parts have embraced 21st-century industries, or become dormitory towns and villages for London commuters. However, little significant change has taken place here to disturb the traditional pattern of rural life in this part of the county since mediaeval times. Blakesley today remains a delightful and virtually unspoilt corner of English country village charm.

The historic combination of farming with rural 'industry' is well demonstrated by noting the, perhaps surprising, fact that in 1698 some 154 people in Blakesley were engaged in lace-making. The two villages are effectively separated by a small stream known as the Black Ouse, which, combined with the word 'leah', meaning a 'clearing in the wood', lends credence to the name 'Black-Ouse-Leah' and, ultimately, Blakesley.

More academic theses on the origins of place names offer less mundane but perhaps rather more fanciful versions of the name's origin; in the Domesday Book (of an era when spelling was not standardised), it was variously 'Baculveslea', 'Blacheslewe', 'Blaculveslea', and 'Blaculveslei'; it has been suggested that these might refer to a black wolf (derived from 'Blaecwulf'), with the stream taking its name from this! The Domesday Book entries do refer specifically to three mills (these being water mills – thus requiring significant-sized streams – as windmills did not appear in Britain until a century after Domesday) and to extensive woodland.

By the mid-16th century the adjacent Blakesley Park in Woodend was recorded as being owned by the Spencer family of Althorp, ancestors of Princess Diana, Princess of Wales; this family continued to own substantial lands in the area over the centuries, and as late as 1902 the then Earl Spencer raised a local Regiment of Yeomanry that, by 1908, was recognised as part of the Territorial Army; its complement included a number of local residents.

As befits Victorian and Edwardian rural communities, an important annual event in the area was the Blakesley & District Horticultural & Agricultural Show, or more simply the annual Blakesley Show. This seems to have replaced the former Wake or Feast, dating from mediaeval times, in the mid-1870s, around the time of the arrival of a new 'Squire' to the village. The population of the two villages was in slow but steady decline from 1871 (when there were 814 people) down to 666 in 1891, 580 in 1931, only 503 in 1971, with just 492 recorded in the 2001 Census.

Even the First World War (the 'Great War') seems to have had a lesser effect on these villages than it did on other communities. Blakesley itself lost just three men in that terrible conflict, while Woodend lost no one – apparently one of only 31 such 'thankful villages' in the country.

The evolution of Blakesley Hall

The Domesday Book contains four separate entries for the owners of land (the King, the Count of Mortain, Earl Hugh, William Peverel) in the Blakesley area, and one of their four estates described therein ultimately developed into that of Blakesley Hall itself. It passed through a succession of holders, including one Norman de St Patric, until Henry III gave it to the Prior of the Hospital of St John of Jerusalem to add to the considerable amount of property in the Blakesley area he already held. In 1509 the then Prior, Thomas Docwra, leased the Manor and Rectory of Blakesley to a John Wattes of Harryngton for 60 years at an annual rent of £30.

The Blakesley Hall estate sat midway between Blakesley and Woodend, as seen here c1900. *Crown copyright*

At the dissolution of the monasteries, the Manor was granted to the then Princess Elizabeth (later Queen Elizabeth I) for life; it is known that she did stay at the Hall, however briefly. In 1554 it was apparently exchanged with John Dudley, Duke of Northumberland, for the Manor and Castle of Tunbridge in Kent. In 1558 it seems to have been briefly restored to the Hospital, but after the order was extinguished by Queen Elizabeth in 1559, it was granted in 1560 to a Thomas Watts. It is not clear whether he was in

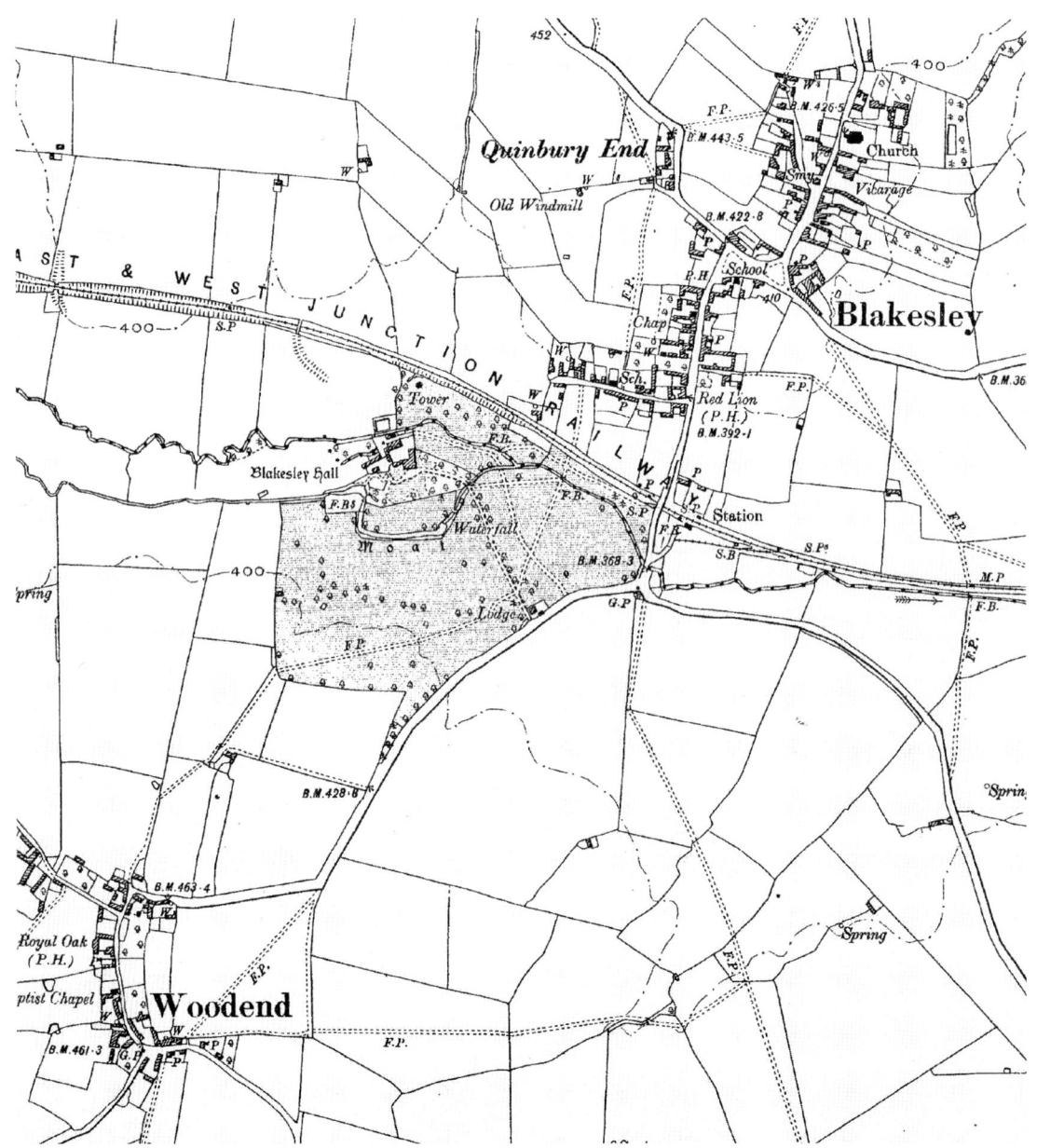

any way related to the earlier John Wattes, mentioned above.

At some point, probably in this Tudor era, a network of 'secret' underground passages was created around the Hall and village, possibly including one between the Hall and a tower in the garden (the latter a 'folly' ruin by the 20th century), presumably as a means of escape during the dangerous intrigues of the period.

The Watts family retained ownership until the male line died out with one Edward Watts; his daughter Mary Penelope sold it in 1721, with other properties in Blakesley, to William Wight of Little Ilford in Essex. His son Henry died without issue in 1793, and the Manor and estate passed in 1823 from his widow to John Wight Hibbit, who had adopted the name Wight. In 1867 he died and in 1876 the executors sold the Manor and estate to one Charles Bartholomew, of Castle Hill House, Ealing.

In reality, this last purchase was for Charles's son, Charles William Bartholomew, who came to live at the Hall with his new bride; the Hall grounds were then of some 25 acres including farmland. It is C. W. Bartholomew who forms the central character in our story; he adopted the title of Lord of the Manor, though was more usually known as the Squire, and over the years he added considerably to the lands held around Blakesley, eventually creating an estate of more than 82 acres. He also extended the structure of the Hall itself by adding to the west wing.

The Hall remained in use by the Bartholomew family for many years, but was eventually demolished in 1957, after being derelict since the sale of the house contents in 1947 and the estate in 1949. Blakesley Hall was really misnamed as it was actually sited south of the Black Ouse and thus in Woodend civil parish, though much of its grounds were in Blakesley, as the dividing Black Ouse stream ran through the estate.

The 'Bartholomew Arms' (once the 'Red Lion') in Blakesley now features the family arms, but with the motto 'Ad Alta'. *Author*

2 The Bartholomew family – engineers

Water, rails and coal

Charles Bartholomew (1806-95), who had arranged the purchase of Blakesley Hall for his son, was a member of a very significant family in transport, engineering and business matters, primarily in Yorkshire, though one tragically almost unknown to the world today.

He had become, inter alia, the Engineer (while still in his twenties), and subsequently Manager (at the age of 34), of the River Don (or Dun as it was known locally) Navigation. He was appointed Engineer to the stillborn South Yorkshire Coal Railway in 1845, as well as to the associated – and more successful – South Yorkshire, Doncaster & Goole Railway and its successors, and was similarly involved with other related local canals and railways in the West Riding of Yorkshire.

He thus became Engineer to the South Yorkshire Railway on 1 January 1848 at the considerable salary of £1,000, in addition to his existing salary for his River Don responsibilities. A 'sting in the tail' was that he was expected to '...devote the whole of his time to the service of the two Companies' in return for this salary, but this was later to cause major ructions.

In due course, he became both Engineer and General Manager of the enlarged 'South Yorkshire Railway & River Dun Navigation', which brought these water and rail interests together into one company in 1850 – an intriguing piece of 'integration' for the time, as both interests were advanced in parallel. However, from 1 August 1858 he surrendered his railway traffic managerial responsibilities, his salary reducing commensurately to £500. His stewardship of the SYR became on occasion somewhat turbulent as there were accusations that railway assets were being diverted into collieries that he (and other SYR directors) partly owned.

He did, at one point in 1859, tender his resignation during one particularly vitriolic battle; however, in so doing he neatly pointed out that not only did 'his' new Wombwell Main Colliery already contribute an income of upwards of £10,000 per annum to the SYR in rail-borne coal movements (which could equally well go out on other companies' railways), but that the SYR would have to give him a 'golden handshake' of £3,000! With his wealth from his associated business activities, Charles had little to fear from such threats; his resignation was, somewhat reluctantly one feels, not accepted.

The railway's evolution (with that of the

Author's collection

The Bartholomew family – engineers

associated waterways) is a truly complex and confusing story; some sections of line were even built along the banks of existing canals or along land 'acquired' by the company, often without Parliamentary authority. Eventually it passed into the hands of the Manchester, Sheffield & Lincolnshire Railway (MS&LR) in June 1864, although the legalities were not completed until 1874.

Some of the peculiar SYR 'traditions' clearly persisted after the takeover, no doubt still being influenced by Charles. In the early 1870s the MS&LR diverted a section of Bartholomew canal – built to bypass a river length of the Don Navigation – back into the river so that they could build a new railway (also without an Act of Parliament) into Rotherham along the bed of the canal, using its existing bridge under a Midland Railway branch!

One of the abutments of that bridge bore deep scars from the tow-rope burns of horse-drawn barges until its final demolition, around a century after the conversion to a railway. Today's local passenger trains just south of the 'new' Rotherham station run along part of this old canal bed (a railway that is strangely susceptible to flooding!) and the remains of one of the earlier canal locks can still be found near the south end of the southbound platform.

Charles was, jointly with Samuel Roberts (also an SYR director), the leading light in The Wombwell Main Colliery Company founded in 1853, whose pit at Wombwell near Barnsley was opened in 1856, as well as several other nearby collieries, including Edmunds & Swaithe Main (which he founded with the Tyas family), and Cortonwood (which he founded with the Roberts family and a number of other partners from his colliery and railway interests). Virtually every colliery in which Charles Bartholomew had an interest was adjacent to either or both of one of 'his' railways or canals.

He crowned his long transport career by being appointed in 1888 as a Director of the newly formed Sheffield & South Yorkshire Navigation Company, created to combine various waterways (uniquely including those that had previously been absorbed into the MS&LR deliberately to prevent such development and competition!) into a cohesive and notionally independent network covering the area of its title.

During those 60 or so years he had transformed

Combining Charles's railway and waterway interests, this distinctive bascule drawbridge carried the SYR's Elsecar branch railway of 1850 over the satellite Dearne & Dove Canal. *Old Barnsley collection (B1340)*

Below The 1880 edition of Charles Bartholomew's treatise on Jesus Christ, records his then addresses as 'Broxholme, Doncaster; and Ealing, London'. *Author's collection*

an awkward part-river/part-canal navigation into a major, vibrant waterway capable of taking significantly increased volumes of goods in much larger craft, as well as developing a small and rather impecunious railway into a thriving secondary line; the South Yorkshire Railway carried more than 1 million tons of coal in 1861.

The archetypal Victorian entrepreneur with a prodigious workload and output, he was a consultant engineer to other collieries, and a co-patentee in 1857 of machinery for rolling railway tyres, as well as being the compiler of a substantial theological treatise of more than 700 pages, *The Life and Doctrine of our Blessed Lord and Saviour Jesus Christ*, published initially in 1854, which ran to a second edition in 1880. He was also involved in a flax mill at Rotherham. His prominence in local affairs may be judged from the survival, in the Institution of Civil Engineers Library, of many safely delivered envelopes sent via the Royal Mail addressed simply to 'Charles Bartholomew, Rotherham'.

Charles was the youngest of four children (all male) of the Rev Thomas Bartholomew (1759-1820) and his wife Elizabeth, the others being Thomas Hamond (born 1796 – see below), James (born 1802) and John (born 1804 but died in infancy). Born at Batley on 9 April 1806, he was educated at Woodhouse Grove Methodist School, Apperley Bridge. He also had a half-sister, Hannah Maria Andrews; although the circumstances here have not been confirmed, this suggests that she may have been a daughter from an earlier marriage of either Rev Thomas or Elizabeth Bartholomew.

Charles was living in Westgate, Rotherham, in 1837, but an urgent house move became highly desirable for this now significant member of the community. It is recorded that in 1838, after a riot at Darfield by the navvies building the North Midland Railway (NMR) – which required the personal intervention of Robert Stephenson '…to protect the Irishmen…' – the houses in Westgate in which some of the Irish navvies lived '…were broken into and searched; and if any unfortunate Irishman was discovered he was dreadfully beaten and ill-used…'

As if this wasn't cause enough, '…the Yeomanry were immediately recalled and together with the civil force, led by the magistrates, they proceeded to West Gate, where the Riot Act was read … as the mob did not disperse, the cavalry received orders to clear the streets, which they quickly effected, and took prisoners of the most active of

The Bartholomew family – engineers

the rioters, who were placed in gaol'! Not the most desirable of addresses!

By 1852 Charles is recorded as living both in Masbrough and at 48, Rock Street, Sheffield. An 1857 Directory records him only in Masbrough, but in this year, sadly now a widower with three children, but with his power and wealth assured, he purchased the brick-built 'exceedingly comfortable family mansion' of Broxholme House and park, possibly from the Hospital of St Thomas, or the estate of its founder Thomas Ellis. Broxholme House had been built by George Broadrick, Town Clerk of Doncaster, at the end of the 18th century, although it may perhaps have replaced an earlier structure; it was certainly extended post-1835, but it is uncertain whether this was before or after Charles bought it.

The house was officially in the Parish of Long Sandall, but was very close to Doncaster town centre, only a few yards north of Christ Church. Over the next 20 years or so he purchased large amounts of land to the north-west of Broxholme, forming a single large tract adjacent to, and intersected by, the South Yorkshire Railway, the River Don, and its 'flood river', totalling in all some 83 acres.

It is suspected that Charles had hopes of developing a major rail and water transhipment, warehousing and engineering centre here to add to his riches, but this seems to have come to nothing. Parts of this land also had a potential strategic value in connection with a possible major re-alignment of the Don Navigation (of which Charles was, of course, Engineer!).

Charles married his first wife, Sarah Watson Linley, on 2 August 1841. Following her death in Sheffield in the first quarter of 1852, he married his second wife, Louisa Mary Hutton, at Tunbridge Wells on 31 January 1871. As with Charles, this was her second marriage, having been born Louisa

Broxholme House and grounds were located in the quality outskirts of Doncaster when purchased by Charles Bartholomew in 1857, but had been nearly engulfed by rows of terraced houses by the time of his death in 1895. *Crown copyright*

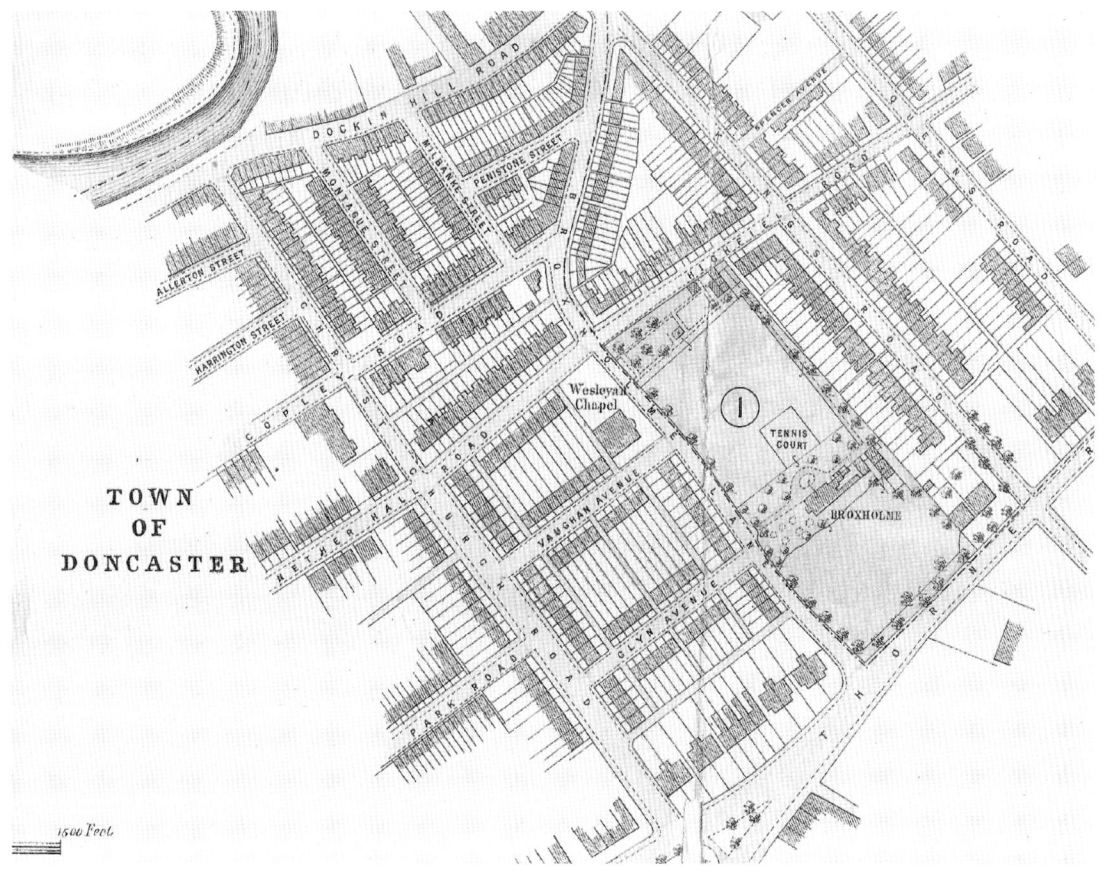

17

The only significant house once owned by Charles Bartholomew that still stands is Lowdale Hall, Sleights, near Whitby. *Noel Barrett*

Mary Copeman, her father being a solicitor, Edward John Copeman. In 1876, however, perhaps as a result of the profits that he would have made from his colliery interests during the coal boom of the early 1870s, Charles moved to Ealing, while retaining Broxholme as his Yorkshire base; he expanded the immediate grounds of the house in 1877.

He had also acquired Lowdale Hall, Sleights, near Whitby, in 1865, where he developed a substantial estate that remained in his possession until his death, after which it was speedily sold as part of his estate (although, curiously, it was not mentioned in his will of 1894). Further research is needed here as to whether the Hall was perhaps bought as a country escape from Broxholme, for his elder daughter Sarah, or whether he was involved in railway and industrial developments in this area.

The date coincides with the opening of the nearby deviation railway from Goathland to Grosmont on the Whitby-Pickering line, and it also suggests that Lowdale may have been bought with monies received following the takeover of the South Yorkshire Railway by the MS&LR. Apparently entirely coincidentally, a much later owner of the Hall had once been an employee of the family's Wombwell Main Colliery Company.

Charles died, a widower, at home in Ealing on 12 January 1895. During his lifetime he amassed considerable wealth, his estate at final probate being valued at £284,680 1s 5d, having been revised downwards from an initial valuation of £290,955 1s 5d (perhaps upon the realisation that the strategic value of his Doncaster lands was not matched by their financial value). This would have been equivalent to about £17 million a century later. The estate included the Rock Street property in Sheffield in which his son 'CW' had been born, as well as others in London, Doncaster, Sleights, and Blakesley Hall itself.

'Bartholomew's Vineyard'

The Bartholomew family is – as already noted – deservedly, though inadequately, best known for its activities in Yorkshire in reconstructing and transforming major river navigations into thriving canals. Charles's eldest brother, Thomas Hamond Bartholomew (1796-1852), was appointed Surveyor and Clerk of Works to the Aire & Calder Navigation (A&C) in 1825; he subsequently became its formal Engineer, and later Manager. The port of Goole, through which most of the A&C's traffic was to flow, opened in this same year.

Thomas married Ann Wood at Bradford on 12 April 1826, and they had three children, Mary Rebecca (born 1828), Thomas Wood (born 1829), and William Hamond (born 1 February 1831). Sadly Ann died in the early 1830s and Thomas married his second wife Hannah (Holmes?) shortly after. He then had two more children, James Holmes (born 1841) and Eliza Anna (born 1842); Eliza died when she was four.

Thomas himself died comparatively young, on

The Bartholomew family – engineers

William Hamond Bartholomew. *John Goodchild collection*

The Hamond Bartholomew family grave in Stanley Churchyard. *Author*

25 October 1852, and was succeeded as Engineer to the A&C, after some considerable soul-searching by its directors, by his son William Hamond Bartholomew at the tender age of 21. He followed in his father's footsteps, becoming General Manager in 1875 and continued in post until 1895. Even then he remained as a 'Consulting Director' with that waterway virtually until his death in 1919 (although in his latter years a degree of senility seems to have made him perhaps more of a hindrance than a help).

These two Bartholomews, father and son, thus influenced engineering on the A&C for an amazing total of 94 years between them. William, though essentially self-effacing, achieved international fame for his works, and presented papers at overseas conferences. His half-brother James Holmes Bartholomew also entered the engineering profession.

William married Maria Wilson in 1860 and they had three children, one of whom died in infancy. He devoted himself to improving the Aire & Calder to an even greater extent than did his Uncle Charles in South Yorkshire – and particularly with regard to its strategic link with the rest of the country and the world, the inland port of Goole.

The town even became known as 'Bartholomew's Vineyard' as a result of his business activities and philanthropy there (for example, he funded the Cottage Hospital). To protect access to Goole for sea-going vessels, William fought – and won – the battle to prevent a (low-level) Humber Bridge being built at that time.

In 1880 William considerably extended his influence over the strategic value of Goole by becoming Chairman of the Goole Steam Shipping Company, and in characteristic fashion he re-invigorated the company so that by 1882 it was advertising services to Antwerp, Dunkirk, Ghent and Rotterdam with nine ships. In 1904 the company was sold to the Lancashire & Yorkshire Railway, later absorbed into the London, Midland & Scottish Railway (LMS) and, ultimately, post-Second World War, the British Transport Commission's Associated Humber Lines fleet.

It is also of note that the Dutch River of circa 1633, one of the earliest major artificial waterways in Britain and constructed by Vermuyden primarily to improve land drainage, linked the

River Don near Stainforth directly with the River Ouse at Goole, and thus provided an existing link via Goole between the two major waterways of the Bartholomew brothers. Waterways called 'Ouse' will, by coincidence, reappear unusually frequently in this story.

The Bartholomews and Stephenson

The Bartholomew family would have come into contact with George Stephenson during the late 1830s when the latter was Engineer to the North Midland Railway then being built from Derby to Leeds. The course of Stephenson's new railway through the Masbrough and Swinton areas required the realignment, as it crossed them, of parts of Charles's waterways (on the River Don Navigation and its satellite the Dearne & Dove Canal respectively).

In the case of the latter, its original, virtually straight, course was diverted into a sharp 'dog-leg' to allow a shorter railway bridge over the canal at the Swinton station and also a lengthy S-curve created to allow the canal to share a cutting with the new railway (with an unfulfilled view to creating an interchange wharf) at Bow Broom, allowing the original 472-yard Adwick canal tunnel to be bypassed in the process.

Stephenson's route also crossed the Wakefield to Castleford (Calder) section of Thomas's Aire & Calder Navigation near Altofts, and ran close alongside its Leeds to Castleford (Aire) section between Methley, Woodlesford and Stourton. The A&C's nominally independent satellite, the Barnsley Canal, was also crossed twice by this railway – at Royston (also requiring substantial realignment of this canal) and at Oakenshaw by Sandal Magna near Wakefield.

The Bartholomew family would have been involved previously in opposing the building of Stephenson's railway in direct competition with their canals, thus initially bringing them into professional conflict with Stephenson, prior to them working together to achieve the necessary waterway realignments. Interestingly, the tables were turned only a few years later when Stephenson was similarly opposing Charles Bartholomew's proposed South Yorkshire Railway in competition with this same North Midland line!

There are remarkable similarities between the Bartholomew and Stephenson families – both were self-made, and pre-eminent in their day (though perhaps on a different scale) in their own transport field (primarily canals and railways respectively), and both developed their own coal-mining and related businesses around their transport corridors. In later years the Bartholomew family members remained particularly proud of their earlier contact with George Stephenson.

Wakefield, Stanley and 'Tom Puddings'

The Aire & Calder's engineering was controlled from 1802 to 1839 from Lake Lock (where

The Aire & Calder Head Office was near Chantry Bridge, Wakefield, until 1851; seen above right is part of Wakefield Kirkgate station, the site of Joseph Aspdin's first Portland Cement factory. *Author*

William was born) at Stanley, then from 1839 onwards at nearby Stanley Ferry, following Thomas Bartholomew's work in replacing the old Calder river navigation between Castleford and Wakefield by a new 4½-mile-long Calder Cut. This reduced the waterway distance between the two towns by no less than 5 miles, and included the construction of a cast-iron bowstring suspension aqueduct at Stanley Ferry over the river.

From 1821 to 1851, virtually throughout Thomas's engineering reign, the A&C Head Offices and Boardroom were adjacent to the mediaeval Chantry Bridge over the River Calder at Wakefield; they then moved to Leeds. Stanley and Wakefield have further, hitherto unappreciated, relevance to our story, as will be recounted in more detail shortly.

It is of note that Joseph Aspdin, who patented Portland Cement in 1824, established his first factory for this immensely strong new material in 1825 in Lower Kirkgate, Wakefield (on the site later occupied by the town's Kirkgate railway station), only yards from the then A&C offices. This site was ideal because of its proximity to both the Aire & Calder and Calder & Hebble waterways. which met at Wakefield, more easily allowing the heavy raw materials in and finished cement out.

This was the same year that Thomas Hamond Bartholomew was appointed as the A&C's Surveyor and Clerk of Works (in effect its 'Engineer' in all but name), and he was thus, in his waterway works, probably the first to use this material on a large scale – and almost certainly ahead of the much-vaunted claims for Brunel's use in his Thames Tunnel works, although Joseph's original cement was quickly improved by his younger son William. Despite two changes of site, remaining close to the A&C, the Aspdin factory in Wakefield remained in production until the 20th century.

William Bartholomew, in trying to increase and improve the efficiency of coal movement on the Aire & Calder, perhaps achieved the more widespread and long-lasting fame in the family through his invention of the 'Tom Pudding' compartment boats, primarily for coal transport, which effectively allowed large numbers of them (19 became usual, with around 35 to 40 tons of coal in each – or up to 22 pans for smokeless fuel) to be formed into a single 'canal train'. These took the coal to Goole where it was transhipped, using his own design of hydraulic coaling-tower-style hoists, into sea-going vessels.

By 1913 more than 1,000 compartments were in use, moving some 1½ million tons of coal annually (as well as other commodities); the system remained in use virtually until the end of the 20th century. The author and his fiancée remember a pleasure trip on Charles's South Yorkshire Navigation in the mid-1970s when our friends'

The A&C engineering base at Stanley Ferry is seen here in the 1950s, with steam tug No 4 leaving the aqueduct with a train of loaded 'Tom Puddings', designed by William. *Mike Taylor collection*

The Blakesley Hall Miniature Railway

Above In July 1973 an empty 'train' of William's 'Tom Puddings' enters Long Sandall lock on Charles's River Don Navigation, en route from Goole, while a laden coal train heads towards Goole along Charles's South Yorkshire Railway. *Author*

Below The Dearne & Dove and the Barnsley canals met physically from 1804 at this junction; they eventually came under the engineering control of Charles and William respectively. *Old Barnsley collection (B1302)*

relatively flimsy craft rapidly had to seek refuge as a 'train' of 17 of William's empty 'Tom Puddings' came into view heading the opposite way, with the compartments, caught by the wind, straggling across the width of the waterway!

The 'Tom Pudding' concept was taken a stage further by William in 1891 when a standard-gauge railway slipway was built in the Newland basin of the A&C at Stanley Ferry, whereby these 15-foot-wide compartment boats could be drawn individually from the canal on one of two huge 12-wheel rail transporters and taken to St John's Colliery (more than a mile away) by rail for direct loading at the screens (still on the transporter) with coal, saving one transhipment; the arrangement continued in active use for half a century, until around 1939.

One long-term objective of the Bartholomews (uncle and nephew), a modern-engineered link between their two major West Riding waterways, was finally achieved through the building of the New Junction Canal. Financed jointly by the Aire & Calder and the Sheffield & South Yorkshire, it finally opened in January 1905, sadly some 10 years after Charles's death. This virtually paralleled the old Dutch River, and enabled a far greater tonnage to be moved.

The Bartholomews and the Heywoods

With such significance in regard to their ownership and control over the production and movement of raw materials and commodities in the West Riding in the early and mid-19th century, it is inevitable that the Bartholomew family would be well known to, and acquainted with, many of the other important families in the area at that time.

A family that was destined to play an intriguing complementary (or contradictory) role to one of the Bartholomews in 15-inch-gauge estate railway development, was that of Heywood, whose prime business activity was in banking. Although certain railway histories have previously mentioned that Charles William Bartholomew and one Arthur Percival Heywood were coincidentally students at university at the same time, no other likely contact between these two families has previously been identified or recorded. However, research has now revealed that the two families were actually remarkably well connected, although the Heywood relationships are truly complex.

An important local cloth-merchant, Benjamin Heywood built Stanley Hall, near Wakefield, in 1802 – close by the Lake Lock engineering base (also built in 1802) of the Aire & Calder Navigation, whose day-to-day management was in Wakefield until 1851. The A&C was initially promoted primarily by such merchants in Wakefield and Leeds to provide adequate transport for their raw materials and finished products to maintain and grow their businesses – well before the coal industry became significant – and Benjamin was one such major shareholder.

Benjamin died in 1822 and his only son Arthur, who inherited his father's interest and shares in the waterway, continued in residence at Stanley Hall until 1836 (when he and his wife Mary Duroure moved to nearby Ackton Hall, which had been left to her). He retained ownership of the former until 1854, when it was sold in a hotly contested auction to William Shaw, the noted railway contractor (who had, inter alia, built Stephenson's North Midland line between Royston and Oakenshaw – near the various Bartholomew waterways – and would thus also be well-known to the latter family); the building has for many years been a Nurses' Hostel for the city's Pinderfields Hospital.

Arthur's eldest sister Elizabeth married Hugh Jones, establishing thereby a Heywood-Jones family line at Badsworth Hall, strategically half way between Wakefield and Doncaster (and home to the famous Badsworth Hunt), while younger sister Mary married Daniel Gaskell (1782-1875), Wakefield's first MP; they lived at Lupset Hall, Wakefield. Arthur and Mary had no children and their estate passed in due course to the son of his youngest sister Hannah Brooksbank.

Benjamin's brother, John-Pemberton Heywood, a barrister, built Wentworth House in Wakefield, living there with his wife until his death in 1835. He is recorded in the 1822 and 1830 Wakefield Directories as a Magistrate and as Acting Commissioner for Taxes. Today the house is the nucleus of the city's Girls High School.

The significance of these Wakefield Heywoods is that both Benjamin and John-Pemberton were shareholders in, and directors of, the Aire & Calder Navigation. Following Benjamin's death in 1822, his son Arthur and his son-in-law Daniel Gaskell became A&C directors in 1823, joining John-Pemberton on the Board. There were thus no fewer than three Heywood family members on the A&C Board (out of twelve!) at the time of

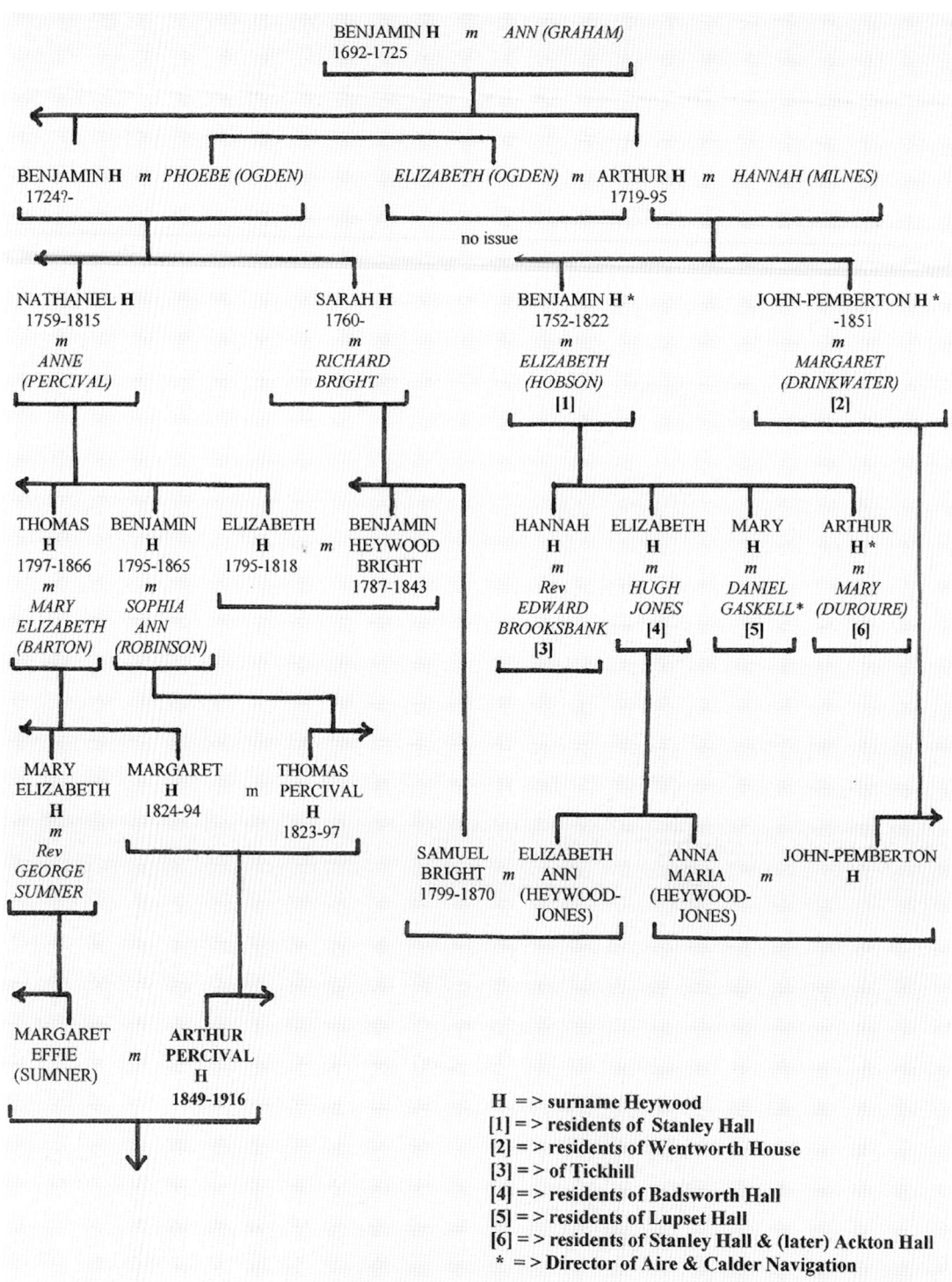

Heywood family connections, showing the links between the Dove Leys and Duffield Bank and the West Riding branches of the family. Only relevant 'connecting' members of the family are shown. Also, siblings, where shown, are arranged to facilitate the display of links, rather than in birth-date order.

their initial appointment of Thomas Hamond Bartholomew as their Surveyor & Clerk of Works in 1825, and for many years thereafter.

Arthur Percival Heywood's grandfather (the first baronet, Sir Benjamin Heywood, Bt) was a second cousin to Arthur Heywood (of Stanley Hall), Mary Gaskell (of Lupset Hall), and Hannah Brooksbank (of Tickhill). Sir Benjamin was also a first cousin to Samuel Bright (son of Sarah Heywood and Richard Bright). Samuel married Elizabeth Ann Heywood-Jones of Badsworth Hall, a niece of Arthur, granddaughter of Benjamin and great niece of John-Pemberton, while her sister Anna Maria married John-Pemberton's son (also called John-Pemberton).

There were other links also through further family intra-marrying. As noted by Howard Clayton in his definitive work on Heywood's railways, 'Like many nineteenth-century families the Heywoods were very clannish, and the various branches of the family spent much of their time visiting each other', in the process facilitating such intra-family acquaintanceships!

As but one further example of the complex interaction between families in the area, the Taylor family, long-time residents of Middlewood Hall, Darfield (and effectively Squires thereof), would be well known to Charles and C. W. Bartholomew, with their direct involvement not only in the same local mining and railway activities, but also through their patronage of Darfield Church (as we shall see). The Taylors were also involved with the Badsworth Hunt (and thus in direct contact with the Heywood-Jones family).

The above identified business and social relationship between the Heywood and Bartholomew families (members of both families duly appearing in the appropriate 'Nobility, Gentry & Clergy' sections of the same local Directories of the time) indicates that C. W. Bartholomew and Arthur Percival Heywood would have known each other prior to their near simultaneous arrivals at Trinity College, Cambridge.

Goats and unicorns

It is clear that the Bartholomews felt a need to establish the credibility of their family in Victorian society in view of their newly created wealth and positions. Charles, in a surviving letter dated 26 August 1859 to his nephew William, says 'I think the motto "Stand sure" is the best that I see you have marked' in discussing a coat of arms for the family.

While their use of a shield featuring the heads of three black goats, and a crest featuring the head of another (but grey), is indeed the arms of the Bartholomew family, this suggestion for the preferred motto creates all sorts of subsequent mysteries in its wake – the 'Bartholomew Arms' inn (renamed from the 'Red Lion' long after the Bartholomew era) in Blakesley uses 'Ad Alta' as the motto on the inn sign (see page 13).

However, a series of stained glass windows, erected in 1900 by C. W. Bartholomew in Blakesley Hall to commemorate all the previous owners through its long and convoluted history, included a panel with specific reference to his father Charles, showing the motto 'Deo Fidens Persistas' accompanying the family arms (see page 85)! This same motto appears, also with the family arms, on a plaque in All Saints Church, Darfield, recording the family's donation of the east window there in 1915.

Burke's *The General Armory* of 1884 gives 'Ad Alta' as the motto for the Bartholomew family as a whole (also for three other families), whilst 'Deo Fidens Persistas' is given only for a Rector named Kinahan in County Down! 'Stand sure' is given for three families (but not the Bartholomews).

The pub would appear to be 'technically correct', while 'Deo Fidens Persistas' appears to be what was used, without formal support, by this branch of the family. Presumably Charles's preference for 'Stand sure' was not adopted! A family signet ring in the archives of the Waterways Museum at Goole features the head of a goat.

A final twist to these mysteries was added by the substantial gate on the main drive of Blakesley Hall grounds, which once featured the symbol, not of a goat, but of a unicorn; although there is no trace of this creature to be found in connection with the arms of any of the families known to have owned the estate, the head of a unicorn is the symbol (being that of the Wombwell family) of the Wombwell locality – whose inhabitants of course indirectly funded the purchase and upkeep of the estate from 1876!

3 Charles William Bartholomew

Early days

Charles William Bartholomew was born on 19 August 1850 at 48 Rock Street, Brightside, Sheffield, into this now increasingly wealthy and significant family of civil engineers and non-established clergy. Known as 'Charlie' to his business partners (perhaps to distinguish him from his father Charles), he was generally referred to as 'CW' around Blakesley – and this latter term will be used throughout the rest of the book to minimise confusion between him and the various other members of the family also called Charles.

CW was the youngest, and the only son, of the three children of Charles surviving beyond infancy from his first marriage to Sarah; his two sisters were Sarah Hamond (born 1846) and Eliza Hamond (born 1847). There are believed to have been six children of the marriage in total (one brother and two sisters being lost in infancy); sadly their mother died early in 1852, leaving Charles a widower until he remarried in 1871.

Nevertheless CW grew up in the lavish and pampered surroundings arising from his father's wealth, including (from the age of seven) Broxholme House in Doncaster, experiencing thereby close contact with the railways, canals, collieries and docks for which Charles (and his cousin William) were responsible.

Charles would therefore no doubt be expecting great things from his only son to complement the industrious characteristics of himself and his brother's side of the family, thereby establishing the Bartholomew name, along with that of Stephenson, as one of those great dynasties able successfully to combine business with civil and transport engineering.

Sadly this hope appears to have been largely unfulfilled and, despite CW's education at Uppingham School, followed by a number of years at Trinity College, Cambridge, it was clear by the time he was in his mid-20s that he was not going to follow as notable or active an engineering career.

Although he was admitted to Trinity College on 10 July 1868, matriculating during the Michaelmas Term of 1869, it took him until 1876 to get his BA degree, with the usual purchase of an MA following three years later.

It has already been mentioned, and it is intriguing in the light of later events, that Arthur Percival Heywood (later Sir Arthur Heywood)

A carbon copy of a business letter to CW from his colliery agents in Sheffield in 1906, recording his name in such circles as 'Charlie'. *Sheffield Archives, Ref NCB 980*

entered Trinity College on 15 February of that same year of 1868, although he was awarded his BA (with First Class Honours) in 1872.

Surviving family correspondence seems to confirm the notion that CW preferred a more 'gentrified' lifestyle to the hands-on engineering of other family members, though he did in later life claim to be a 'not now practising' civil engineer. It often happened in wealthy Victorian families that, upon a first son's marriage, the father would secure a suitable estate for the young couple, together with adequate financial means to maintain the appropriate lifestyle.

It is no surprise therefore that in 1876 Charles arranged the purchase of Blakesley Hall for CW, this coinciding not only with the completion, at long last, of his BA, but in celebration of his marriage to Lucy Isabella Ussher at St Luke's, Cheltenham, on 19 August (CW's 26th birthday); it could well be that the Hall was the incentive from his father to get him to work hard enough to get his degree!

Lucy was the daughter of Lt Col Edward Lee Ussher; she was born 'at sea in the Indian Ocean' about 1855. Interestingly, 1876 was also the year in which Charles himself moved his main place of residence from Broxholme to Ealing – and CW was recorded on his marriage certificate as then living at the latter. Blakesley was certainly a long way from the homes and activities of other family members – and far from their industrial base too!

There is no implication that father and son did not get on together; on the contrary, the provisions of Charles's will and the extent of, and sentiments expressed in, the memorials by CW to his father after his death suggest a very close relationship. The desire of Charles and his nephew to establish the family name in the late-1850s, through such things as securing a coat of arms, also lends weight to the idea that Charles might not have been too unhappy to have a son who would play the part not of hands-on engineer, but of established country squire, to the hilt!

Interestingly in this respect, CW fell wholeheartedly into the role – he was not only Lord of the Manor of Blakesley, but also Lord of the Manor of Sharnbrook, Bedfordshire, and it was noted in his obituary in the local press that, in due course, '…both … estates benefited greatly by his open-handed generosity'.

Blakesley Hall, as seen from the south-east before 1912, but after CW had extended the west wing. *Charles Simpson collection, courtesy of Sir William McAlpine*

The Blakesley Hall Miniature Railway

Businessman

Much of this side of the Bartholomew family's capital and income was derived from their shares in various South Yorkshire collieries, one of the principal ones being The Wombwell Main Colliery Company. Following his father's death in 1895, CW inherited those interests to add to the token shares he already held, giving him personally an additional 3,005 of the 6,014 issued £20 shares, plus 622 of the 1,350 issued £100 shares, in that company.

His father's business activities had been so extensive and in so many fields that, coupled with the tragic early deaths of his siblings prior to his father's death, this meant that CW became, by the standards of the time, a very wealthy man indeed; this enabled him to enjoy a rich 'playboy' lifestyle with only minimal involvement in direct business activities, preferring to delegate this to his agents.

As with Lowdale Hall, CW obviously felt no need to retain Broxholme House or the 83 acres of land at Doncaster amassed by his father. They were auctioned on 24 September 1895, the agents, in typical fashion, making great play of the land as being of 'exceptional value for building purposes'. This was no doubt true as regards the land associated with the house; from a 'gentrified' setting distantly surrounded by other great houses with their own extensive lands at the time of Charles's purchase, it now stood solitary and faded, almost engulfed by encroaching densely packed rows of working class terraces.

However, it is unlikely that CW's capital benefited significantly, other than from the sale of the house, as no building had taken place on any of this land by the time of the Ordnance Survey revision of 1904. Much of the land near the rail and river routes still remained undeveloped a century later, being in a flood plain, although the house was soon demolished in favour of yet more terraced rows covering the immediate grounds.

The family connection with Yorkshire is perpetuated through the existence of Bartholomew Street, West Street and Frederick Street in Wombwell, which were created in CW's era. The first nowadays consists of a number of terraced rows, some stone-fronted, others all-

Begrimed miners trudge through Wombwell Main Colliery yard, ignoring the 'Barnsley British Co-operative Society' horse-drawn cart, with its load of bottled 'Pure Mineral Waters'. *Old Barnsley collection (585)*

Looking down Bartholomew Street in Wombwell, at its junction with West Street; the former 'corner shop' carries a stone 'Alexandra Terrace 1902', placing it firmly in CW's era. *Author*

brick, most of which were originally built and owned by the Wombwell Main Colliery Co.

The top-end house, formerly the 'corner shop' at the junction of the first two streets, and the only building to carry a 'Bartholomew Street' cast-iron street nameplate, also carries an 'Alexandra Terrace 1902' building stone. (West Street and the slightly later Frederick Street derive from CW's younger sister Eliza's marriage to the Rev Charles Frederick Cumber West; they had two children before her early death.)

A surviving share certificate of the Edmunds & Swaithe Collieries Company, issued in April 1879, is signed by C. W. Bartholomew as 'Secretary', and by Charles and C. W. Bartholomew as 'Members of the Company'. This was in connection with turning this operation into a limited liability company with eight subscribers; these included Charles (CW's father), CW himself, Sarah (CW's elder sister) and the Rev Charles West (married to CW's other sister Eliza), although the younger members had only a token shareholding. The Tyas family held the remaining half of the shares.

In 1904 CW funded a huge and magnificent east window in the new chancel for St Mary's Parish Church, Wombwell, in memory of his father and two late sisters. He also contributed £200 towards a new organ and £1,000 towards the chancel building itself. As with many things connected with the Bartholomews, there is a fascinating story here about this (and another) rare documented example of their philanthropy in and around Wombwell itself. Charles Bartholomew's will of 1894 refers to '…all my rights in respect of the Presentation to the Rectory and Parish Church of Wombwell … To my said son Charles William Bartholomew…', as well as to similar 'rights' in connection with the livings associated with the sister churches at nearby Darfield and Worsborough.

Thanks to the assistance of Joan Robinson of

Wombwell Heritage Group, and the Dean of Trinity College Chapel, the Rev Dr Arnold Browne, it has been established that CW's father had purchased, for £5,500, the advowson (ie right of presentation) of part of the Parish of Darfield (which then included Wombwell), with 'the Masters and Fellows of Trinity College Cambridge' holding the remainder. In 1884 he offered, in a letter to the College dated 25 July, to either buy their part himself for £1,000, or alternatively sell his part to the College for the same sum of £5,500 that he had paid, although nothing seems to have resulted at this time.

In 1864 part of the Darfield parish was assigned to the church of St Mary, Wombwell. One direct implication of all this for our story is that it shows that it was Wombwell Church that had thus provided the direct connection and avenue by which, in 1868, CW's entry to Trinity College as an undergraduate had been facilitated (and thus his closer contact with Arthur Heywood ensured)! With his inherited (part-)right of presentation at Wombwell still intact in 1904, CW clearly also had little choice but to be a significant benefactor to the new chancel works; he is not recorded as attending either the laying of its foundation stone or its subsequent consecration.

However, it appears that, after this, CW quickly set the wheels in motion to divest himself of this responsibility, and the *London Gazette* of 20 February 1906 records (in a weighty three-page description) that, with effect from this date, the King, Edward VII, had approved (as head of the Church of England), inter alia, the transfer of responsibility for these Bartholomew family portions to the Master and Fellows of Trinity College, thereby giving them the sole patronage.

It is therefore all the more curious to find that, as late as 1915, CW funded yet another stained glass east window, this time in Wombwell's 'mother' Church of All Saints, Darfield, '...in affectionate remembrance of Charles Bartholomew of Doncaster Civil Engineer and Patron of the Rectory of Darfield...' (see page 86). It may simply have been conscience arising from the combined effects of his son being away at war, him being now quite ill, and a realisation that it was 20 years since his father had died, although it demonstrated that his personal interest in stained glass remained undiminished.

There is, however, nothing simple about the stained glass work itself, which is perhaps even more elaborate than that at Wombwell, featuring scenes depicting Saints associated with northern Britain, two on either side of the central panel of Christ.

In 1910 Wombwell Main Colliery was the largest single employer in the area, with 1,082 underground workers and 239 surface workers, while Cortonwood employed 545 and 230 respectively; there were also coking plants and other related activities. Wombwell Main produced a noted hard coal used by both the British and French navies. However, Edmunds & Swaithe Main collieries had closed by 1896, the final decision apparently being taken by CW himself.

In the 21st century it is not always easy to appreciate the almost total influence on workers' lives that such a dominant industry could have from the mid-19th century. For example, between the 1880s and the 1930s more than three-quarters of the jobs in Wombwell were in the various pits, and most of the rest were dependent on them.

As indicators of the harsh life, it is recorded that in the 1870s a case of wife-selling occurred there, while during the Great War years a group of miners were arrested and fined for buying each other rounds of drinks in a local inn, such being illegal at that time!

However, the Bartholomew collieries appear to have suffered more than their fair share of serious incidents, and Charles in particular seems to have been considered to be less generous than the more locally based, and very active, partners (such as the Roberts family with Wombwell) in making provision for the dependants of those lost in such accidents.

Several of these were caused directly by reliance at the coal face on candles, still all too common throughout the coalfields decades after the invention of the safety lamp independently but simultaneously by Stephenson and Davy (the Bartholomew collieries seem generally to have used Stephenson lamps, which gave a brighter light).

Poor industrial relations of this kind seem, by consequence or coincidence, to have left a very long-term legacy, as the principal 'flashpoint' colliery that led to the bitter 1984-85 stand-off between the miners and the Government of the day was Cortonwood, by then the last surviving pit in which the Bartholomews had been part-owners; it was finally closed by the National Coal Board in 1985.

A poignant consequence of this particular strike was the ending, in 1986, of the last remnants of William Bartholomew's 'Tom Pudding' operations, although their usage had been in decline for some time.

Squire

While the new Squire of Blakesley Hall would no doubt have wished to become fully involved in local affairs and to perform to the full the expected role of philanthropist to the neighbourhood, there was but little sign of this during the first years of CW's tenure. One small example does emerge from The Blakesley Boys School records for 9 August 1889, which state that '…C. Bartholomew Esq and C. W. Bartholomew Esq have jointly subscribed 30/- towards the School Museum'.

A village Reading Room may also have been a 'jointly subscribed' activity with his father, as it seems to have dated from 1887 (and was itself magnificently restored by the local community in 2003). It was only after his father's death on 12 January 1895, when he came into possession of the Blakesley Hall estate, that CW found the financial freedom, and the resources, to indulge himself in the provision of much-needed amenities for the village.

Well before his similar activities in Yorkshire, he had the chancel of Blakesley Church completely rebuilt and extended in 1897 in memory of his father and his two mature sisters who had died relatively young (Eliza in 1883 and Sarah in 1892), although he used a 'Victorian Urban Gothic' style, quite out of keeping with the rest of the building (it must be admitted that after 100 years or so it has mellowed into closer harmony with the original!), together with a new organ chamber, organ and church clock. He provided new stained glass windows – CW was clearly an enthusiast for these, both secular and ecclesiastical.

CW was elected to the first Blakesley Parish Council in 1894, being Chairman thereof from 1907 to 1911 and again in 1915. He provided such things as a room for the Blakesley Band to practice in, an entirely new water supply for the village in 1902, and a cricket pitch with pavilion. He also invested in property in the village, buying and renovating the Dower House in the early 1900s, and the Priory in 1913.

He built a pair of lodges flanking the entrance to the Hall grounds, one in 1895 and the other in

St Mary's Church, Blakesley, with the heavily rebuilt chancel funded by CW in memory of his father and sisters.
Author

The Blakesley Hall Miniature Railway

1905, these being initially occupied by estate or Hall employees. In 1912, having funded the enlargement of the village school to accommodate girls, CW acquired the old girls' school and had it converted to act as the Village Hall.

CW instituted a new tradition of opening his Hall grounds for the revamped Annual Show of the Blakesley & District Horticultural Society, as this event appears to have commenced around the same year that CW came to Blakesley, although possibly the Hall grounds may not have been the venue before the 1880s.

Not surprisingly perhaps, CW became President of the Show Committee and, after his death, his son James took over this role. The Hall grounds were opened for any suitable cause for celebration, one of the more notable being for James's 21st birthday, as well as annual treats for the village schoolchildren.

He was a Justice of the Peace, as well as a supporter of local enterprise and initiative. In 1912-13, for example, he supplied one of his own cars, converted into an open truck with a canvas tilt, which the then landlord of the Red Lion used to start a short-lived bus and carrier service to Northampton in competition with the railway.

'Knight of Grace'

CW especially allowed the use of the grounds for various ambulance competitions, maybe remembering its earlier history as a Hospital. Excellent records exist of one such series of annual tournaments, for staff of the Great Central Railway, and will be described later. The local school records note that on 14 June 1913 'By the invitation of Mr Bartholomew, the school troop of Boy Scouts were allowed to watch the St John

A postcard sent personally by CW to his Wombwell friend John Robinson, showing him with 17 of 'our boys' from his Hospital outside Blakesley Hall during the Great War. Note the embossed Hall lettering on the card.
Joan Robinson collection

Ambulance competition at the Hall today…', presumably one of a regular series.

During the First World War, CW established a convalescent home in a house in the village for wounded soldiers, and well over 400 passed through; his daughter Ivy and her friends helped with the nursing. It was known as 'The "Bartholomew" Military Auxiliary Hospital at Blakesley'. The Hall itself was not used directly for this purpose, although CW certainly entertained the patients there on suitable occasions.

CW was honoured by being made a 'Knight of Grace of the Order of St John of Jerusalem in England' on 15 June 1917, unusually without having previously been a 'Serving Brother' of the Order; sadly the records as to whether this was in recognition of these convalescent home activities, or the Ambulance Competitions, or both have not survived.

Family man

Despite the splendours of their new marital home at Blakesley, the relationship between CW and Lucy was not a happy one and remained childless; it failed relatively quickly. Although she is recorded in the 1881 Census as resident with CW at what it, strictly correctly, called 'Woodend Hall', she left Blakesley some time in the 1880s. This was no doubt aided or precipitated by its sudden renewed isolation as a result of the withdrawal of passenger train services through the village in 1877.

The 1891 Census records her in London, but by the 1901 Census she was in Beckenham, Kent, 'living on [her] own means', still as Lucy Bartholomew. It is presumed that CW (or more likely his father) provided a 'lump sum' financial settlement upon their separation, as there is no provision of an annuity or any other bequest for her (or even any reference to her) in either his (or his father's) wills. She long outlived CW and died, aged 87 and still retaining her married surname, at Croydon in the latter part of 1942, never having remarried.

CW's second partner was Sarah Ann Floyd. She was not a native Blakesley girl, but came from Byfield – a rather larger village some 7 miles to the west – both villages being located on the East & West Junction Railway (E&WJR) line. She was born there on 22 April 1863, the daughter of James Floyd, a Byfield 'Shoemaker Journeyman', born in 1818. Her mother was Mary Ann (née Lawrence), born 1819, who had married James Floyd in December 1840. She was thus 44 when she had Sarah Ann; sadly she died in December 1867, when Sarah was only 4½ years old – mirroring CW's own loss.

The 1881 Census lists Sarah as a 'domestic servant', living at the same address in Banbury Road, Byfield, as her widowed father James; it is presumed that she 'kept house' for him, as well as working for others in this capacity. Blakesley's temporary isolation was eased in early 1885 by the re-introduction of passenger trains through the village, once again linking it directly with Byfield.

Sarah became the cook at Blakesley Hall and thus came to CW's attention; some 13 years his junior, she was in due course discreetly dispatched to a 'finishing college' to be educated in the ways of her new station in life. This liaison would not be publicly approved of in late-Victorian society and the family may therefore now have found maintaining or establishing relationships with other 'gentry' (such as Sir Arthur Heywood and his family) difficult.

In keeping with common practice of this Victorian moral stance, CW and Sarah appear to have partly withdrawn from personal involvement in Blakesley from the late 1880s until around 1900. The Hall and grounds were let to Lord Penrhyn over much of this period as a hunting lodge each season, although CW at least must have spent some time there as he was, as already noted, elected to the Parish Council in 1894.

A life-long devoted couple, Sarah and CW had two children, Ivy and James, both being born in the London area. Ivy was born on 11 July 1890 at 5 Mall Road, Hammersmith; she was registered at birth as Ivy May Bartholomew Floyd, but the formal record entry was such a mess (both mother and father – together with his occupation – being wrongly recorded as Annie Floyd and Charles William Floyd, Mechanical Engineer, respectively!) that CW and Sarah had to make a 'Statutory Declaration' in 1912, correcting the entry.

James was born on 12 June 1892 at 1 Lyncombe Villa, Broadway, Ealing, his name being registered as James Floyd. His mother's occupation was given as 'Housekeeper', and he was presumably named after Sarah's father. In 'final' form, neither Ivy nor James had the identity of their father registered. As both births were during this 'absent' period, they may have been living in Ealing with CW's father at this time.

The Blakesley Hall Miniature Railway

CW and his second partner Sarah in later life. *Doreen Birks collection*

In due course Sarah changed her surname by Deed Poll to Bartholomew, and this change applied also to Ivy and to James. This produced the curious feature for Ivy of her name (having been Floyd) becoming, strictly, Ivy May Bartholomew Bartholomew!

Perhaps because of these initial problems with the surnames of his partner and his children, CW, in his will, threatened future generations via the female Bartholomew line who '...omit or refuse or neglect to assume such surname ... or shall afterwards cease to use such surname then and in every such case my Blakesley Hall Estate shall go and be held in trust for the Prior and Order of the Hospital of St John of Jerusalem in England'!

The moral niceties of the time, which led to these entries or omissions, were exemplified when CW presented James with a copy of grandfather Charles Bartholomew's treatise on Jesus, presumably to celebrate his Confirmation; the author now owns this copy, in which CW has written, in his own hand: 'To James Bartholomew from the Son of the Compiler October 1905. This read in remembrance of He who loved us and gave his Life for us'. Note how CW has here, neatly but deliberately, not admitted in writing that James is his son!

Curiously, the 1891 Census records Sarah in Northamptonshire, but both CW and Ivy (not yet a year old) as being in Hampshire; perhaps Sarah was nursing her father at this time, as he died less than three months later. CW had returned fully to Blakesley by the turn of the century with his now 'established' partner and children – and had also inherited his father's substantial wealth in 1895, allowing something of a fresh start. The 1901 Census has the whole family (CW, Sarah, Ivy and James) at Felixstowe, but this may simply reflect a seaside holiday.

A 'local pillar of society' would be expected to uphold strict moral standards. The delivery of a new railway locomotive for the estate from the local Bassett-Lowke factory in 1909 provided an excuse for their staff to be invited to a cricket match, followed by 'a meat tea' at the Hall. The Squire advised them '...to take an interest in their work, and in their moral conduct, to keep to the "straight and narrow track", like a model locomotive'.

However, there have been persistent stories of CW's interest in other village ladies, despite his devotion to Sarah; as with most such tales involving those unable to offer their own version of events, they seem to have grown in successive tellings – to the point where allegations featured in several 'gossip' articles in the *Sunday Telegraph* newspaper in the early 1990s. It is, of course, possible that such activities – maybe even involving Sarah upon her arrival as the Hall's new cook – contributed to Lucy's departure.

With an engineering background, it is no surprise to learn that CW installed a well-equipped workshop at the Hall in the former stable block, this being presided over by his able estate engineer, Alec Wyatt (one suspects that, unlike his fellow student Arthur Heywood, CW did not make much use of his own equipment himself!).

Being interested in the modern energy of electricity, CW also arranged the early installation of his own electric light plant for the Hall and estate, this being (like most things connected with the estate) also looked after by Alec Wyatt (and his son Percy); mains electricity did not reach the village until 1931.

A mischievous streak in his character is supposed to have led him to wire up some of the house doorknobs, particularly those leading from the toilets and bathrooms, to the electricity supply, thereby giving any unsuspecting visitor an electric shock as they tried to leave these rooms! The workshop equipment remained in place, though perhaps not in use, long after CW's death, as village historian Philip Kingston was able to borrow some of the lathes, courtesy of Sarah, during the Second World War.

Godfather

CW, as the local Squire, also had an 'extended family' by virtue of being a godparent to several local people. One of the most notable was Charles Simpson, born on 4 March 1906, the son of CW's doctor (who was not the local village doctor, but lived at Towcester). Charles R. H. Simpson's future interests were clearly influenced both by CW and by what the latter achieved in miniature railway terms, as he was subsequently to rise to significant heights in various amateur and professional railway fields.

Once involved in supervising the fitting of the engines to the R101 airship, he rose to become Works Manager for AC Cars, before joining the famous locomotive builder, Beyer Peacock. Here he was involved in sales, shipment and testing abroad of that company's articulated Beyer-Garratt locomotives. He became a '…director, partner and manager of the Locomotive Publishing Company…' (as he described himself), as well as editing *The Locomotive Carriage & Wagon Review* for a period. In 1961 he became an Assistant Editor for *Engineering*.

An Associate Member of the Institution of Locomotive Engineers, Charles Simpson was an accomplished model locomotive builder; his prowess in the modelling field was recognised in 1974 when he was elected the first President of the then newly formed '7¼in Gauge Society'. He recorded then that 'In my view, the 7¼in gauge is the ideal size', suggesting that what he had grown up with at Blakesley did not find favour with him.

Because of his interests and his close and frequent contact with Blakesley as he grew up – '…prior to 1919, and to a lesser extent afterwards, I spent a lot of time at Blakesley Hall' – his recorded recollections (though sadly few in number) are of inestimable value in assisting the compilation of the story that follows. He was also most meticulous in terms of accuracy. Where he was an actual observer to an event, his description would be wholly accurate, but where he is reporting something second-hand he would record carefully that this is what he had been told or had understood.

Historian, farmer and man of the 20th century

CW, mindful of the history associated with the Hall and no doubt still determined to create an aura of a long-established family, put together a small museum in the extended west wing. To quote CW directly from a short 20-page history of the village he produced:

> 'In the Museum, amongst other specimen [sic], have been placed the Legs of the Bedstead on which Queen Elizabeth, at that time "Princess Elizabeth" slept, when in residence at Blakesley Hall, (about the year 1552,) the Princess occupying the principal bedroom in the N.E. wing. The Rocking Chair belonging to George Stephenson (the Father of Railways). Nelson's relics. A piece of Valencienne lace worn by Charles I. when he was beheaded. Relics from the South African War. Human Sacrificial Bowl from

Abeokute, Lagos, West Africa and many other interesting articles of virtu [sic].'

Truly a cosmopolitan, if somewhat macabre in parts, collection! His extensive library included such things as a rare copy of the Domesday Book.

Further information on the engineering and railway elements of CW's collection was given in *The Model Engineer & Electrician* for 5 July 1906:

'He is possessed of many relics of the great George Stephenson, amongst which may be mentioned a favourite chair, a slide rule, and a chronometer. In addition, he has a large collection of models connected with various engineering schemes in which he has been interested, and also several models of early railway coaches and trucks, some of which were used in the House of Commons during the Parliamentary fights incident to the introduction of railways in this country.'

One of the '…models connected with various engineering schemes…' was undoubtedly the wooden model of the workings of the Wombwell Main Colliery, which his father had maintained and continually updated, first in Yorkshire and then in Ealing.

The '…several models of early railway coaches and trucks…' were not merely a sentimental attachment to some of his father's possessions. CW was an out-and-out railway enthusiast. There were prints of railway engines from various periods on the walls of many rooms – after his death many of these were relegated to the upstairs walls at the back of the Hall where the 'secondary' bedrooms were situated – and his railway activities (as we shall see) were ultimately to go far beyond such mundane objects (once he was freed from the financial restraints imposed by his father).

He imported some relatively exotic livestock to the estate, including Zebus cattle and Jacob sheep. In 1892, when the Society's Annual Show was at (relatively) nearby Warwick, he became a Life Member of the Royal Agricultural Society (an organisation with which the Heywood family were also closely involved), though he does not seem to have taken any active part in its running.

One interesting event occurred in 1903 when he obtained somewhat dubious 'permission' to close the public footpath linking School Lane in Blakesley and Woodend through his estate on condition that he replaced it with an alternative route. This closure, some 27 years after his acquisition of the estate, must have been not simply to remove public right of access to his lands, but also to create a suitable route for the Squire's new 'toy' by avoiding his new railway coming into contact with a public right of way.

There were other significant works undertaken too in the park in the late 19th century (though well before there was any serious thought of a railway there); a 'millstream' some half a mile in length was created feeding from the natural stream through the park, but running on a gentler gradient to and round the southern boundary of the gardens. The family enjoyed relaxing moments fishing or punting on this short waterway (a still surviving wide flight of steps led to the 'landing stage'). It is probable that this feature made use of what had once been the old course of one of the mill races for the mills recorded in the Domesday Book.

One suspects that, in view of the family's involvement in the major canals of Yorkshire, CW would be particularly delighted to have his very own, if rather short, 'canal' in his grounds – and even more that it was fed by an Ouse waterway! As

Philip Burt, owner of the Blakesley estate, examines a now dry waterfall in the Hall grounds, constructed for CW in artificial 'Pulhamite'. *Howkins & Harrison*

the water was by this stage several feet higher than the brook itself, it allowed the installation of a series of artificial waterfalls, forming an attractive addition to the formal gardens.

These extensive water features were developed for CW by the noted landscape architectural firm of James Pulham & Son, which undertook work for many famous gardens, including Battersea Park, Sandringham and other Royal Palaces. The company used an artificial stone, called 'Pulhamite', made of Portland Cement and clinker, often mixed with fossils, and laid in strata over a hollow framework to replicate natural stone features.

There were four generations of James Pulham involved in the business, and their use of Portland Cement seems to have commenced virtually concurrently with Joseph Aspdin's patent, suggesting that those two families were acquainted – and therefore, quite possibly, also with CW's uncle, thus leading to the commission at Blakesley.

This material was used extensively, including the routes for Blakesley's cascades and waterfalls, which date from the late-1890s; this was probably one of the last such applications. A century later these functioned as well as ever following periods of heavy rain, the flow still supervised by various animals including a fox entering its earth and an ever-watchful crocodile, all in this same material! Further features, including 'stone' seats, terracotta bridges and walls, etc, were added around 1907 (by which time this newer material had itself become known as 'Pulhamite'). Another proprietary artificial stone product, known as 'Hitch bricks', was used by Pulham, but in a grey 'dressed stone' hollow breeze block form, to build the watercourse channels and the walls surrounding the Hall gardens on the estate.

Supporting CW's modern approach to everything, later phases of work even resulted in bungalows being built, in the estate grounds and in the village, in the same 'Hitch bricks'; these stand a century later as strong and clear as when they were new. Unless one examines the material quite closely, all these structures look to be built of high-quality dressed natural stone, rather than this early form of 'breeze block'.

In addition to the works for the new waterway around the south side of the Hall, the Black Ouse stream itself was also re-routed on a straight course over a distance of some 400 feet on the north side, taking it further away from the Hall's outbuildings, probably to provide a better supply to the gas producer plant.

CW was very much a man of the 20th century, with a keen interest in the emergent motor car and the developing potential of the internal-combustion engine in general. Not only a pioneer in the use of petrol engines in railway locomotives, as we shall see, he was also an exceptionally keen and active motorist.

Fate helped him to find and pursue this interest with vigour. In October 1895 Sir David Salomons arranged the first ever motor show – at his Broomhill estate near Tunbridge Wells – a location familiar to CW as his father's second marriage had taken place there. Some 10,000 visited the event, and Salomons arranged another show at the Crystal Palace only seven months later. Thus, just as CW became extremely rich from the death of his father that January – and the sales of the Lowdale and Doncaster properties in September – the world of motoring was opened up to him.

He added a large extension to the western end of the old stable block (by now the workshop) as a garage able to hold six cars, with a turntable therein to avoid reversing the cars in or out. For many years he was the only person in the area to own a car (or rather cars, as he had at least three at this time).

'Who's Who in Motoring' in the 'Motoring Annual' for 1906 records:

'Bartholomew, C. W., Blakesley Hall, near Towcester.
Cars: 12hp Humber, 12hp and 28/36hp Daimlers,
is interested in railways, mechanics and electricity.
Has driven 15,000 miles.
Clubs: Royal Societies, Society of Arts, National Union, Junior Conservatives and the Automobile Club of Great Britain and Ireland (Founder Member).'

He was indeed a Founder Member of what became the Royal Automobile Club, being elected a Member of the Automobile Club of Great Britain on 15 December 1897, just one week after the Club was formally inaugurated. However, this initial interest – and his continuing hands-on involvement with motor vehicles – does not seem to have led him to have any active role in its running or development; he seems simply to have used it as his London Club – with subsequent intriguing literary consequences.

CW with some of his early cars outside Blakesley Hall: '...no gentleman (it was said) thought of having fewer than three cars...' at this time. *The Institution of Civil Engineers Library*

Despite apparently having little social contact with Yorkshire, CW is recorded as being a member of the Yorkshire Yachting Club, although no record has been found of any active participation.

His business responsibilities with, inter alia, The Wombwell Main Colliery Company, particularly following his father's death, obviously took him to Yorkshire regularly. He also sought to ensure that the next generation of the family had the necessary knowledge to maintain their business activities. While CW had been to Trinity College, Cambridge, with its long traditions and high academic reputation, James was instead dispatched in 1911 to a very different environment to learn, at the sharp end, about the industry providing the family's income.

He returned to his father's city of birth to attend the then nearly new University of Sheffield (founded in 1905) for a three-to-four-year 'Diploma Course in Mining'. This had a strong practical bias and required 50 per cent of the time of a 'Day Student' to be spent at the University, the remainder at a colliery – no problem with the latter, of course, the family's collieries being only some 10 miles from Sheffield!

This course would lead to a 'Colliery Manager's First Class Certificate'. As the University's Calendar records that 'This course has been recognised by the Home Secretary under Section 9 of the Coal Mines Act, 1911', it is presumed this new need for an appropriate qualification to manage mining was the reason for this break in Bartholomew family tradition.

While at university, James would have lodged with the Wombwell Main Colliery Manager, Charles Elliott, at Wombwell Hall, there being then a close friendship between the two families (this was to change dramatically later). James represented his father in Wombwell at this time; on 30 June 1913 (very soon after coming of age) he laid the foundation stone for the new tower of St Mary's Church, towards the costs of which CW contributed.

The Great War started just as James finished his third year, requiring his presence elsewhere for that time; there is no record of him (then or later) receiving a degree, which would have been Bachelor of Engineering (Mining). He subsequently entered the legal profession. CW's own business activities were, however, somewhat curtailed during the war as the Government took control of all the nation's collieries; they were not returned to their owners until the 1920s, after CW's death.

The spring of 1917, though in the tragic depths of the Great War, was a very busy time for the Bartholomew family as both James and Ivy were married. James married Charlotte Mabel Hempson (born 1891) at Gatton Church near Reigate during the spring, while Ivy was married at Blakesley Church to Cyril Douglas Birks (born 1890 – and usually known as Douglas) on 7 June; the latter event was a cause for local celebration, with the whole village involved.

At the time of these events, both men were in the Army on active service, James being then a Captain and Douglas a Lieutenant. It is recorded that 'Mrs C. W. and Mrs J. Bartholomew visited the [village] school together with Captain James Bartholomew' in March 1918, and this may have been the first occasion, in view of his wartime duties, that James was properly able to introduce his new wife to the local community.

'My Fair Lady'?

Because both weddings were in wartime, their celebrations were inevitably muted in comparison with the major celebration a little earlier in the Bartholomew household for the coming of age of James – his 21st birthday on 12 June 1913. Those events were spread over several days, including Thursday 19 June 1913, which featured a large attendance of guests including family friends, business colleagues and village worthies.

The most notable guest on the 19th was George Bernard Shaw, the famed playwright and philosopher, then approaching the height of his popularity. His attendance should be considered exceptional and an honour indeed, as he did not celebrate such events at all – he did not attend friends' weddings, nor did he mark birthdays in any way. He once commented: 'Why should I celebrate Shakespear's [sic] birthday? I do not even celebrate my own'!

Shaw had arrived in London from Dublin in 1876 – the same year that CW's father moved to Ealing, and CW married and moved to Blakesley. He was six years younger than CW and both families had a non-conformist church background; however, the friendship almost certainly came from their mutual – and highly active – pioneering interest in motoring, coupled with a similar, if somewhat impish, interest in new scientific discoveries.

CW was, of course, an established (Founder) Member of what became the RAC, while Shaw

The 21st birthday party for James, with guests, outside Blakesley Hall on 19 June 1913. James is standing (centre) behind his seated father. To James's immediate right is Charles Elliott, Manager of Wombwell Main Colliery, while to his left is George Bernard Shaw. Wombwell Heritage Group collection

was granted Life Membership of the Club in June 1908; both men frequently used the Club as a base when in London, the latter at least having a pre-breakfast swim on such occasions.

The contemporary Shaw biographies published over the period 1911 to 1942, despite their lengthy 'name-dropping' generally, appear to make no reference to him visiting Blakesley or knowing the Bartholomews (nor indeed, later – after CW's death – Bassett-Lowke, although he certainly stayed at least twice with the latter at his famous Mackintosh-decorated house at 78 Derngate, Northampton). Shaw was a leading light in the Fabian Society (which was how he came to know Bassett-Lowke), but neither CW nor James were members.

However, Shaw's biographers concentrate on his literary, theatrical and political circles, almost completely ignoring his other interests. A published letter by Shaw to his confidante, Mrs Patrick Campbell, dated Tuesday 17 June 1913, appears to make no reference to his imminent visit to Blakesley on the coming Thursday, but mentions that 'If you will come on Thursday [ie the day of James's party] I will not come up until Friday, though I ought to', the strange grammar suggesting that significant 'editing out' has taken place.

A further letter of his, as published, written the following day, also makes no mention of Blakesley, but this too may have been considerably edited for publication. Accepting these uncertainties, it is tempting to speculate on the extent to which the plots of certain of his plays happen to reflect circumstances in Bartholomew family life.

For example, his play *Pygmalion*, written by 1912 and first performed at the Hofberg Theatre in Vienna in 1913 (and also in Berlin the same year – coincident with James's party – but not performed in England until 1914), features a working-class girl taken and educated, by a man 20 years her senior, in the graces of upper-middle-class families of the time so that she could pass muster in such society – more or less exactly what had happened with Sarah.

Shaw's idea for loosely developing the Greek fable about Pygmalion and Aphrodite into a stage play has been claimed to date back in 1897, although the letter from Shaw to Ellen Terry, upon which this claim is based, is hardly conclusive of this. 1897 was also the year that CW and Shaw are likely to have first come into regular contact via the new Club that was to become the RAC. Conversations with CW there would easily give Shaw the opportunity to know of Sarah's transformation, which took place in the 1880s. The original script contains the words '…we can walk to a motor bus…', placing it clearly in, or just after, the late Edwardian era, by which time the two men would be 'old acquaintances'.

Was Sarah Bartholomew thus, at least in some part, the spark, or the role model, for Eliza Doolittle – My *Fair Lady* – the title of the highly successful musical by which the somewhat expanded plot of *Pygmalion* is today better known? Obviously the London setting is very different from rural Blakesley, as Shaw had one of his lady actor friends in mind for the stage role. A Blakesley village lady who was taken to tea with Sarah Bartholomew in about 1945 has recently described her as then being a '…charming but somewhat confused old lady who didn't have any particular accent…', which suggests that her rural dialect had been eradicated. Is it also pertinent that CW's late two mature sisters, commemorated by him in the churches both in Blakesley and Wombwell, were called Sarah and Eliza?

Family fortunes after CW

CW died on 29 April 1919, his funeral being on 5 May. There was a large turnout for this, including the pupils from the village school, as well as seven representatives of his partners and managers in the various coal-related businesses. His estate at final probate was valued at no less than £335,899 5s 1d. – still a massive sum by today's standards – but considerably less than that of his father's estate (such a sum in 1915 would have had a value today of £14 million, but by 1919 it would only be the equivalent of £7 million as a result of wartime inflation).

To satisfy the legal niceties, the final probate was granted on 11 September 1919 to Sarah Ann Bartholomew 'spinster', as well as James Bartholomew, Richard Donald Bain (the last-named – then HM Assistant Inspector of Mines – had also featured in the probate for CW's father's estate), and a solicitor. The will was comprehensive, retaining the feature found in his father's will of leaving many things in trust for future generations, rather than as outright bequests.

The Hall was thus not left to Sarah, although she had the right to continue to live there 'during the remainder of her life'. She remained involved in village affairs – as did James – and she still wielded considerable power and influence. The annual Show was not held during the Great War, and was not revived until the early 1920s; unfortunately heavy rains washed it out in both 1931 and 1932, leading to it again being discontinued until 1944.

In the 1940s two events affected the Bartholomew fortunes. In 1944 a Miss Dorothy Elliott (the daughter of the late Charles Elliott, former Colliery Manager), the Secretary of The Wombwell Main Colliery Company, representing one of the major sources of capital and income to the family, was found guilty of embezzling the then huge sum of £91,630 from the company, and its associated coking operations, between 1936 and 1943. She received a sentence of six years penal servitude. That scale of financial loss almost ruined the company and decimated the family finances – she reappears later in our story. After the fraud was discovered, the colliery company was forced to sell off many of the houses it owned in Wombwell, including those in Bartholomew Street, just to raise some cash for the company to keep it afloat.

Then, on 1 January 1947, the National Coal Board came into being, taking over the assets of all private colliery companies, including of course those part-owned by the Bartholomew family, through nationalisation; the family received a substantial sum of money in compensation, but a sum drastically diminished from what it should have been because of Dorothy's escapades.

On the eve of nationalisation, the Wombwell Main Colliery Company's Vice-Chairman of Directors was CW's son James (by now Major James Bartholomew MBE), while James's son Charles Edward was also a director; just as in 1853, the Bartholomew and Roberts families were still in sole control of the company.

By 1947 Sarah was 84 and, in view of her deteriorating health, it became prudent for son James to move his mother to his own home, then at Saham Toney Hall, Watton, Norfolk; she died on 26 January 1953, aged 89. The contents of the

The Blakesley Hall Miniature Railway

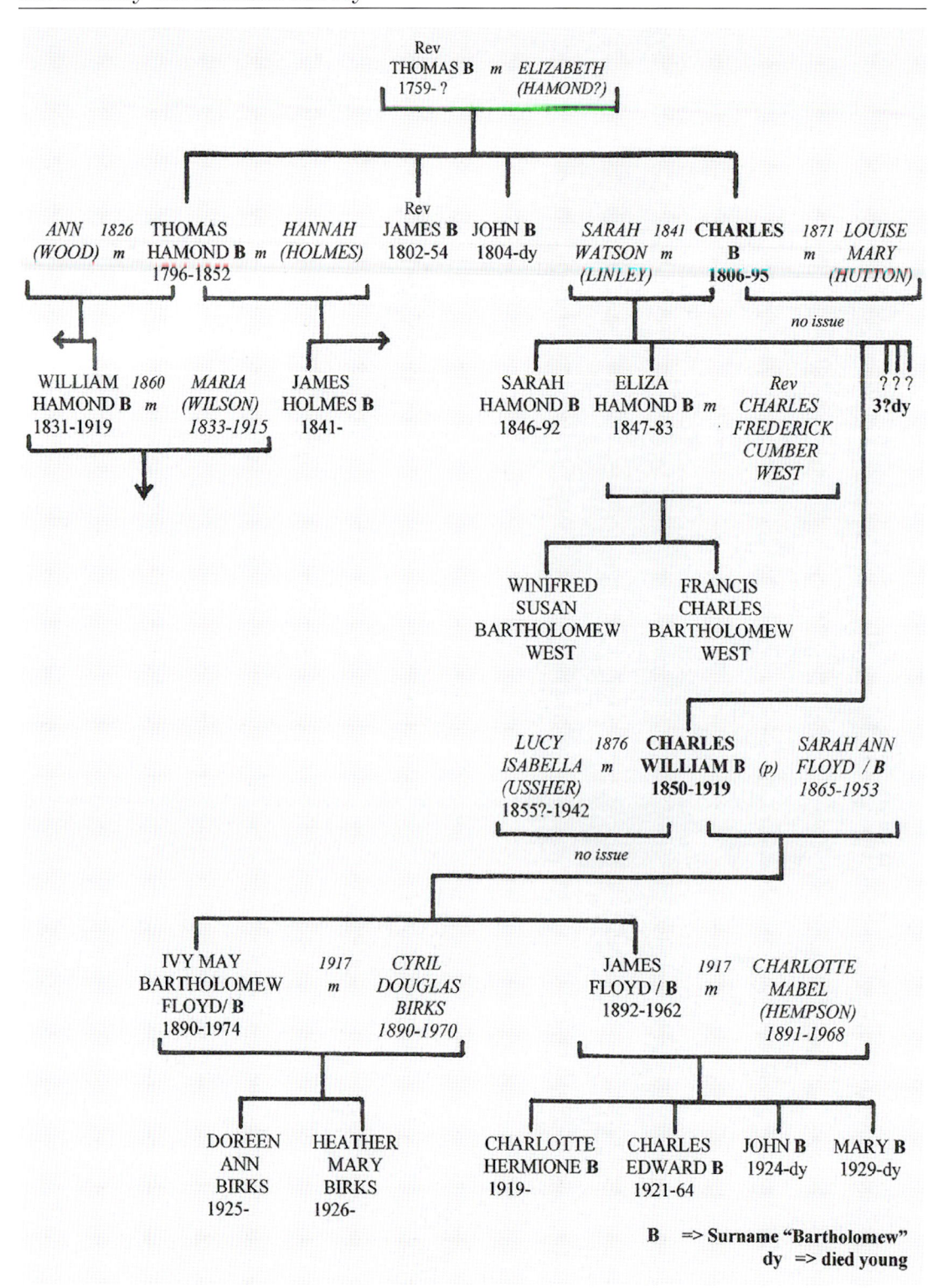

```
                          Rev
                          THOMAS B  m  ELIZABETH
                          1759-?       (HAMOND?)
    ┌──────────┬──────────┬──────────┬──────────┬──────────┐
                          Rev
ANN   1826  THOMAS    HANNAH    JAMES B   JOHN B    SARAH 1841 CHARLES 1871 LOUISE
(WOOD)  m   HAMOND B m (HOLMES) 1802-54   1804-dy   WATSON m     B      m   MARY
            1796-1852                               (LINLEY)   1806-95      (HUTTON)
                                                                        no issue
WILLIAM  1860  MARIA    JAMES          SARAH       ELIZA        Rev             ???
HAMOND B  m   (WILSON)  HOLMES B       HAMOND B    HAMOND B  m  CHARLES         3?dy
1831-1919     1833-1915 1841-          1846-92     1847-83      FREDERICK
                                                                CUMBER
                                                                WEST
                                              ┌──────────────────┐
                                         WINIFRED            FRANCIS
                                         SUSAN               CHARLES
                                         BARTHOLOMEW         BARTHOLOMEW
                                         WEST                WEST

                              LUCY      1876  CHARLES        SARAH ANN
                              ISABELLA    m   WILLIAM B  (p) FLOYD / B
                              (USSHER)       1850-1919       1865-1953
                              1855?-1942
                                  no issue

        IVY MAY        1917   CYRIL              JAMES      1917   CHARLOTTE
        BARTHOLOMEW     m     DOUGLAS            FLOYD / B   m     MABEL
        FLOYD/ B              BIRKS              1892-1962         (HEMPSON)
        1890-1974             1890-1970                            1891-1968

              DOREEN    HEATHER        CHARLOTTE   CHARLES    JOHN B    MARY B
              ANN       MARY           HERMIONE B  EDWARD B   1924-dy   1929-dy
              BIRKS     BIRKS          1919-       1921-64
              1925-     1926-

                                              B  => Surname "Bartholomew"
                                              dy => died young
```

Charles Bartholomew's family tree (including other waterway/engineering members).

The cover of the sale brochure for Blakesley Hall in 1949.
Anne & John Weekley collection

Hall featured in an eight-day sale from 23 September to 1 October 1947.

The 'Residential and Agricultural Estate' (as described by the auctioneers) itself was offered separately; it was finally auctioned on 7 September 1949 at 3pm at the Angel Hotel in Northampton. Sold initially to the Hesketh family, it then passed through other ownership where few changes were made, the Hall itself remaining empty until the by then ruinous shell was demolished in 1957.

To complete the recording of this branch of the Bartholomew family, we should note that James and Charlotte Mabel had two children, Charlotte Hermione (born in 1919, shortly after CW's death) and Charles Edward (born in 1921); the latter attended Trinity College, Cambridge, like his grandfather, although the Second World War cut short his attendance there. Two other children, John, born in 1924, and Mary, born in 1929, died within days of their births, while Charles Edward died in 1964. James died in 1962 and Charlotte Mabel in 1968.

Ivy and Douglas had two children, Doreen Ann, born in 1925, and Heather Mary, born in 1926. Douglas died in 1970 and Ivy in 1974. Bearing in mind one of the strange provisions of CW's will, it is perhaps surprising that neither Doreen nor Heather had 'Bartholomew' as a Christian name. However, their second names (Ann and Mary respectively) combine to commemorate their great-grandmother – Sarah's mother – Mary Ann Floyd (née Lawrence). The direct family line from CW is continued through Heather's children.

4 Railways large and small

The 'Shakespeare Route'

The earliest form of transport in the Blakesley area was the carrier's cart; in 1849 there were carriers to Northampton on Saturdays and to Towcester on Tuesdays, and further 'services' followed. However, Blakesley was about to be linked, if somewhat humbly, to the growing national railway network.

The new line's impecunious existence in its early years was to have a profound and long-lasting effect on the future of the Bartholomew family and its members by playing a major part not only in the break-up of CW's marriage, but also in his meeting his second partner – and on the circumstances that in due course surrounded the building of a miniature railway at Blakesley, and on its continuance for many years even after the Squire's death.

On 23 June 1864 an Act of Parliament authorised the construction of the East & West Junction Railway (E&WJR) from the Northampton & Banbury Junction Railway at Greens Norton, near Towcester, to a junction with the Stratford and Honeybourne branch of the Great Western Railway at Old Stratford, passing through Blakesley en route; certain additional running powers were also granted. The share capital authorised was £300,000, with powers to borrow £100,000.

The first sod was cut by Lady Palmerston at Towcester on 3 August 1864 in the presence of her husband, who was then the Prime Minister. Sadly such a prestigious presence at the inauguration did not confer success, and a further Act was required in 1866 to double both the original share capital and the borrowing powers. However, the company was unable to raise the necessary monies and work had to be suspended until adequate finance could be secured.

The first section from Fenny Compton to

An invitation to subscribe for E&WJR Debenture Stock. *Author's collection*

Kineton finally opened on 1 June 1871, followed by Kineton to Stratford and Fenny Compton to Greens Norton (this last section passing through Blakesley), both on 1 July 1873 – although not without another Act allowing further funds to be raised. The vast majority of the earthworks were built to take double track, but only a lightly laid single line could be afforded, with passing places as necessary – one of these was at Blakesley.

In keeping with the struggle to raise the original finance, the line did not prove a success and, despite the passing of yet another debenture-authorising Act, the line passed into receivership on 29 January 1875. Things were so bad that on 31 January 1877 passenger services had to be suspended – an almost unheard-of occurrence in Victorian times. They were not to be resumed until 22 March 1885.

The passenger service through Blakesley was thus suspended a bare few months after CW and his new wife moved into Blakesley Hall in August 1876, and for more than eight years an awkward and tedious journey by horse or horse-drawn carriage would be required to reach the main-line network. Fortunately it was not necessary to have to go as far as the London & North Western Railway's main-line station at Blisworth, since the Northampton & Banbury Junction line was still providing its (somewhat limited) passenger service through Towcester.

This comparative isolation must have proved too much for Lucy, however, contributing to, if not causing, the break-up of the marriage. Contrarily, the restoration of the local passenger services in 1885 facilitated CW's second partner, Sarah, moving from Byfield, where she had been 'in service' and had kept house for her father, to Blakesley.

Despite some references saying otherwise, CW does not seem to have been a Director of the E&WJR (or its successors), but there is evidence that he was a holder of E&WJR Debenture Stock by 1900; there may have been an ulterior motive in his holding of this stock, as we shall see later!

There was no doubt, however, that CW was regarded as a significant personage by this complex, if impecunious, network of railways. He was recorded as being among the few local dignitaries present at the cutting of the first sod for the long-awaited Towcester to Olney link by the nominally separate Stratford-upon-Avon, Towcester & Midland Junction Railway on 15 December 1887.

The hand-to-mouth existence of the E&WJR extended to its locomotive and carriage fleets, which included a motley collection of cast-offs from other railways. Apart from a couple of early French locomotives, there is evidence of some desperation when it is realised that the company used, albeit briefly, a standard-gauge 'double Fairlie' (a cancelled order from a Mexican railway!), while in the following year of 1877 it ran for an even shorter period the only 'single Fairlie' to run on a British standard-gauge line – one of these two was almost certainly the first loco with Walschaerts valve gear to run in Britain.

The E&WJR and its related companies had even resorted, on occasion, to hiring in locomotives from the famous 'Boulton's Siding' at Ashton. Of the three (or possibly four) hired, the company broke one and defaulted on the payments for the pair! Matters did improve and, although purchases of second-hand locos were made from the LNWR and the London, Brighton & South Coast Railway, a number of new Beyer Peacock ones arrived too, including a series of double-framed 0-6-0 tender types.

An important event, both for the E&WJR and for CW, was the opening of the 'London Extension' main line of the Great Central Railway in 1899 through from Annesley to Marylebone. Not only did this cross (and connect with) the E&WJR at Woodford, just to the west of Blakesley, where a large locomotive depot and sidings were created, but it also offered CW a fast and direct passenger train service from Woodford to Sheffield, close to the heart of his colliery operations in South Yorkshire. His Wombwell Main coal deliveries to Blakesley Hall also came this way!

One still-surviving village tale about CW concerns how apparently he sometimes used to be allowed to drive the main-line passenger trains, and that one night he pulled up beyond the platform at Blakesley and had to reverse back a few yards. A passenger, coincidentally one of his own employees, demanded irately at the cab steps, 'What bloody fool is driving tonight?', only to be confronted by his boss!

On 1 August 1908 the Stratford-upon-Avon & Midland Junction Railway Act was passed, which amalgamated the E&WJR line with other local lines with effect from 1 January 1909. The Northampton & Banbury Junction joined the new company on 1 July 1910, following a further Act of 29 April 1910. The new management team rapidly

The Blakesley Hall Miniature Railway

Above An S&MJR 'Beware of Trains' sign, as found at line crossings (including those adjacent to the Blakesley miniature railway). *Author*

Below The author's career has involved the modern guided bus concept, so the LMS 'Road-Railer' Karrier bus is of particular interest to him. Views of it actually in service are rare, but here it is about to leave Stratford for Blisworth via Blakesley. *Author's collection*

brought order and even near prosperity to the newly formed company; this was perhaps exemplified by the new company's telegraphic address in Stratford – 'Regularity'!

The S&MJR adopted the slogan the 'Shakespeare Route' and applied this to everything from the humble luggage label to timetables and posters (though not to rolling stock). The First World War brought increased traffic to the line, which became part of the LMS with effect from 1 January 1923.

Two highlights of innovation on this little line may be mentioned. First was the pioneering demonstration, no doubt witnessed by CW, on 28 June 1912 of an electrical system – the RAILOPHONE – whereby a signalman was able to talk to train crew and indeed even to halt remotely a steam-hauled train in full flight. Second was the operation, for a few months in 1932 under LMS auspices, of a Karrier (of Huddersfield) 'Road-Railer' bus providing a connection from the West Coast Main Line at Blisworth, through Blakesley, to Stratford on the railway, then continuing on the highway to the railway-owned luxury Welcombe Hotel there.

This vehicle had a Cravens (of Sheffield) 26-seater body, and was registered UR 7924. Effectively a carefully thought-out adaptation of a road bus, it had both road and flanged rail wheels and a gearbox with high and normal ratios for rail and road operation respectively. Although primarily intended to provide a through link to and from the Welcombe Hotel, it did call en route for passengers at the ex-S&MJR station at Stratford, from where the only known eye-witness account by a genuine passenger records '…I entrained for a fast, but ear-shattering journey back to Blisworth, calling only at Towcester…'

It was not entirely successful, the 'Road-Railer' service running (non-stop) through Blakesley only from 23 April until some time in June, when it is believed that problems arose with the front axle; it was officially withdrawn from 2 July 1932. How the single-line staffs were exchanged at loops such as that at Blakesley is not known – perhaps the 'conductor' performed the task, using the either-side central doorways.

With the 'Road-Railer' failure, and therefore no 'through' LMS service for most of the time, the elite passengers for the luxury Welcombe Hotel needed to interchange at Stratford, and the buffet at the LMS's Stratford station was thus graced with facilities of rather higher quality than would perhaps normally befit a 'country' station.

The Second World War again brought a significant, if temporary, growth in traffic, and the line was nationalised into the British Railways system with effect from 1 January 1948. Closure of the passenger services soon followed, the last such through Blakesley being on 5 April 1952 (official closure was from 7 April). Freight continued for a few more years until the line through Blakesley was eventually closed completely from 3 February 1964, the tracks being lifted over the following year and a half.

(For want of anywhere more appropriate to record it, and in view of this section being primarily concerned with standard-gauge railways, it will be mentioned here that the 1929-built Great Western Railway 'Hall' Class 4-6-0 tender locomotive No 4909 *BLAKESLEY HALL* was not named after the Northamptonshire Hall, but after one built in 1590 that still stands near Yardley, some 4 miles east of Birmingham city centre.)

15-inch pre-history

While the last quarter of the 19th century appears to have been the start of 15 inches as an accepted gauge, it actually has a history going back into the mists of time in connection with mining. The

Although slightly blurred, this is the best early view located that shows the S&MJR station at Blakesley together with the 15-inch miniature railway station. *R. M. Casserley collection*

47

choice of such a gauge in a mine may have been determined locally by the difficulties in hand-cutting the access tunnels.

The earliest claim for a 15-inch-gauge line of which the author is aware was in the George & Charlotte Mine at Morwellham in Devon, which has been quoted (as a 15-inch wooden way) to date from the 18th century. This deployment of the gauge was purely for commercial and industrial purposes, an approach to be expounded much later by Arthur Heywood. It has been claimed that the Norris Locomotive Works of Philadelphia in America built a 15-inch locomotive for Japan as early as 1854, but evidence is that this was actually of around 2-foot gauge.

The earliest substantiated 15-inch-gauge locomotive is PEARL, a sandwich-framed 2-2-2 built by Peter Brotherhood around 1859-62, and preserved today at King's College, London. Brotherhood lived in Chippenham, deep in Great Western territory, and the external detail of the model included certain major visual characteristics of GWR broad-gauge engines of the period, giving it a rather old-fashioned appearance.

It does not appear to be an exact model, but has a close technical resemblance to a batch of six express locomotives built by Robert Stephenson & Co for the Midland Railway in 1852 as its Nos 130-135. Detailed drawings of this particular design featured in the 1856 *Imperial Cyclopaedia of Machinery* and the model is almost exactly quarter-scale to these in all dimensions except in the gauge; as such it looks very small indeed in comparison with later 15-inch models. The noted early railway modeller J. N. Maskelyne, while the first to suggest the dimensional similarity of PEARL to the MR design, '…came to the conclusion that it represents no particular prototype, and that the proportions in detail are not altogether satisfactory…'

Perhaps the need to fit fully working inside cylinders and valve-gear of the appropriate size caused the correct 14⅝-inch gauge to be widened to a more manageable 15 inches. This idea of adapting a full-size design into a slightly 'freelance' model (representing '…no particular prototype…') was to be the precursor to the approach of virtually all subsequent 15-inch locomotive designers. Such a 'freelance' approach was not to prove particularly popular, especially in the gauges above and below 15 inches – model engineers Waller Martin & Co asked in one of their adverts, 'Do you wish to make or buy a correct Model Locomotive, one that IS a Model, and not a strange and wonderful combination of several types of engine?'

However, while these examples were indeed of 15-inch gauge, and the first such loco was of freelance miniature outline rather than minimum gauge, it is highly unlikely that they – or any other early examples – had any influence whatsoever on what was to come.

The Heywood influence

Arthur Percival Heywood, later Sir Arthur Heywood, was a 'Gentleman', but with an amateur engineering passion, his grandfather having been granted a baronetcy for his support of the 1832 Reform Act (Percival – a common forename in this branch of the family – was the maiden surname of his great-grandmother).

Born on Christmas Day 1849 at Dove Leys in Staffordshire, Arthur Percival Heywood entered Trinity College, Cambridge, in the same year (1868) as C. W. Bartholomew. Unlike CW, however, he completed his course – with distinction – in the normal timescale.

It should not be forgotten that social position was taken very seriously in this era. Heywood, eldest son of a 'Gentleman' and baronet (even though a recently created one), had been at Eton, while CW, eldest child (and only son) of a new-monied 'Engineer' (though also an extremely rich, influential and propertied businessman), had 'only' been to Uppingham. Despite their common interests and simultaneous arrival at this same small college, this distinction could ordinarily have kept them apart.

However, as we have seen, the two families were closely connected through business and transport activities in the West Riding. Both having a common amateur interest in railways, they were, in the years that were to follow, to conceive, develop, pioneer, use and establish along diametrically different paths virtually all the key components and options for 15-inch-gauge railways in all their many and varied forms – and which were to sustain that concept in its entirety for the next 100 years.

It would appear from CW's later actions that, whether on a personal or an engineering basis, he was either totally disinterested in, or disagreed wholeheartedly with, what Heywood would seek to achieve with his railway developments, and in due course, perhaps deliberately, approached everything in as opposite a fashion as he could, thereby establishing the parallel miniature railway to counter the latter's minimum gauge ideas. It is therefore necessary to understand Heywood's approach, so that CW's contrary actions can be placed in context.

Arthur Heywood sought to determine by practical experiment what he felt was the minimum gauge, given the technology available at that time, for a railway system able to perform useful work, including the carriage both of goods and passengers. After initially experimenting with 4-inch-gauge and 9-inch-gauge railways at the family estate at Dove Leys in Staffordshire, he had moved into his own home (as with CW, provided by his father upon his marriage) at Duffield Bank, Derbyshire, with his new wife Effie, in 1872.

He concluded that '…stability of this 9in line was perfect enough so long as persons did not attempt to ride on the ends and edges of carriages and wagons, but man being an article of approximately standard size, it is clear there must be a minimum gauge which will be stable enough to be independent of such liberties.'

In 1874 he began to lay down at Duffield Bank a line of his chosen 'minimum gauge' – 15 inches, '…as the smallest width possessing the necessary stability for practical use…' – with fearsome gradients (as steep as 1 in 10) and equally fearsome curves (down to 25-foot radius). The names of sections of the railway suggested various family locations, including 'The Plain of York', which seems likely to relate to the West Riding family branches (as their various residences gave splendid views out towards the Plain of York – just as Duffield Bank gave splendid views out over the Derwent Valley).

The latter's first locomotive, understandably named *EFFIE*, was completed in 1875. From this point he developed locomotives and rolling stock to their ultimate, logical conclusion in accordance with his specific principles. He had studied C. E. Spooner's work on small-gauge railways (notably the Festiniog) in some detail, which suggested that a width of around 2½ times the gauge would be stable for railways of 2-foot gauge. He believed that he could better this with the even smaller gauge, as he agreed with Spooner's view that the practical vehicle width did not reduce in proportion to the narrowing of the adopted gauge; thus choosing the minimum possible gauge would allow a proportionately larger load.

All his locomotives after *EFFIE* conformed to a fairly standard design, though differing in size and number of wheels; they had all wheels coupled, with a flexible wheelbase and an equal overhang at each end. Launch-type fireboxes helped in producing such a symmetrical design of chassis, while cabs were deemed impractical in comparison with the shelter afforded by a stout mackintosh! Even the valve-gear was chosen to keep parts as high off the ground as practicable. These locos had a standard width of 3ft 10in – 3.1 times the 15-inch track gauge.

Clearly such engines could in no way be considered as miniature replicas of full-size locomotives, but had a unique – and rather old-fashioned for their time – character quite unlike anything else. With their flexible wheelbase and lack of carrying wheels, remarkably sharp curves and vicious gradients (such as those at Duffield Bank) could be negotiated with comparative ease.

His carriages and wagons were similarly designed to make maximum productive use of this 'minimum gauge', open and closed bogie carriages progressing even to dining and sleeping cars. Thus he developed carriages with an overall width of some 42 inches – 2.8 times the track gauge.

Heywood's wagons, their loads being less predictable than passengers, were of slightly lesser width, 3 feet (2.4 times the track gauge), and were arranged to have removable boxes (open top and bottom) on their flat bases, allowing loads of similar weight but different densities to be carried on the same wagon at different times through judicious use of these interlocking boxes.

This multi-purpose principle extended to his recommendation of the use of pairs of these wagons as independent 'bogies' coupled directly together under large loads, their boxes being replaced by what he called 'swivelling carriers' (or bolsters).

William Hamond Bartholomew's 'Tom Pudding' compartment boats as transported by rail to and from Stanley Ferry adopted Heywood's principle of using two independent trucks coupled together with the load resting directly on, and straddling, each truck – rather than them being bogies under a full-length body frame. It is tempting to speculate that, in developing this transporter idea in 1891, William enlisted the aid not only of his uncle Charles (with his extensive standard-gauge railway experience), but also of Arthur Heywood through the Heywood family connections with the A&C.

Bartholomew 'maximum width' rather than Heywood 'minimum gauge'! One of William Bartholomew's 15-feet-wide 'Tom Pudding' compartment boats, having come by standard-gauge railway with 40 tons of coal from St Johns Colliery, is lowered into his A&C Navigation at Stanley Ferry. *Old Barnsley collection (B1075)*

However, Bartholomew rather disproved both Spooner's and Heywood's ideas about the improved proportional load-width to reduced-gauge argument, with his compartments being 3.2 times wider than the (standard) track gauge; this shows that Heywood's conservatism was still failing to determine the true limits and take proper practical advantage of the 15-inch gauge. (With modern materials and bogie suspension systems, the 15-inch-gauge Ravenglass & Eskdale Railway re-took this ratio lead for the minimum gauge a century later, with its 'Maxi' carriages being more than 3.4 times wider than the gauge.)

Heywood made valiant efforts to interest others in his minimum gauge ideas, including the military, through a series of 'Open Days' and the like at Duffield Bank. The first of these had coincided with the 1881 Annual Show of the Royal Agricultural Society (of which his father, Thomas Percival Heywood, had been elected a Life Governor in 1844-45), held locally in Derby that year.

Despite all this activity, only one 'commercial' Heywood railway was built – the Eaton Railway serving the Duke of Westminster's estate at Eaton Hall near Chester, which resulted from one of Heywood's Open Days at Duffield Bank in 1894. This was the year before Charles Bartholomew died; had this major Open Day at Duffield Bank been exactly one year later, just as CW inherited his financial freedom, the entire course of 15-inch estate railways might perhaps have been dramatically different – and less interesting! However, as we have seen, the timing of the first motor show by Sir David Salomons was perfect for CW, and an alternative way of pursuing an estate railway would be needed to arouse his interest.

Heywood succeeded to the baronetcy in October 1897, upon his father's death – which rather changed his family and related responsibilities, and thus the amount of time he could devote to his 'amateur' activities. Indeed, as head of the family he moved to Dove Leys as his formal home. Here he continued development on a further 15-inch line for this estate.

After one last major 'fling' at Duffield Bank in 1898, he did continue to hold lesser 'Open Sessions' there for invited guests. The final such event was from 20 to 22 August 1903, by which time a new 15-inch cause was rising. As Howard Clayton notes, 'By the time the Eaton Railway was completed in 1896, the future of the Heywood system was doomed. Already the first motor cars were spluttering their way along the roads; the petrol engine had arrived, and it was plain to see that the day of the "minimum gauge" railway was over.'

Unaccountably, Heywood completely ignored the potential both of this new power and new mode of transport, but not so CW, who, with his recently inherited money, had actually now himself built a quite different kind of 15-inch estate railway – one that was to prove the real catalyst for its development throughout the 20th century.

The Cagney influence

Heywood had been the British exponent and advocate of 15 inches as the ideal minimum gauge for practical narrow-gauge railways, able to carry both goods and passenger traffic. In contrast, the influence in America was to establish the role of the passenger-carrying miniature railway for pleasure, with locomotives and some of the other features being miniature replicas, in the style of those on the full-size railway, and in a variety of gauges to suit different circumstances.

Commercial needs ultimately demonstrated here too the particular suitability of the 15-inch gauge (or thereabouts). It was this pleasure role, not the commercial one of Heywood, that was to dominate the British scene in this gauge, and it was C. W. Bartholomew who was, with his Blakesley railway, to pioneer, acquire and develop the cause of the 'permanent' miniature railway in Britain from these American temporary exhibition origins.

It is therefore necessary to understand the complex principles behind the American products to appreciate how CW could initiate such dramatic developments in Britain. Although the full story is highly complex (and still has many uncertainties), it may be useful to record the principal facts as currently understood, as these may help to establish the origins of particular locomotives and carriages in Britain (and particularly those at Blakesley).

The catalyst for this considerable activity in America was Timothy G. Cagney, a member of an entrepreneurial family in such fields as property speculation and development, ticket agencies, and legal and banking services, as well as some 'showmen' activities.

In about 1885, roughly contemporary with Heywood's mainstream development work, Peter and Thomas McGarigle of Niagara Falls, New York, came up with the concept of a model railway of sufficient size that it could carry passengers as a recreational activity. Their initial product – of 9½-inch gauge (one-sixth scale) – was purely for their own family's pleasure and not intended as a commercial production item. Having a significant and partly railway-based engineering business, the McGarigle Machine Company, they were easily able to develop a design of small steam locomotive.

The Cagney and McGarigle families knew each other through the Irish-American community. Timothy realised the amusement park potential of such a miniature railway – and also the potential of Miss Winifred McGarigle, whom he married in 1887. In May 1898 Timothy Cagney publicly ran the McGarigle's family train on a freight depot site of the Lehigh Valley Railroad, in an effort to secure investment support for a company to market such a product.

The Miniature Railway Company (of New Jersey and New York) was duly incorporated in 1898 by Timothy Cagney, with his brothers David and John, as well as the McGarigles; the company name sometimes appears (technically incorrectly) with 'Railroad' rather than 'Railway'.

A very early 12⅜-inch 'Cagney' train at Island Park, Easton, Pa, with its youthful driver. The old-style loco carries the number '2002'. This line was on an island in the Lehigh River, accessible only via the Lehigh Valley Railroad. *Keith Taylor collection*

In line with their established aggressive business practice, most references to the new company also referred to the 'Cagney Brothers'; the terms were virtually interchangeable in catalogues and letters. The locos and coaches were built at the McGarigle 'machine shops' at Niagara Falls, which opened in 1898. Little time was now lost and a 12⅜-inch-gauge loco was developed, based on what was a typical, but even then old-fashioned, American 4-4-0 tender locomotive, some one-third greater than the company's original one-sixth scale 9½-inch example.

Before the end of that year, a line of this gauge was in operation at the Trans Mississippi Expo at Omaha. The Chairman of the New York Central & Hudson River Railroad Co, Chauncey M. Depew, was moved to write to The Miniature Railway Co in January 1899, describing a ride on its Omaha Exposition line as '...the best Lilliputian representation of the Great Railway System of the United States in existence'.

This early loco at Omaha was apparently branded as No 890 of the Union Pacific Railroad Co, with cow-catcher, headlight and a representation of the traditional shallow-roofed wooden cab. Thus far, the miniature trains had only developed from a gauge of 9½ inches to 12⅜ inches. However, the early work had demonstrated a number of limitations of these, and a more modern-looking 15-inch-gauge version followed, to be quickly copied in 12⅜ inches as well, both probably in 1899. Officially, the locos were described in their catalogues as being '...of the standard eight-wheeled American type'; the smaller version was designated as Class C, with the larger as Class D.

It remains unclear as to how Cagney and McGarigle decided upon their 'new' gauge of 15 inches; there is a remote possibility that the idea came indirectly from Heywood, as the opening of his Eaton Railway in the mid-1890s provided much publicity for it. However, the first Cagney train to reach Scotland (in 1901) was reported to be running on 14½-inch-gauge track (double 7¼ inches and very close to one-quarter full-size). Certainly Cagney's 15-inch gauge as a standard was less 'definitive' in the USA than it became in the UK – as examples at 15½ inches and 16 inches (and probably also 14½ inches) are also known, while 7½ inches was (and is) also a common gauge.

In 1893, a New York Central & Hudson River Railroad Co 4-4-0 loco, No 999, had captured the imagination of the American public with a claim for a world speed record of 112mph achieved over a measured mile on 10 May hauling the 'Empire State Express' (a claim subsequently hotly disputed, it must be said, by British recorders of train speeds!).

No 999 was anything but a 'standard ... American type', having, by USA standards, huge driving wheels (their 7ft 2in even requiring small splashers above the already high running plate) and a three-side-window arch-roofed wooden cab. Built specifically for high speed, it was in due course rebuilt with smaller (5ft 10in) driving wheels for continuing use on the 'Empire State Express'.

However fanciful the speed claim might have been, this was just the sort of stimulus needed to create enthusiasm for miniature railways in the USA, the Miniature Railway Company being directly involved in the development and operation of many of these lines.

Several of the miniature locos inevitably appeared in America with the legend '999' on the cab-sides, but the company itself did not claim any such resemblance in its catalogues; it is also notable that none of the various Cagney locos that came to Britain in the early 1900s carried the '999' identity, and this spurious link seems to be a fairly recent phenomenon here (long after their original disappearance from the British exhibition circuits).

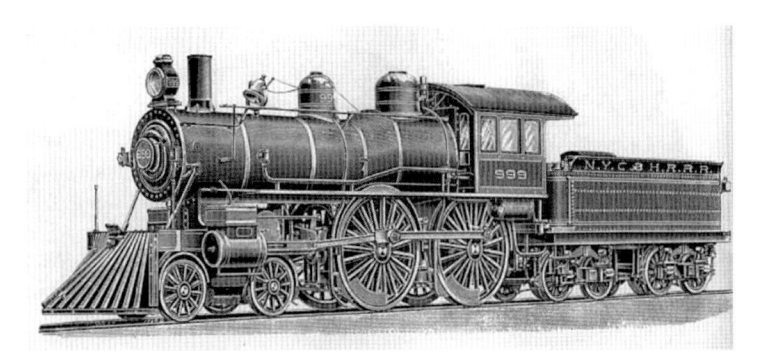

New York Central & Hudson River Railroad Co 4-4-0 No 999, for which a world speed record of 112mph was claimed while working the 'Empire State Express' on 10 May 1893. It needed splashers for its original 7ft 2in wheels, unusual for American locos.
Keith Taylor collection

Railways large and small

The '999' legend as applied to Cagneys endured for many years. Here the author's elder son Peter poses on a 22-inch Class E Cagney of 1905, so branded, in Florida in August 1986. *Author*

Strangely enough, there was a 15-inch-gauge model design available in the USA that did bear a close resemblance to the Buchannan-designed classes that included 999, with their three-window cabs and large driving wheels. Accurate scale drawings and castings for the rebuilt smaller-wheeled version were available at the turn of the century for 3½, 4¾, 7¼, and 15-inch-gauge versions from an engineering firm, Olney & Warren; at least one is known to have been built in 15-inch gauge.

The design was itself enlarged in 1903 (confusingly with the same class designations), although its production launch was delayed until the 1904 St Louis World's Fair. By 1904 a new 22-inch-gauge Class E had also been produced (though few of these were built – mainly in 1904 and 1905). In all cases, the coupled driving wheels were proportionately far too small (scaling out at only about 4 feet) compared with those on the real No 999 – but were eminently suitable for (relatively) lower speed and greater pulling power.

Among the complications are that the McGarigles, though possessing a substantial engineering facility, did not have a boiler shop; boilers were made instead initially by the Armitage-Herschell Co, which went bankrupt in 1899 but continued to function in receivership; eventually the work was taken over by the Herschell-Spillman Co (and still later by Spillman Engineering). The design work for every 'Cagney' loco was by Peter McGarigle.

Loco origins were identified by a cast-iron smokebox door ring, with supplier, address and building date cast therein. The Cagney Brothers ticket and property address moved from 301 Broadway, New York City, to 407 Broadway during 1902, the numbers on the ring changing accordingly, although the MR Co office remained at the Cagney's home at 395 Ogden Avenue, Jersey City. The McGarigle shops built the first 'improved Class D' (with heavier frames and a longer wheelbase) and the first of the new Class E locos in 1904.

Sadly, a rift was to develop between the families. One issue was the pressure of the St Louis Fair in 1904, as the Cagneys felt that Miniature Railway Co needs should take precedence over the McGarigles' other work. However, it would also appear that the Cagneys were accused of 'false advertising' at this time, leading to the loss of the company's New Jersey Charter, which did not please the McGarigles.

The Cagney brothers thus took the patterns and tooling for these new designs and established a new shop and sales business of their own in Jersey City, producing their first locos there in 1905; for the first time, therefore, the words 'Cagney Brothers' now appeared on loco smokebox rings.

The McGarigles, maintaining a long engineering association with the Herschell-Spillman Co and its successors, continued to build the earlier and lighter Class C and D models, but with the latter company's name and its North Tonawanda (New York) address on the smokebox ring (they were of course fitted with Herschell-Spillman boilers!).

In simple terms, therefore (and in particular relevance to our future story), 'Cagney' locos built between 1898 and 1904 would actually have been marketed by the Miniature Railway Co, were built by the McGarigles, and probably had their boilers supplied by Armitage-Herschell (while bankrupt)! It is possible that very similar machines, marketed by Herschell-Spillman, might have been built entirely by them around this time.

After 1904, most, if not all, locos from these various suppliers had 'wagon-top' boilers with raised firebox crowns; these came mainly from Herschell-Spillman, although some of the boilers for Cagney's own production (possibly only the last batch of about 1924) were made by Cousins of Jersey City.

The aim of the Miniature Railway Company was to provide a complete railway product; hence a 15-inch Class D loco was supplied with bogie tender on which the engineer (or driver) rode, as well as a complete train of ten four-wheeled carriages, each seating two adults (or four small children) face-to-face. The complete outfit turned the scales at 2,450lb (the loco, tender and each carriage weighing 1,000lb, 200lb and 125lb respectively). Locomotives were not supplied on their own!

(The Class letter designation actually referred not only to the gauge, but also to the complete train rather than just to the locomotive – hence a Class D loco would be supplied also with Class D carriages, irrespective of the type of carriage involved.)

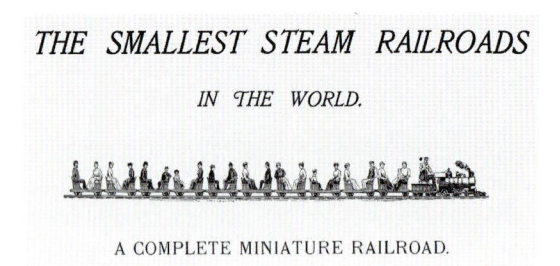

THE SMALLEST STEAM RAILROADS
IN THE WORLD.

A COMPLETE MINIATURE RAILROAD.

The Cagney catalogue, 1902-3.

The 15-inch-gauge four-wheeled carriages were only 21 inches wide (hence their inability to seat more than one adult abreast); this was a consequence of the first 15-inch-gauge locos and carriages being simply created using earlier 12⅜-inch components on extended axles (their bodies being even narrower). The McGarigles also seem not to have appreciated for many years what Heywood had determined by experiment at the start of the 1880s – that up to 2.8 times the track gauge on 15 inches would still be stable for passengers. These early carriages had simple and crude axle bearings.

At some time around the turn of the century, the original four-wheeled carriage (or, in American parlance, 'car') design with two facing seats was supplemented by two new carriage designs. One, the 'Small Gold Medal Special Car', featured the same underframe and running gear as the original design (now designated the 'Small Regular Style Car') but with curvaceous and decorated panelled sides and 'finely upholstered back and seats'; these were designed to be easily taken apart and re-assembled, no doubt for travelling showmen's use.

In addition, a wider, bogie, carriage was introduced in 1902, in time to first appear in the company's 1902-03 catalogue, known as the 'Large Gold Medal Special, Adjustable Canopy Top Car' (the terms 'Small' and 'Large' referring to four-wheeled and bogie cars respectively). This had two compartments, upholstered in similar fashion to the 'Small Gold Medal Special Car', but now with a total rated capacity of eight adults or 12 children each. The adjustable-height canopy '…can be placed to any height desired, up to 7½ feet from track to top of canopy', which was, of course, also removable entirely.

With these bogie cars the Cagneys finally took advantage of the stability afforded by the 15-inch gauge to widen the bodies to 3 feet, compared to the 4-wheelers' 21 inches; hence the doubling of adult capacity per seat. Heywood had been using 3ft 6in-wide carriages for more than 20 years at this time, but he did so on a prepared, stable trackbed, whereas the Cagney equipment would often be used on a rough or poorly consolidated base.

In contrast to the ten four-wheeled carriages available as a train (with their total rated capacity of 20 adults or 40 children), a complete train of these new bogie carriages consisted of three cars with a rated total capacity of 24 adults or 36 children. The bogie carriages weighed 370lbs each, making a three-coach train of 1,110lb on 12 axles, compared to the 1,250lb for ten four-wheeled cars on 20 axles.

Although the Cagney vehicles are often thought of as rather simplistic and crude, they claimed some technically advanced features for the time; as early as 1902-03 the Cagney catalogue records that its carriages were now '…complete with the Finest of Chilled Steel Ball Bearings', long before British standard-gauge railways adopted such aids. Cynics might suggest that these would help make up for the inadequacy in pulling power of the little locomotives!

There has been some question as to whether ball bearings were actually used in carriage axlebox journals or merely for the kingpin bearings on bogie tenders and carriage stock (these latter were long known from surviving equipment); however, the 1902-03 catalogue notes further that 'With Class D ... we deliver ... 10 Small Fancy Pan-American Ball Bearing Cars, or 3 Large Fancy Pan-American, Adjustable Canopy Top Cars, fitted complete with Ball Bearing Trucks'. This directly re-affirms that four-wheeled cars were indeed fitted with ball bearings in the axleboxes at this time, there being nowhere else for such bearings to be used!

Recent archaeological research on original 1902 and 1903 Cagney carriage running gear, during restoration work in connection with the subject of this book, has finally revealed that their use at that time was actually even more extensive than might be expected today. The 1-inch-diameter axles ran in ball-bearing races fitted inside simple cast-iron boxes; single ball bearings were also used, one at each end of each axle, acting as simple, if crude, thrust bearings against the end cover plates.

The truth has proved difficult to establish as, not only have few survived, but most Cagney carriage axleboxes have been extensively modified over the years. Their fitment thus appears to have been short-lived; there is no mention of them in the 1901 catalogue, and later-built carriages (post-1904?) appear to have reverted to plain bearings.

It would appear that the ball bearings, at that stage of their development, were not robust enough for the job and most such axleboxes were subsequently modified with plain bearings, the ball-races having partly disintegrated. As noted in

Below Cagney 1903 carriage axleboxes, showing the remains of the outer sections of their original ball-races; these were later modified to plain bearings. *Author*

Right A well-worn, but original, Cagney carriage wheel-set of 1903, showing the single ball thrust bearing in the axle end. *Author*

The Locomotive Magazine for 15 October 1906, '...for use on journals of railway rolling stock ... the employment of ball bearings for such purposes is practically impossible owing to the limited amount of surface in contact, which tends to crushing of the balls...' without the use of hardened steels – and Cagneys only had 'chilled steel' available.

Business continued to develop, including a thriving export trade, particularly to South America, but Timothy Cagney's death in 1917 proved a significant blow, although the remaining brothers carried on the business. Further blows were to follow. It is often, but incorrectly, claimed that in 1923 a change in US Federal legislation required two-man crewing of steam locos, which forced the introduction of a steam-outline petrol-driven loco. However, no specific Federal legislation has ever affected miniature railways there.

What actually happened was that, concerned by the growing numbers of incidents, including small-boiler failures, a number of individual states encouraged the formation of the 'American

55

Society of Mechanical Engineers' (ASME). One of its first tasks was to create a set of codes governing the design and construction of boilers generally, and – far more importantly for miniature railways – establishing a uniform set of rules to licence those who operated such boilers.

As more individual states accepted the ASME codes, the employment there of cheap-labour students or retired people to drive steam locos became impossible. Since virtually all such licensed operators were members of the Brotherhood of Operating Engineers, their wage rates and employment conditions rendered steam-worked miniature railways uneconomic overnight. Within a year steam production had ceased and Cagneys were, none too successfully in comparison with what had gone before, producing internal-combustion locos instead.

The McGarigles' workshops finally closed in 1929, while the Cagney operation was eventually dissolved in 1948, by which time some 1,300 locomotives had been produced. Even then, however, the 'Eagle Locomotive Works' in due course acquired the remaining parts, foundry patterns and blueprints from the Cagney family.

Two 'Cagney' railways were in operation in Britain in 1901, both promoted by an American, Captain Paul Boyton. A 12⅜-inch-gauge line operated at the Military Exhibition at Earls Court, while a 14½-inch (or 15-inch) Class D operated at the Glasgow Exhibition. These two lines heralded the arrival of the true commercial miniature railway in Britain, albeit in temporary form.

Boyton also operated a line at Alexandra Palace from March 1903 to April 1904, which may have used the equipment he ordered from the Miniature Railway Co on 10 December 1902, by a letter that featured in the company's 1902-03 catalogue; this letter makes it clear that by now Boyton was only ordering bogie car sets. He had now ordered 11 complete sets in total, for use both in the USA and abroad, and the earlier ones would certainly have had four-wheeled carriages.

This letter also shows that Boyton was then paying about $1,000 for four complete train sets, two of Class C, ie 12⅜-inch gauge, and two of Class D, ie 15-inch gauge. Further Cagney lines, perhaps supplied by a W. H. Bond, operated later at Crystal Palace and Southend Kursaal. Others followed in due course, possibly 'recycling' the stock and fittings from these early lines.

In the catalogue for the Military Exhibition at Earls Court in 1901, in extolling the virtues of its 12⅜-inch-gauge miniature railway, it was suggested that the '…average speed is about 10 miles an hour, from which it will be seen that on country estates a miniature railway may be used for many purposes besides that of amusement'.

The Railway Magazine subsequently reproduced this sentiment almost exactly. C. W. Bartholomew, as a keen 'railwayist' (as they were then known), would have read this, and had also probably seen at least one of the 1901 exhibition lines, and compared it with what he knew well of the 'minimum gauge' alternative offered by his erstwhile student colleague Arthur Heywood.

The most active miniature railway engineer in Britain, Henry Greenly, was undoubtedly less impressed by the way the Cagneys achieved their success – in 1909 he recorded that the '…steam engines … of the "American" type … do not appeal much to the artistic side of one's nature…'!

However, none of this initially prompted any action by railway enthusiast – but motor car fanatic – CW. Something else would be needed before the first true miniature 15-inch passenger-carrying estate railway in Britain would be born.

The first railway at Blakesley Hall

The first railway at Blakesley Hall was actually not a miniature railway at all but an extensive model railway, created by the Squire for his son James (at least that was the excuse!).

The magazine *Model Engineer & Amateur Electrician* (without whose recording of the miniature and model railway scene through time our knowledge of such history would be much the poorer) in its issue of 1 May 1902 gave a full and detailed description of 'A Model Clockwork Railway' that CW had installed for his son James '…for his amusement during the last Christmas holidays' – which neatly dates this railway to the latter part of 1901.

The railway, situated in one of the Hall's outhouses, at the western end of the generating plant, consisted of tracks, turnouts, sidings, turntable, one station and one junction station, to a total of 200 feet, with signals, electric light, bridges, viaduct (5 feet long), tunnels, footbridge, covered way, electric bell connections between stations, cranes and telegraph poles; curiously there is no mention in the magazine article of the gauge adopted.

Railways large and small

The Blakesley Hall model railway, with its pioneering use of scenery.
The Model Engineer & Amateur Electrician, courtesy of West Riding Small Locomotive Society

The track and rolling stock were all supplied by W. J. Bassett-Lowke & Co of Northampton, a company that will reappear frequently in our story. At that time (1901) it was supplying quality 'standard' items from continental firms such as Bing and Carette, the first design ordered specifically to Bassett-Lowke requirements not being delivered until 1902. The initial Blakesley railway stock consisted of:

> '...two express 4-wheel coupled bogie locomotives, two 4-wheel coupled goods engines, one shunting engine, one dining bogie car, one sleeping car, one postal guard's van, one saloon car, one saloon carriage, one Swiss verandah car, three 4-wheeled coaches, one brake van, with passengers and guard, and one live-stock carriage.
>
> The "goods" department comprises four GN coal trucks, one 4 wheel bogie rail truck, one timber carriage, one goods van, one covered-in truck, one petroleum tank, one brake van, one travelling crane, one ambulance wagon, one armoured truck with three guns, and overhead and ordinary cranes.'

In the light of later events regarding liveries of the miniature railway locos at Blakesley, it is of note that the only British railway specifically identified in this description is the Great Northern (although the Bassett-Lowke catalogues of the period suggest that, at the time the Blakesley layout was built, no other British railway company livery was actually available for the described 'coal trucks').

Further examination of these catalogues for the availability, at these dates, of the range of stock listed above also allows, by a process of elimination, the surmise that the layout would have been of Gauge 1 (1¾ inches between rails), although the photographs do perhaps suggest something larger.

The cuttings, tunnels and bridges were '...designed and modelled out of clay and moss...' by George Bailey, one of the estate staff. All credit to him and to CW, as its provision was quite significant for the time, and the Blakesley model railway must count as one of the first such to have 'proper' (if still rather crude) scenery; this may have been the reason for its appearance in *The Model Engineer*.

There were also display models in the Hall itself. When the contents of the Hall were sold in September/October 1947, a number of locomotive models were included; whether they were from this layout or perhaps its successors (if any) – or some of the display models – is not known. The number was not as large as might have been expected, and the layout itself does not seem to have been included, suggesting that much of it had already left Blakesley (possibly for Wombwell in 1942, as is mentioned later); individual lots included a 'Quantity of models', a 'Box of Toy Railways', and 'A model L&NWR Railway Engine'.

What is clear is that CW's attention for 'model' railways was almost immediately diverted elsewhere – to bigger things!

5 The miniature railway arrives

In the beginning?

Given CW's obvious interest in motor cars from at least 1897, it is actually rather intriguing that he decided to adopt any kind of railway at the start of the 20th century for his relatively small estate, instead of perhaps developing early forms of motor 'estate cars' and lorries for the purpose.

CW may perhaps have been influenced by his erstwhile student colleague Sir Arthur Heywood to adopt a 15-inch-gauge railway, but it is far more likely that Heywood played no direct part whatsoever in the selection. CW had no need of Heywood's idealistic concept of '…shewing how a much smaller annual tonnage than has been hitherto deemed worthy of a railway may be profitably thus conveyed'. Initially at least he was interested neither in 'tonnage' nor profitability – indeed not in goods of any kind – nor even of a useful railway.

While Heywood obviously started his railway development as soon as he acquired his wife and estate, CW had made no such attempt more than 25 years later, obviously preferring the 'playboy' lifestyle (including, later, motor cars). The contrast in starting age in such an interest would be followed by a similarly contrasting type of estate railway. The only real commonality between the two men would be the gauge – and, as we shall see, this was by coincidence rather than by design. CW, however, would achieve more – and longer-lasting – developments in just eight fast and furious years from 1902 to 1910 than Heywood achieved in his 30 main years of development from 1874 to 1904.

The earliest surviving reference to an outdoor railway proper for CW would appear to be in the notes of one of the planning meetings early in 1903 by the committee for that autumn's Blakesley Show in which 'Mr Bartholomew said that he would have a new model railway in working order by the show day and hoped that the committee would help him to carry out the arrangements'.

The reference to 'new' was previously thought to infer that, at the 1902 show, James's indoor model railway had been an attraction to Show visitors. However, as we shall see, the 15-inch line's first locomotive was built in early 1902 and the carriages would also appear to date from early that year. This suggests that a short 15-inch line – perhaps on a different course entirely – was operational for the 1902 Show (and thus the above reference would be to this, not to the indoor railway).

The building of James's new indoor model railway for Christmas 1901 seems to have been almost perfectly mistimed as the two immediately successive issues of *The Model Engineer & Electrician*, which followed that Christmas, showed that others were developing far more exciting types of 'model' railway. That of 1 January 1902 carried a brief description and a fine full-page sepia plate of the recent 10¼-inch Pitmaston Moor Green Railway of the Holder brothers, but CW was undoubtedly even more influenced by an article in the very next issue – that of 15 January.

This carried an illustrated feature on a model railway of a quite different kind constructed earlier in his garden by a Mr E. W. Payne '…for the amusement and instruction of his little 5½-years-old daughter and her friends…', showing the daughter actually riding in and driving the loco. Although somewhat crude, this was infinitely superior to any indoor clockwork model railway!

Of 14-inch gauge (almost exactly one-quarter full-size), it featured an attractive home-built largely-wooden 0-4-0T steam-outline loco, initially mechanically hand-driven but intended in due course to be '…propelled by a small electro-motor…'. The other key difference compared to

The Blakesley Hall Miniature Railway

Above This full-plate picture of the Pitmaston Moor Green Railway appeared in *The Model Engineer* for 1 January 1902; an enclosed 'ride-in' carriage for children is at the rear of the train. *The Model Engineer & Amateur Electrician, courtesy of West Riding Small Locomotive Society*

Left Was this the final 'spark' that provoked the Blakesley railway? This 14-inch line was built by Mr E. W. Payne for his daughter – she is leaning out of the cab of the home-built loco in this picture from the 15 January 1902 issue of *The Model Engineer*. *The Model Engineer & Amateur Electrician, courtesy of West Riding Small Locomotive Society*

the very few other existing 'garden' railways (of narrower gauge) such as that at Pitmaston Moor Green was that this was a miniature toy train primarily for children. Thus by the time the article on CW's own indoor model railway for son James appeared in this magazine in the 1 May 1902 issue, it looked very mundane and insignificant in comparison with these.

Not a man to be upstaged in any way, how could 'playboy' CW quickly regain the initiative? Ivy and James were already around twice as old as Mr Payne's daughter and something 'bigger and better' was needed now for the children of CW! (Although Heywood's children did operate, and play with, the Duffield Bank Railway, this was

The miniature railway arrives

The first of the 30 typical bar-framed Baldwin 2-6-0s as supplied to the Midland Railway in 1899 for use in the Yorkshire coalfield. *Author's collection*

more an aside or a result than a cause.) The recent Exhibition railways at Earls Court and Glasgow suggested an answer. Not only could the Cagneys supply him with such a product, but they could also do so very quickly.

As their catalogues of the time repeatedly pointed out in true salesman style, 'We have a limited number of Miniature Railways on hand…', implying that immediate supply would be no problem. To be 'biggest and best' from this Cagney source – at this time – would mean 15 inches; thus would the gauge be chosen, without any direct influence from Heywood.

While there may be some puzzlement that CW would condescend to feature an American loco for his 'state-of-the-art' model railway in 1902-03, Britain had just (in 1899 and 1900) become a significant importer of American-built locos for several main-line railways (20 for the Great Central, 20 for the Great Northern and 40 for the Midland – all 2-6-0s – together with three 0-6-2Ts for the Barry Railway and two 0-8-2Ts for the Port Talbot Railway).

They were needed to handle a crisis in the movement of coal from British collieries – something of which CW would be all too well aware, as it was affecting the profitability of his pits, particularly as it was those three English lines collectively that were his vital lifelines. It may not be too great an exaggeration to suggest that these American loco imports might have saved CW's financial fortune!

Seventy of the 2-6-0 imports were built by Baldwin (with ten from Schenectady), and all featured typical American bar frames, the former also having high running plates, bogie tenders, etc. This 'invasion' could well have foretold (but didn't – for another century!) a turning point in loco sourcing here. Thus a Cagney 4-4-0 would be a good model compromise for one of these 'Moguls' – arguably then the most modern, or at least innovative, locos in the country! Even the Pitmaston Moor train illustrated in *The Model Engineer* was led by an American-style (though British-built) loco. It could also be that at this time, in exercising its comprehensive running powers over the E&WJR, the Midland ran these on occasions through Blakesley, thereby further attracting CW's attention.

The article on Mr Payne's line showed how track could be constructed so as to '…interfere as little with the garden as possible, and great care has been taken … to prevent it being an eyesore to anyone whose taste lies more in the direction of flower gardening than model railways.' The method adopted formed '…a good representation of ordinary railway ballasting, and at the same time a good garden path', allowing such even to be in the lawns and gravel driveways close to the Hall, and thus acceptable to the likely circles of eminent visitors.

Philip Kingston, who grew up in the village and knew many of the people long connected with the estate, wrote in 1981 that 'The first track layout included two circular tracks, one making a circuit of the gardens…', and also that '…the circular track through the gardens was [later] removed to accommodate some ornamental features…'. The reference to 'gardens' indicates the area close to the Hall within the Pulham watercourse and 'back wall' area.

Although this reference is non-contemporary, Kingston had access to sources with then-contemporary knowledge unavailable today; a fuller version of this reference is given later. If CW did order and receive his Cagney equipment

61

quickly during 1902, and if he did initially install a Payne-type 'garden' line for Ivy and James, then this could indeed have been sited in the gardens, as suggested by this reference.

The idea of a garden line being operational by August 1902 is indirectly supported by one piece of surviving physical estate ephemera – and even hints as to the possible location of part of its route – as will be revealed right at the end of our story.

From toy (?) to estate railway

While Bassett-Lowke had supplied (though not at that time manufactured) virtually all the components for James's model railway, he was not then in the business of providing for passenger-carrying railways – indeed, he had possibly not even considered the idea at this time. In any case CW's estate railway was to change very rapidly from the original large-scale ride-on children's toy into a line with a clearly defined role in the functioning of his estate. It was in due course to display his own completely new and modern approach, merging the New World miniature passenger trains of the Cagneys with the goods-carrying ideas of the smallest of continental European industrial narrow-gauge lines.

CW had an advantage in railway terms over the other estate railway owners: his major part-ownership in a number of Yorkshire collieries and coking plants meant that he already effectively owned not merely narrow-gauge equipment, but also standard-gauge steam locomotives, wagons and track, as well as being a substantial customer of several of the main-line railway operators and suppliers. His contacts with this industry were thus substantial and influential.

CW also had one absolutely clear advantage over Sir Arthur Heywood (both at Duffield Bank and at Dove Leys) and the Duke of Westminster (at Eaton) in planning a railway: his residence and grounds lay directly alongside the local standard-gauge railway, including access to the nearby passenger station and goods yard. No public road or other person's land intervened, except for a sufficiently wide road overbridge right at the station itself – which had already allowed through his private footpath from the Hall to the station.

The Blakesley Hall Miniature Railway would thus be able to provide a useful and direct connection between the Hall and the local station at Blakesley on the East & West Junction Railway. It was this key factor that enabled CW to transform his new line, in a few short months, from just being a 'toy' into serving a serious purpose, both for passengers and for goods, between the 'main-line' station and the Hall.

For a private estate line, it was to become also, as near as such could be, a line for the enjoyment of the public in their recreational activities at every reasonable opportunity. Once again CW would pioneer a type of railway operation that would be commonplace half a century ahead – and one that Heywood seems to have largely ignored.

It was remarkably short, the length of the original 'main line' from station to Hall being only just over a quarter of a mile; even at the longest extent of the whole line (around 1910), it just failed to reach an end-to-end length of half a mile.

The Squire, being (conveniently) a stockholder in the relatively minor E&WJR, was easily able to secure its agreement to his 15-inch-gauge line passing through its road overbridge (No 25) at the western end of Blakesley station, thereby providing direct access for passenger, and later goods, interchange between the two railways.

The layout of the line

Despite CW's claims as a Civil Engineer, he does not seem to have taken the trouble to produce a plan of the estate or the railway in any form. The Ordnance Survey, unfortunately for history, surveyed the village and estate in 1900 (shortly before any part of any railway was built) and does not seem to have updated its plans until long after the railway disappeared.

Even the Royal Air Force seems not to have undertaken an aerial survey that included the estate until early 1947 (when three such were carried out in quick succession) – by this time the last sections of the line had been derelict for at least five years and few traces remained. More recent colour aerial photographs also fail to reveal any signs of railway alignment on the estate, except where such may be still in use as agricultural vehicle wheeltracks or regular animal paths.

The line also underwent several major, as well as minor, changes during its life as its function changed from purely pleasure passenger operation to the addition of serious coal and farm transport. The one piece of contemporary quantified information that does exist is a gradient survey of the 'main line', as it then stood in 1909, undertaken by the leading model and miniature railway designer of the age, Henry Greenly.

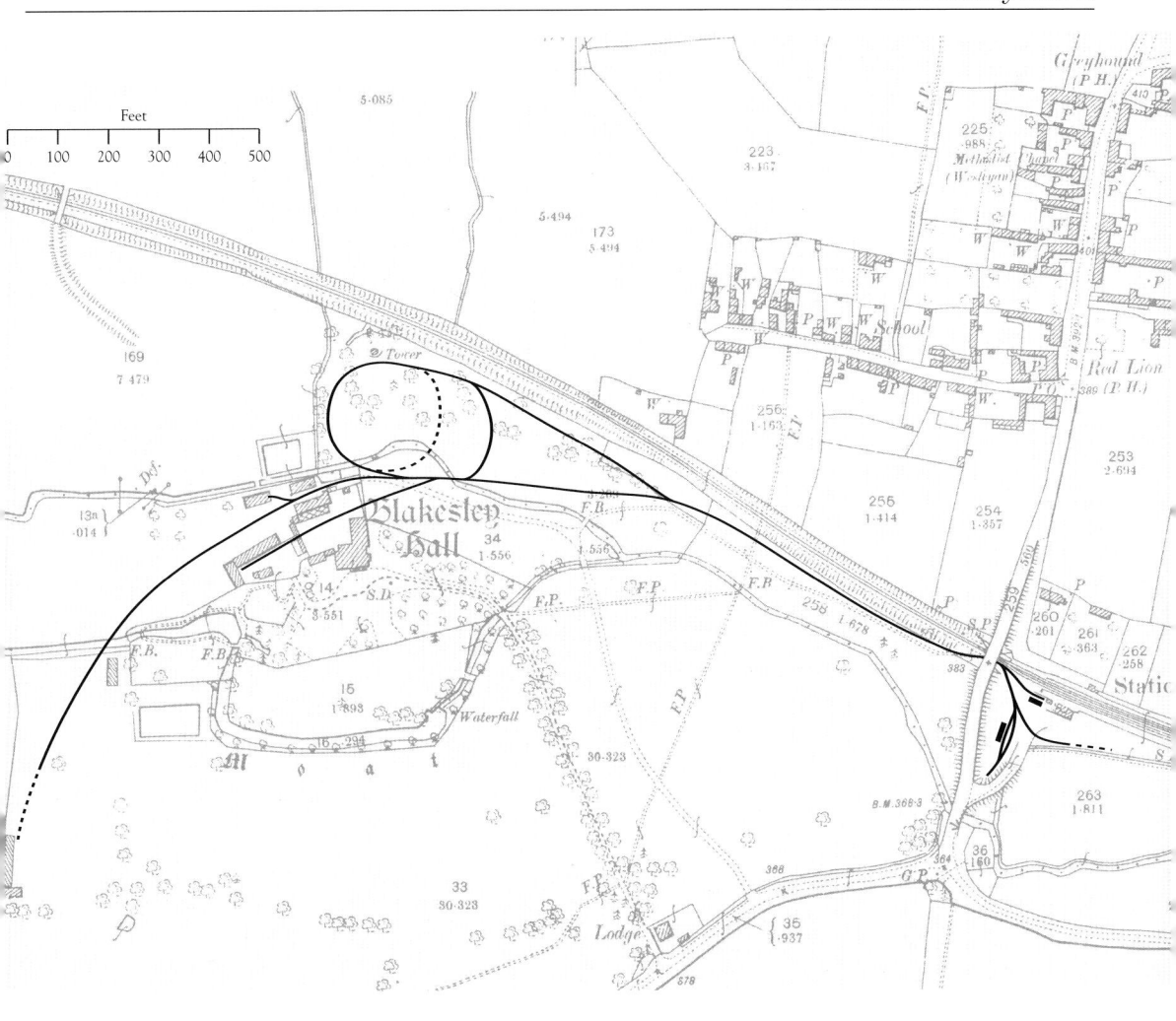

The miniature railway arrives

A sketch of the line's probable layouts, superimposed on an Ordnance Survey map of c1900; not all of the lines existed simultaneously, and the broken lines are conjectural. Later buildings relevant to the railway have been sketched in. *Map Crown copyright*

In researching the railway's layout we find, not for the first – or last – time in this study, misleading information repeated in more than one secondary source, in a way giving it an aura of spurious reliability. The only previously published plan of any part of the railway is of the area around the main-line station, and two publications with near impeccable pedigrees (including local railwayman and enthusiast Arthur Jordan's 1982 history of the S&MJR line) have carried virtually identical sketches purporting to show the 15-inch layout here.

Yet both sketches are hopelessly wrong in showing the 15-inch line veering sharply to the south just west of the railway station overbridge, having apparently ploughed straight through the remarkably solid embankment carrying the southern road approach to this overbridge! The former was still easily disproved more than 60 years after the line closed, by virtue of the remains of the 15-inch line's cutting alongside the standard gauge line (as well as distant photographs), while the latter is disproved by clear contemporary photographic evidence that both railways passed through the single bridge arch. (The second reference – which is probably copied from Jordan – replicates the Jordan layout, but manages to compound the errors by referring to the line as the 'Blakesley Mill Tramway'!)

In view of these errors, some doubt must exist about these sources' interpretation of the 15-inch layout in the goods yard by the station. Nevertheless, Jordan (as well as his father and

63

mother, both of whom worked for the S&MJR) did know the line and its stations very well, and one must assume that the layout shown in his sketch is reasonably accurate in principle, even though the positioning and detail is wrong.

By the end of the 20th century most evidence of earthworks, bridges and structures had disappeared without trace. With the aid of photographs, Greenly's gradient survey, and a sketch of the line as remembered in its latter days prepared by Philip Kingston, the author spent several days during 2004 minutely exploring the estate, helped by Philip Burt, the estate owner, long-time resident of the 1905 Blakesley Hall Lodge Ann Weekley, and several other local people; he was able thereby to draw up a reasonably sound sketch of the likely layout.

This exploration initially suggested something unthinkable, that there was something wrong with Greenly's 1909 survey: the line as measured by him was far too short. Indeed, his measurements suggested that it was shorter than the straight-line distance between the two furthest points on the railway known for certain from photographs!

However, it was eventually realised that his survey was entirely accurate, and that the ephemeral nature of parts of the Blakesley system had misled every subsequent researcher – initially including this author – and the extension built in 1909, and thus surveyed by Greenly, was itself extended with a hitherto undocumented (but curiously well-photographed!) extension in 1910.

Being almost entirely built in the grounds of a single estate, with a Hall surrounded by grazing farmland, there were quite a few fences and walls through which various parts of the line had to pass. Thus five or six sets of gates, often of wrought iron, were provided, normally kept closed against the railway.

The former locations of some of these gates have been of particular help in identifying the lines' course. Being so significant, it is surprising that – with the exception of the very ordinary one at the station leading towards the goods yard – they appear in no photographs; however, their approximate positions are recorded on the layout sketch. Remarkably, one impressive set of these survived into the 21st century.

It may seem curious that, with such a large estate potentially available, the complex pre-1909 railway layout seems to be somewhat squeezed 'into a pint pot', with comparatively tight curves and circuits, etc, at radii of around 100 to 150 feet. However, it must be appreciated that the greater part of the estate was by no means level, as would be shown by the fearsome gradients on the two later extensions towards the farm buildings.

Also, while much of it was valuable grazing land for CW's exotic livestock, the area used for the major part of the railway was effectively a flood meadow for the Black Ouse stream and thus far less suited to farm livestock needs.

Contemporary viewpoints

With no contemporary map or plan of the line surviving, it is useful first to refer to written descriptions in contemporary authoritative sources. Even the few photographs do not help as much as they might, as the ability to turn engines means that one is not quite sure which way they are pointing!

Also, the layout underwent changes around 1904-05, both to complete the original 'fun' sections and immediately afterwards to fit it for the coal traffic, and then a major upheaval occurred in 1909, ready for the arrival of the new steam-outline petrol locomotive *BLACOLVESLEY*. Just to trap the unwary, further changes occurred also after 1909. Fortunately there are two useful descriptions of the early line, both dating from 1906 (ie in its 'intermediate' period).

The follows is from an article in *The Locomotive Magazine* for 15 May 1906:

> 'The track at present laid down is over half a mile long, including several branches. Starting from the engine sheds, or Hall terminus, there is a good and practically straight run (crossing the river once), for about a quarter of a mile to the East & West Junction Ry Co's Blakesley station…
>
> The two platforms are close together and joined by a private way. At the station there are points connecting with the goods yard, and it is there that the transfer of coal, coke, etc, takes place. The private station is a pretty structure with booking office, used generally by the family and their friends, whilst on certain occasions trains are run from the station to the Hall, and vice versa, in connection with the various functions held in the park. The line is fitted with telephone and electric light, and is worked with Sykes' electric signals on a similar system to that used at the St Enoch Station, Glasgow.
>
> From the Hall terminus there are also other tracks through the park, one of which is

a circle passing twice over the river amongst chestnut trees by an old ruin. The other track leads off the top side of the circle, and, wandering between an avenue of chestnut and other trees, joins the main line about 200 yards on the way to the railway station; from there a "triangle" is run off the circle, and by this arrangement it is easy to turn an engine or carriage without the use of a turntable.'

The Model Engineer & Electrician for 5 July 1906 confirms much of the above, but also provides some additional information (it is probable that this periodical's reporter here was Henry Greenly himself):

'The miniature railway … connects the East and West Junction Railway with the Hall in a more or less direct line; the track also includes a circle which passes through a well-wooded part of the estate, and joins the main line between the Hall terminus and the railway station. Here a "triangle" is formed so that it is quite an easy matter to turn an engine or coach without resorting to a turntable.

The road is constructed of flat-bottomed (Vignole's section) rail, 12lbs per yard, laid to 15 ins gauge on pressed steel sleepers. The gradients are not severer than about 1 in 100, and to do this several cuttings and embankments are necessary. The main line is about a quarter of a mile long, but with the circle and branches over double this amount of railway has been laid down and at the time of my visit further work was in progress. The presence of a stream also necessitates several bridges. These are of the girder pattern…'

Fortunately the (undated) photographs illustrating these two articles show parts of the track layout not seen in any other illustrations. The photographer(s) concerned must have been particularly active to provide such a range of otherwise elusive views of this little line.

Village historian Philip Kingston wrote in 1981, from his own lifelong local knowledge and that of other villagers who had contemporary knowledge, supporting the above descriptions:

'The first track layout included two circular tracks, one making a circuit of the gardens, a second one crossing the brook at two points and passing an old ruin near the local "main" line. The third track was a straight quarter mile from the engine sheds at the back of the Hall to the East and West Junction Railway Station on the line from Blisworth to Stratford on Avon.'

There is a further 'contemporary' description of the line that appeared in 1938 (virtually at the end of the line's active life), when Ing Dr W. Strauss published (in German) a comprehensive review of the evolution of small-gauge railways, with much emphasis on those in Britain, entitled *Liliputbahnen*. He claimed to have visited many of the lines during a tour of Britain in the 1920s and 1930s. It is known that Greenly visited Strauss's father in Berlin in 1922, and would thus have known also the younger Strauss.

Few copies of the original work survive as it suffered from Nazi displeasure in giving too much credit to Britain for such railway development! His description of Blakesley appears far more consistent with the earliest days of the line than would be expected from the dates of his tour, suggesting that the account is second-hand. While it provides little additional information about Blakesley to that contained in the earlier articles, one particular sentence is of interest:

'Geschickt angelegte Schleifen an den Enden der Zweiglinien ersetzten besondere Drehscheiben und vermittelten ein schnelles Umstellen der Zuege, ohne erst die Maschine abkuppeln zu muessen.'

An English-translation edition of this work, published in 1988, offers this as:

'Skilfully arranged loops at either end replace turntables and allow the trains to be turned swiftly without uncoupling the engine.'

This translation, if accurate, might have helped identify the terminal layouts at each end of the line; however, a more literally precise translation of the original would be:

'Cleverly arranged loops at the ends of the branch lines replaced special turntables and permitted quick rearrangement of trains without having to uncouple the engine first.'

This shows that Strauss was referring not to 'either end' of the (main) line, but quite specifically to 'the branch lines' ('Zweiglinien'), which may be interpreted as the circuit and triangle lines. In addition, 'Umstellen' does not really imply 'turn', and could even suggest re-marshalling. The original Strauss description thus seems not inconsistent with the earlier ones.

Tracing the 1906 layout

Together the 1906 articles do provide a good insight into the railway's infrastructure. Combining these descriptions with interpretation of photographs and site visits, what follows is believed to be substantially correct in principle, if not in exact detail, for the railway as it stood at that time.

As noted earlier, with one distant exception all the structures on the standard-gauge E&WJR line had been built for double track, although only a single line had been laid. This meant that, even though there was a passing loop in Blakesley station itself, the two lines converged back into single track in time to allow sufficient space under

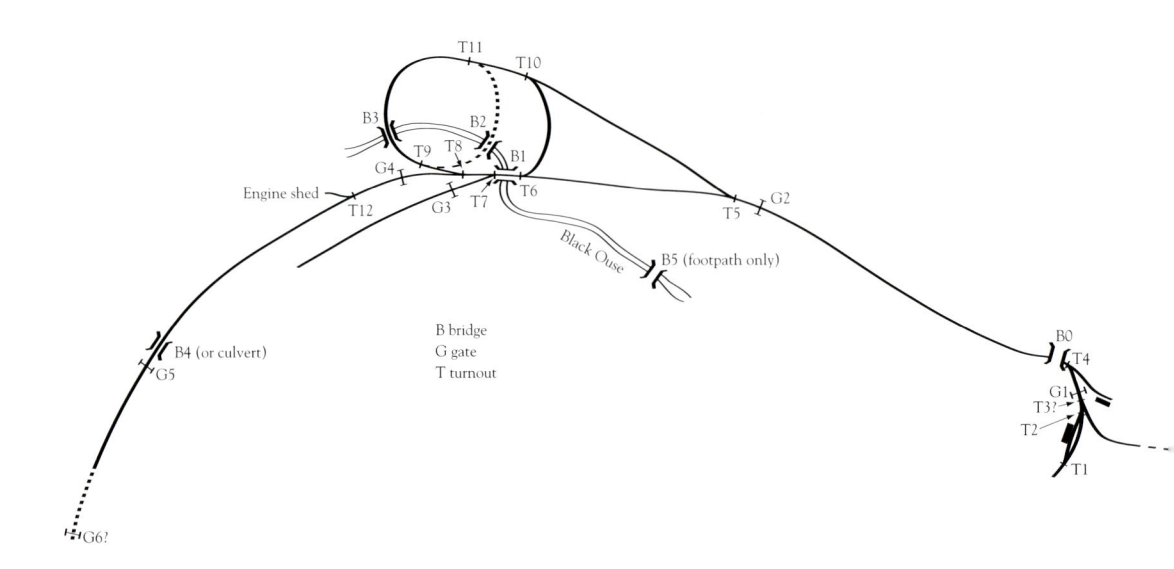

Above A sketch plan of the line with turnouts, bridges and gates marked and identified, as described in the text.

Left The original short-lived 15-inch station and run-round loop by the approach road to Blakesley E&WJR station in about 1904; the Cagney has a full train of three bogie carriages, and James Bartholomew is on the footplate. *J. Wyatt*

The miniature railway arrives

this bridge (shown as B0 on the accompanying sketch) for a footpath from the Hall to pass through on the south side. A simple iron post-and-bar fence, later partially hidden in laurel bushes, separated the footpath from the standard-gauge rails. The miniature line was in due course able to be put through the same bridge on the course of this footpath.

Originally (from late 1903) a small station building and single wooden platform alongside a single track and loco run-round loop capable of accommodating the Cagney and three bogie coaches (some 60 feet in length) served at this end of the miniature railway. The platform and run-round loop (with turnouts T1 and T2) were sited roughly parallel to the main road above, in the enclosing 'V' formed by the joining of the embankment for the main road and the station approach road.

As the original intention of the line was purely for passengers, it made great sense for this layout to stay tucked into the side and get as close as physically possible to the road connecting Blakesley and Woodend villages. However, in readiness for the commencement of the miniature line's goods traffic from the standard-gauge yard in 1905, the entire layout here needed to be considerably modified.

A new single-track stub for the passenger trains was constructed, roughly at right-angles to the original, parallel and very close to the track of the westbound standard-gauge platform. The miniature line's original wooden platform and station building were moved, revamped in 'rustic' style, and placed on the south side of this track.

The stub finished just before the E&WJR corrugated-iron oil and lamp store. A wooden walkway across its end directly linked the platforms of the two railways; this layout now meant that passengers transferring between trains had a much shorter walk. The E&WJR station building interior could itself only be accessed direct from the westbound standard-gauge platform, not from the yard, although the main pedestrian route thereto was at the far (eastern) end of this building.

A turnout (T4) was put in just on the east side of the road bridge B0 to provide access to the new passenger station; the original route could then be transformed into a long siding for the goods yard. One way of doing this would have been to take a

A construction train with petrol loco *PETROLIA* stands on the spur into the new 15-inch station during the winter of 1905/06, while the old route to the original station awaits conversion to link into the standard-gauge goods yard.
Charles Simpson collection, courtesy of Sir William McAlpine

Looking down the approach road to the S&MJR station after closure, on 23 May 1964, a slightly sunken depression running across its course locates the former route of the 15-inch line into the goods yard. *Leslie Freeman (Transport Treasury LRF 1872)*

new turnout off the former passenger station loop, with a line running straight across the approach road, and then alongside the standard gauge siding. As far as is known such a turnout (T3) and route was never provided, although this would have retained run-round facilities at this end of the line.

Instead, the straight section now immediately off the end of turnout T4 was retained as far as the 'farm' gate (gate G1) that protected the (unsurfaced) E&WJR station approach roadway.

Below Road bridge No 25, from Blakesley village to Woodend, crossed the E&WJR line at the west end of Blakesley station. Ex-LMS 4F No 44567 is on an eastbound goods train on 15 March 1952. The trackbed of the 15-inch line (with sleeper hollows visible) is behind the iron fence on the left. *H. C. Casserley (76289)*

Inset At least one of these bridge weight restriction signs was on bridge No 25, and as the 15-inch line passed through it, it can be regarded as a sign on the miniature railway! *Author*

However, rather than the line curving to the south en route to the original 15-inch station, a completely fresh layout was now created for the goods traffic.

The former right-hand curved tracks were simply lifted and turned, so that the siding now headed east. It crossed the unsurfaced station and yard approach road, finally turning once more slightly to the left to run close and parallel to the single standard-gauge siding on its northern side, although recollections suggest probably for only about the length of one standard-gauge wagon. There was a small weighbridge with wooden 'office' outside the standard-gauge station building on its south side, but the 15-inch line seems not to have passed over this.

With both tracks at ground level and virtually all transfer traffic being inbound to the Hall, the smaller 15-inch wagons would be easy to load from the standard-gauge ones. Most of the 'new' track required for this work would have come from the

The only significant earthwork on the line was the cutting parallel to the E&WJR line. The remains were still clearly visible in 2004, seen here looking west. *Author*

original station and loop layout, although there are two photographs of 1905 that show a works train loaded with new wooden sleepers en route to the yard to undertake these changes.

This new layout made it impossible for a loco to run round either passenger or freight trains at this end of the line, except by hand-shunting, but there is no direct evidence of any replacement loop.

Leaving the single-track 1905 station, passenger trains passed over the trailing turnout T4 from the goods yard spur. Following the squeeze under the road bridge B0, where the course was shared with the existing footpath, the line entered a long, virtually straight, narrow and shallow cutting, immediately adjacent to the E&WJR fence-line.

After an initial climb at around 1 in 110, there was a local summit in the cutting (about 2 feet deep at this point) and the line then dropped, initially at 1 in 156, before easing to near level until it crossed the course of the old public footpath from the village (closed by CW to public use in 1903 before the railway opened – but still in use for the estate). It then swung slightly away from the E&WJR line, before passing through a gateway (G2) in a field fence.

The footpath from the station had in the meantime pursued a roughly parallel but more southerly course before coming back alongside the miniature railway by this gateway. The footpath now veered off sharply to the south on its own, before crossing the Black Ouse stream on its own bridge (B5) and joining what was known as the 'back drive' round to the rear of the Hall.

A turnout (T5) here provided access, from around 1905 to 1909, to the right to the '…track … wandering between an avenue of chestnut and other trees…', which continued roughly parallel to the standard-gauge line, while the 'main' miniature line struck off in a generally west-south-westerly direction towards the Hall at 1 in 330 down before becoming level.

Further on, this 'main line' crossed the Black Ouse on its own bridge (B1). This bridge is probably the most-photographed part of the whole railway (though infuriatingly always from roughly the same spot and in the same direction!). Shortly before this bridge, another branch trailed in from the right at a turnout (T6).

This branch, which also existed probably only between 1904-05 and 1909 at most, was the 'triangle' link to the 'wandering' track, although primarily it acted as the eastern part of an extended 'circle' (as described later). Equally shortly after this bridge, a facing turnout (T7) separated the line into two routes.

The line to the left crossed the 'back drive', passing diagonally through a pair of wrought-iron gates (G3) in the long and remarkable 'Hitch brick' wall parallel to the 'back drive' and forming the northern boundary to the Hall gardens. It then continued past, and close to, the north-east corner and rear of the Hall, allowing guests arriving by train to have direct access thereto, although, curiously, no actual station or platform was ever provided here – '…one just tumbled out…', as it has been vividly and delightfully described by a family member and regular passenger!

This line also, after 1905, allowed coal to be delivered directly to the Hall and to the greenhouses. It is suspected that this line might once have continued further, up a short but quite steep gradient, into the courtyard of the former stable block, now used in part as the workshop, with CW's new garage for his motor cars at the far end; if so, this section had gone by the mid-1920s.

The right-hand line from the turnout T7 to the west of the stream bridge B1 ultimately gave access to an extended 'main line' after 1909, but initially simply continued through a gateway (G4) and,

Above This is the 'back drive' to the Hall, and the flood meadow, looking east towards the village in 2004. The stone wall is the northern boundary of the Hall gardens, and the wrought-iron gateway (G3) shows the course of the line to the rear of the Hall. The railway bridge over the stream (B1) was on the site of the present occupation bridge (middle left). *Author*

Below A rare view of the rear of Blakesley Hall, looking south-east; the railway branch was just out of the picture to the left. *Alfred Newton & Sons, courtesy of National Monuments Record (BB98/02338)*

passing close to the gas producer plant, led straight to the engine shed; although always so known, it was in practice also used for the carriages.

In 1904-05 a facing turnout (T8) was provided to the right, before gateway G4, giving access to the western side of the circle. This led either, within a few feet, to a trailing turnout (T9), which brought the other, eastern, part of the circle in

The circle line passed close to the old mediaeval Tower. *Alfred Newton & Sons, courtesy of National Monuments Record (AA97/05589)*

from the right, or this turnout T9 was sited immediately before turnout T8 (it is uncertain which layout might have applied here). Both of these sections of the circle featured bridges over the Black Ouse (B3 and B2 respectively).

Returning to the turnout T6, which trailed in before the first bridge (B1), and following this 'triangle link' on its northern course, it curved gently to the left before meeting up with the 'wandering' line at a trailing turnout (T10). This line continued to a further trailing turnout (T11) where it joined the circle coming in from the left from turnout T9.

The line continued beyond turnout T11, passing close to the south side of the old Tower before curving back round to the south, where it became the western section of the circle. Unlike the original layout at the eastern end, other than by making use of the parts of the circle and triangular layout, there were no loco run-round facilities at this end of the line.

Although the circle and branches formed an apparently fiendishly complex layout (probably easier to understand from the sketches than from the above written description), it was actually all rather clever. Not only was it possible to run directly onto or off the circle from or to almost any direction, branch or other location on the railway, but it was also possible to operate trains on the tight circle independently of any activity on the rest of the railway. Thus the children could still have fun while the day-to-day work continued.

Bridges, turntables, etc

Although the footbridge (B5) over the Black Ouse for the (non-public) footpath linking village and Hall had been built with substantial estate 'standard' hollow breeze-block 'Hitch brick' abutments (the piers of which still survived intact and immaculate as late as 1984 – and in 2004 were still extant though partially collapsed), those for the railway were built on quite different – and much less sound – principles!

The railway's original bridges crossing the Black Ouse were simple beams of former flat-bottom railway or tramway rail, extending well beyond the bank sides, spaced at 15-inch centres with a wide wooden decking on which the steel sleepers and rails were then laid. Not only were these bridges somewhat flimsy, but so too were their 'abutments'. Rather than true abutments, these were simply horizontal wooden planks with a wooden upright at each end, embedded in the stream to help stabilise the banks at these locations. They would have rotted away in time, leaving no trace today. It is difficult to be sure that even these were actually provided at all the railway bridges, however engineeringly unsound this may appear! (The current 'farm' bridge on the site of bridge B1 has long beams considerably overlapping the stream banks and no abutments or bank stabilisers.)

While probably adequate for the relatively lightweight passenger trains, CW as a civil engineer may have considered the bridges too

The Blakesley Hall Miniature Railway

Above The original 15-inch railway bridges had simple wooden planking on a pair of beams – no ballast was used. *Charles Simpson collection, courtesy of Sir William McAlpine*

Below A fortuitous photograph taken before 1905 of bridge B1 being rebuilt with proper side girders, not yet properly in place (although the track is already ballasted). The Cagney is crossing with a test train of slightly incomplete bogie carriages. *Postcard (postmarked January 1905), Tony Harden collection*

light or crude-looking for the coal trains he wished to introduce between the standard-gauge sidings and the Hall. Thus by 1904 some rather attractive steel side-beams were added to the edges and 'normal' ballasting extended across bridge B1. Bridge B2, for some reason, survived in original condition until its removal some time after 1914, while bridge B3 was possibly built new with steel side beams in 1905.

That this was additional, rather than replacement, material for bridge B1 is evident from a 1904 photograph of the Cagney and train standing on this bridge with a new beam not yet properly fitted but angled at 45 degrees alongside. Proper abutments were never provided at any of the railway bridges.

The corrugated-iron engine shed contained three tracks, the access being by a track fan. Despite the reference in *The Model Engineer & Electrician* to the ability to turn stock '...without resorting to a turntable', there was in due course a loco turntable outside this shed. This allowed locos still to be turned after the triangular layout was abandoned in 1909.

There are indications that this turntable was relatively flimsy (perhaps home-built), and was probably only just long enough to accommodate the 9ft 8in wheelbase of the line's last – and largest – locomotive. (This railway turntable should not be confused with the well-publicised one for motor cars sited actually within their garage – this latter is believed to have been still in situ in 2004, hidden under a layer of concrete.)

Although the course of the railway passed through a number of fences and walls by means of gates of varying character, the line itself was unfenced except for the short distance on one side where it ran close to the standard-gauge route. Here an iron-railing fence separated the two railways, even where the 15-inch line actually ran on the unused part of the main-line trackbed; this commonplace fencing of the period became augmented over the years by a considerable growth of laurel bushes intertwined around it.

The formation

One reason why it is difficult today to find traces of the railway alignment is the rather unusual – indeed quite pioneering – construction method adopted by CW for the trackbed. Most railways at that time used a comparatively thin ballast bed on a precisely engineered and levelled formation of cuttings and embankments.

The Cagney on the eastern side of the circuit with two bogie carriages, having just crossed bridge B2. A shallow natural cutting and a deep ballast bed make a near-level line. The Hall garden wall is visible to the right in this view looking east. *Charles Simpson collection, courtesy of Sir William McAlpine*

Heywood had adopted this philosophy – and also adopted the then common approach even of main-line railway companies to ballasting by using ash, or '…red furnace cinder…', as he called it, at Eaton; this gave a rigid, somewhat punishing, ride quality. CW rejected this approach entirely and used proper high-quality stone ballast, providing much-needed resilience.

Apart from the relatively long cutting near the station, very little was done at Blakesley to prepare true earthworks as Heywood did. Instead, the alignment was chosen to utilise convenient shallow depressions as low cuttings and thereafter a relatively deep ballast bed (such as is commonplace on main-line railways today) was used to create an even line, which was at its shallowest in such a small cutting, and deepest where an embankment would otherwise be needed.

This was also a speedy (and cheap) method of construction, requiring the minimum of preparation. The method was adopted also for all subsequent extensions and modifications to the line. This ensured a well-aligned and well-drained railway; it also effectively raised the datum of the lower parts of the line a few inches higher – useful on a line built largely in a flood meadow.

However, upon abandonment of any section it meant also that there was much good-quality ballast aggregate available for easy removal for other purposes (which is what happened), while the lack of significant earthworks ensured that what was left returned quickly to the natural contours, leaving behind little or no trace.

The track

The track material is most unlikely to have come from the USA with the loco and carriages, as British manufacturers of such abounded. Many British companies also acted as agents for continental manufacturers of industrial small-gauge railway equipment, as well as supplying such directly themselves.

As recorded in *The Model Engineer & Electrician*, the track consisted of relatively light rail (12lb to the yard) on pressed-steel sleepers. While no further details of what was actually used have survived, it is interesting to note that Heywood had concluded that 'In regard to the most suitable length of rail, I have found 15ft very convenient for weights up to 18lb per yard'. There is significant circumstantial evidence, curiously provided by the design of the line's bogie carriages, that this length was adopted at Blakesley.

As an example of what could be obtained, the 1899 catalogue of Arthur Koppel of Berlin offered formed steel sleepers of similar (but not identical) cross-section to that found at Blakesley, as well as a range of rail sections and weights. The nearest corresponding to 12lb per yard would be Koppel's 65mm high (at about 6kg per metre section, or 12.1lb per yard); however, they supplied this in 5-metre lengths, rather than the 15 feet thought to have been used at Blakesley.

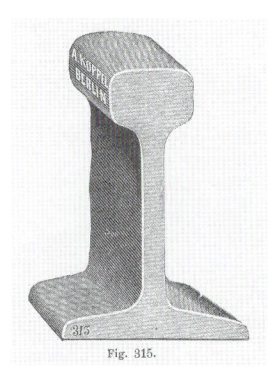

The approximate cross-section of the relatively tall and narrow rail used at Blakesley, weighing 12lb per yard. The actual supplier is unknown. *Arthur Koppel Catalogue, 1899*

Although commonplace for the time, the rail section at Blakesley was somewhat different from the more recent usual rollings of this weight. It had a deep but narrow head, with a similarly narrow base, but a high web. Such a cross-section was particularly suitable for low-speed temporary track where sleeper spacing might be excessive, and it could easily be curved without special tools. This vertical strength was also to prove handy in 1904.

A post-lifting photograph of the section under the E&WJR road bridge at the station shows evidence of conventional deep wooden sleeper hollows there, and a photograph of an engineering train in the line's early days shows new wooden sleepers en route to some layout remodelling work; perhaps the steel sleepers were proving unsuited in places to the line's unusual ballasting technique.

The standard German work by Ing Dr W. Strauss published in 1938 records that the Blakesley line '…hinsichtlich Maschinen und Oberbau ganz nach amerikanischem Vorbild eingerichtet' – or, in the 1988 translation, '…was based on American practice as far as the engines and permanent way were concerned' – but the section therein on Blakesley is believed to be 'second-hand' and unreliable. If the track material had come from Germany and Strauss had been aware of it (bearing in mind the nationalist situation in Germany at the time), it is inconceivable that he would not have made great play of this.

The article in *The Locomotive Magazine* says 'The road … is constructed with flat-bottom rails on iron sleepers', which if correct would suggest a Heywood-style road. Fortunately there are good early photographs of the Cagney on an original-style bridge, and this clearly shows pressed-steel sleepers, so *The Locomotive Magazine* is wrong in this respect. Although not to Heywood's design, the Blakesley track of 15-foot-long rails on metal sleepers was certainly the early-20th-century contemporary equivalent thereof.

Pressed-steel sleepers and 12lb rail would, of course, be available 'off the shelf' for the narrow-gauge lines used in and around coal mines of the period. With CW's shareholding and directorship of several Yorkshire colliery companies, it would be perfectly logical for all the fixed infrastructure (bridges, rails, sleepers, ballast, etc) to be sourced by this means – and perhaps even to be installed 'ready to run' by their employees or contractors.

This light weight of rail and sleepers was really intended for hand-worked lines, and thus also featured correspondingly sharp turnouts and tight-radius curves for the associated short-wheelbase wagons. This set the style of the early BMR track layouts – and influenced the nature of the locomotives and rolling stock used on it. Though intended for hand-worked industrial lines, it was a perfectly satisfactory track for Cagney-weight stock (the Cagney catalogues offered either 8lb- or 12lb-per-yard rail as suitable).

It is believed that the post-1909 extensions were built largely using the rails and sleepers from those sections abandoned in preparation for the arrival of the new loco in that year, although the larger-radius turnouts would be new material; indeed, the length of the extensions was probably determined by what was available here!

Amazingly for such a short line with, initially at least, but one locomotive, it appeared to be fully signalled. Once again CW had looked to the technological future by installing Sykes electric banner signals – a design still used extensively on the national network a century later. Great play was made of this comprehensive state-of-the-art signalling in contemporary reports in the railway and engineering press.

However, *The Model Engineer & Electrician* rather gives the game away by indicating their true, rather more mundane, function by reporting 'Electric signals … are used to indicate the positions of the points. These are illuminated at night by electric lamps.' For at least one turnout (T5) there were two banner signals, suggesting they were used here to indicate whether or not each line was clear for a train to proceed (ie as true signals) rather than as point indicators.

It seems possible that there were other exceptions in that there were signals of this same pattern that seemed to protect 'blind' sections of route such as the passage beneath the E&WJR road overbridge near Blakesley stations – and, much later, the blind corner (nowhere near any pointwork) by the farm manager's bungalow.

All pointwork was operated by simple local weighted hand-levers, adjacent to the points; some of these were connected also to the Sykes banner signals. A photograph taken in 1904 of the Cagney and carriages shows clearly that trains 'pushed through' the trailing turnouts with their weighted levers, rather than needing them to be set for the particular direction.

The line was also fitted with telephones – presumably to allow visitors arriving by standard-gauge train to 'call up' a BMR train to the Hall – and with electric light. No evidence of lineside lighting appears in the photographs and it is assumed this was restricted to the station and signals.

6 Locomotives and carriages

The Cagney locomotive

Although both of Boyton's 1901 Cagney-operated lines closed at the end of their exhibitions in that year, neither of them provided the equipment for Blakesley. The Earls Court line was of the wrong gauge and its Class C loco had the earlier wooden-style cab. Charles Simpson recorded, in a (subsequently published) 1973 letter, about '...the 15-inch-gauge American 4-4-0s [sic] at the Glasgow Exhibition (1901)' that '...I have always understood that these were the engines [sic] acquired by Mr Bartholomew for the Blakesley Hall Railway...'

However, this could not be the case; this statement is a good example of Simpson's recording precision mentioned earlier – he does not claim that Glasgow was the source, only that he understood it to be the source. The Glasgow line was probably of the right gauge, although there is some doubt as to whether it was 15 inches – The Model Engineer of 15 October 1901, usually meticulous in recording dimensions, stated 'The gauge of the track is 14½in...'). However, it had four-wheeled carriages of the 'Gold Medal Special Fancy Car' pattern. (Perhaps the track for the imported 15-inch-gauge train had been laid as 15 inches between rail centres – a problem to recur at Cleethorpes some 70 years later.)

Also, the Glasgow Cagney was recognisably different and of earlier build, having a sheet-steel cab and lacking the four fixing studs on the smokebox front, used on such locos from 1902, including that at Blakesley. Anyway, the Blakesley loco had '1902' cast on its smokebox ring, thereby confirming that it could not be from the Glasgow line.

There was an exhibition at Wolverhampton from May to October 1902, which featured two Cagney lines, one of 15-inch and one of 12⅝-inch gauge; the latter was almost certainly from Earls Court and the former may have been from Glasgow. It is, however, just possible that this Wolverhampton 15-inch line could have provided the train for Blakesley, but without photographic evidence to show its carriages, this cannot be substantiated. All the later exhibition lines in Britain (including those in 1903), while also having locos similar to that at Blakesley, had different carriages.

It is therefore probable that CW obtained his train of one 4-4-0 steam locomotive and ten 'Small Regular Style Cars' direct from the USA. If the idea was prompted by Mr Payne's 14-inch railway as illustrated in The Model Engineer for January 1902, it could well have been ordered new by CW from America, delivered and installed by mid-year, and thus appear as the 'model railway' just before the celebrations for King Edward VII's Coronation in August 1902 and the Blakesley Show in September.

Lest this be thought an impossibly short timescale, in 1898 the Lynton & Barnstaple Railway had invited tenders for a new 2-4-2T in February, and ordered one from the Baldwin factory in America in April. The parts were fabricated in May, and it was shipped, partly completed, in time for reassembly and steaming by the beginning of July of that year! On this basis, the supply of a completely standard 'off the shelf' Class D Cagney plus train, similarly manufactured on the eastern seaboard of the USA, would have presented no problem.

However, if the garden line did not exist, the train could instead have been nearly new but second-hand (perhaps arriving in mid-1903); if so, it could all have come from one of the Cagney-operated lines, perhaps with Boyton acting as agent. As CW would be unlikely to accept second-hand equipment for his new toy, this is considered unlikely.

The loco was obviously a Class D, and certain photographs clearly display the building date '1902' on its smokebox door ring. This date ensures that it was a 'true' Cagney, sold by the Miniature Railway Co (then at 301 Broadway, as shown on its smokebox ring – thus significantly dating it to the early part of 1902, just after the article about Mr Payne's line appeared in *The Model Engineer*), built by the McGarigles at Niagara Falls, and with a boiler by Armitage-Herschell! Neither name nor number was ever carried by the loco, while the tender, though originally unmarked, was, in due course, branded 'B M R'; whether this stood for Blakesley Miniature or Model Railway is unclear.

Although the Class D Cagney locomotive appeared, to the casual glance, to be a highly standardised product, it underwent a fair amount of evolution during the years of its production, as indicated earlier. The photographic evidence confirming the building date of the one at Blakesley as early 1902 allows some details of its design to be deduced fairly easily, although there remain uncertainties. The dimensions quoted below are taken from the 1902-03 catalogue, which would seem most likely to correspond to the Blakesley machine.

The Class D Cagney 4-4-0 poses on the circuit, while the ladies shelter from the sun. *Charles Simpson collection, courtesy of Sir William McAlpine*

The cylinders are quoted as 2¼ inches in diameter with a 4-inch stroke, and the driving wheels of 10¾-inch diameter. The 14-inch-diameter steel boiler was rolled from quarter-inch steel, with 18 tubes 1 inch in diameter and 24 inches long. However, an advertisement in 1923 for the disposal of what may have been the actual Blakesley loco gives its cylinders as 3 inches in diameter (which may simply indicate a re-bore), with 22 boiler tubes (which may indicate a more significant rebuilding). The frames were conventional plate frames of three-quarter-inch steel. Stephenson's valve gear was used. The dome was above the firebox, with whistle and safety valve mounted thereon. A sandbox was on top of the boiler itself and a traditional American railroad bell sited between it and the chimney.

The loco weighed 1,000lb, of which around 800lb was on the driving wheels. Normal working pressure was probably around 120lb per square inch, the boiler actually being tested to 400lb per square inch. It was supplied with water via a single Korting 'Universal' injector on the left-hand side, together with a feed pump on the right.

It was (like most other Cagneys, and in line with full-size American practice) painted black, although this was handsomely and dramatically offset by unpainted 'blued steel' boiler cladding (including the smokebox), boiler bands and dome – these latter items remained thus unpainted throughout its time at Blakesley.

To simplify manufacture, many of the components were castings and certain structural practices, which would not be tolerated with a full-size locomotive, were perpetrated; for example, the smokebox was simply a forward extension of the boiler barrel. The cow-catcher (or 'pilot') was a fabrication, rather than a casting as used on later examples, while the cab components of the Blakesley loco were castings. The running boards either side of the boiler were also castings, while the chimney had a simple flange at the lower end and a small bead at the top.

The unsprung bogie tender had a water capacity of 25 gallons. Cagney tenders are known to have been fitted with ball bearings to their bogie kingpins from 1902. The overall length of loco and tender together was 9ft 6ins, while the height to the top of the 'Smoke Stack' was 36 inches.

Unlike other Cagney tenders in Britain, the Blakesley one was fitted with wide wooden footboards on either side to allow the driver to straddle the tender body, leaving the footplate area clear to work in; with the obvious woodworking expertise available at Blakesley, these would have been made and fitted there.

Simple bar couplings were fitted front and back. They were fixed via a pivoting joint to the loco and tender and had an elongated 'male' eye at the other end to fit into the 'female' pocket of the carriage couplings. Mudguards rather than splashers were fitted above the spoked driving wheels (with their integral cast balance weights), while the bogie wheels were of disc pattern.

The Class D 15-inch-gauge design was simple and robust, but definitely suited to short, amusement-park-type lines rather than long runs, though the catalogues suggest its suitability '...on a straight track from 50 feet to 100 miles'! The latter would be somewhat painful for the engineer (driver) as the bogie tender on which he rode had no springs! It was built in the expectation of minimal maintenance, and of being looked after by somewhat unskilled staff; it is presumed that Alec Wyatt at Blakesley gave it rather more attention than was expected!

The carriages

The Blakesley carriages were four-wheelers of the 'Regular Style' type – ten of these would therefore have accompanied the loco. It is the carriages that effectively 'spoil' one idea, in that Boyton's letter of December 1902 to 'Cagney Bros, Miniature Railroad Co' includes his comment that one Class D 15-inch set is not identified as to its specific destination but '...please ship to my care, Manchester, England, via American Line'.

This could fit with it being for CW – except that the letter also makes it clear that these sets required 'Canopy Adjustable Top Cars', ie bogie cars. As already noted, so far as has yet been proven, no 15-inch-gauge railway in Britain other than the BMR had 'Regular Style' four-wheeled Cagney carriages, although the original 12⅜-inch-gauge Earls Court exhibition line had the significantly smaller version of these for that gauge.

Close examination of the surviving pieces of running gear from the Blakesley carriages indicates that they were delivered with the '...Finest of Chilled Steel Ball Bearing...' axleboxes, since their design is absolutely identical to those recently obtained in some surviving original US-operated boxes – again supporting an early-1902 build date.

The exact dimensions of these coaches pose some slight mystery as no drawings (or indeed four-wheeled 15-inch cars!) are known to survive. While the Cagney catalogues state that they had a length of 6 feet, the same catalogues record that their packing cases for transhipment had an outside length of only 5½ feet! Working from photographs of Blakesley and the dimensions of surviving 12⅜-inch-gauge four-wheeled cars, it would appear that they had an underframe length of some 56½ inches – identical to that of the 12⅜-inch cars, which had a wheelbase of 3ft 1¼ inches.

No photographs are known of these carriages in four-wheel form at Blakesley. These Cagney four-wheelers had an exceptionally long fixed wheelbase, owing to the need to accommodate the upper portion of each wheel beneath a seat so that it did not protrude into the intervening footwell. As the Blakesley track layout after 1904-05 featured quite sharply curved industrial pointwork really designed for short-wheelbase wagons, it was quite unsuited to such long-wheelbase vehicles. However, for a 1902 garden line and for the layout as it stood in 1903 (without the circle lines), these carriages were probably just useable.

A Cagney four-wheel 'Regular Style' carriage, as delivered to the Blakesley line. *Cagney Catalogue, 1902/3*

Thus these long-wheelbase coaches would, shortly after delivery, have been found to be quite unable to negotiate the tight curves on the new circle and the sharp turnouts, having a high tendency to jam or derail, while with short-wheelbase bogies the problem would be solved. This theory is supported by a comment in the 1906 article in *The Locomotive Magazine*, which notes concerning their rapid conversion to bogie vehicles, 'By this means the fixed wheelbase was considerably reduced, and gave much better running on curves and the circle tour…'.

CW (or his advisors or suppliers) thus made a serious and apparently quite costly long-term error in choosing the older four-wheel carriage version rather than the newer bogie design; perhaps the idea of accommodating 40 children with the four-wheeled set rather than only 36 with the bogie set swayed the decision.

However, with the latter not only would the rebuilding work have been unnecessary, but a significant increase in adult train capacity would actually have been achieved, while the child figure was in theory the same – up from 18 adults or 36 children (only nine four-wheeled cars were used to form the rebuilt train) to 24 adults or 36 children – as a result of the wider carriages.

Anyway, nine of Blakesley's ten four-wheeled carriage bodies from the 'set' were used to create three bogie coaches, each seating six adults or 12 children. Although bogie coaches were hardly new in Britain, they were rare around Blakesley! The impecunious E&WJR/S&MJR alongside had only four- or six-wheeled carriages until 1910, when it acquired a second-hand bogie carriage from the Midland Railway (followed by two others in 1912). CW was well ahead of the field (albeit locally) here!

The bogies for these rebuilt carriages were home-built at Blakesley with very simple elm side frames 2⅛ inches deep, 2¼ inches wide and 28 inches long, providing a wheelbase of a mere 12½ inches, a very basic 23-inch-wide wood-plank 'stretcher plate' joining the two side frames together with a 20-inch-diameter steel ring on top to act as a bearing surface for the bodywork. The original Cagney axleboxes and the approximately 7½-inch-diameter wheel-sets from the four-wheelers were re-used. (These dimensions are only approximate – the largely complete sole surviving bogie is of slightly different dimensions – including the wheelbase – on each side!)

The four-wheel carriage bodies were then placed and fixed, complete with their original wooden side-bearers, on new home-made steel underframes consisting of inverted 12lb to the yard flat-bottom rail of the standard type used at Blakesley. It could thus be that the whole idea for creating bogie carriages in this way, each with three four-wheel-carriage bodies, came from the ready availability of suitable rails of just the right length to create such underframes.

Although the whole structure sounds somewhat flimsy, in practice the framework of each of the original four-wheeler bodies would hold the rails securely in line laterally. There is no sign of the framework sagging during the long lives of these carriages, despite their considerable unsupported length between the bogie centres (although of course their carrying capacity was minimal).

These inverted rails on each side were spaced and joined to each other by stretchers above each

The Blakesley Hall Miniature Railway

The bogies at the extreme ends of the rail underframes made the new carriages look exceptionally long and frail. James is driving the Cagney, supervised by Percy Wyatt. *Charles Simpson collection, courtesy of Sir William McAlpine.*

bogie; in due course the ends of the rails were also joined together by curved wooden stretchers, bolted through the existing prefabricated fishplate bolt holes. However, there was a small gap between the headstocks of each four-wheeler body; this avoided the seat-backs touching.

It is suspected that the 'inner end' coupler pockets were removed, and that the two 'outer end' coupler pockets were relocated onto the underside of the new end underframe stretchers. The flexibility in the structure thus created allowed the whole framework to twist slightly, helping to make up for the lack of suspension between the bogie frames and the underframe.

The 20-inch-diameter steel discs on the bogies (the sole surviving bogie retains the slight marks of such a disc of this size) provide the clue as to how the estate staff developed the swivelling mechanism for them, as this dimension was standard for the 'circle plate' of the swivelling fore-carriage of a horse-drawn brougham or landau of the time; the long experience of local custom and practice with such vehicles in this rural area was simply applied to the railway's carriages.

The carriage bodies were left painted in their original lined deep red livery (described by someone who rode in them as brown/maroon), with the upper parts of the seats in a cream finish. A near-identical deep red was then used for the bogie framing, the axleboxes and hornways being in black.

One suggestion that has been made elsewhere is that there was a significant width restriction somewhere on the railway, preventing the use of vehicles wider than 2 feet, which would thereby have precluded Cagney bogie cars; however, as will be seen shortly, some of the railway's own wagons were significantly wider than 3 feet – and, indeed, a train of 3-foot-wide Cagney 'Gold Medal Special Adjustable Canopy Top Cars' did operate at Blakesley, however briefly.

The Cagney locos were very small machines for their intended work. Although supplied with ten four-wheeled carriages or three bogie carriages, these were really at the limit of the loco's hauling power on even moderate gradients, unless the run was sufficiently short that the boiler could recover between trips.

It is perhaps significant that many of the photographs of Cagney-hauled trains at Blakesley show trains of only two carriages, which supports the suggestion that the gradients, even on the original sections, were too much as a general rule for the Cagney with a fully laden three-coach train.

The Blakesley Hall Miniature Railway

Squire Charles William Bartholomew shows off the American Cagney locomotive and train on his Blakesley Miniature Railway. The original painting, commissioned by the Squire, once hung in Blakesley Hall. *F. Moore painting, courtesy of Robert Kingston*

The Blakesley Hall Miniature Railway

Above Charles Bartholomew as a young man, and his first wife Sarah Watson (Linley), parents of C. W. Bartholomew. *Doreen Birks collection*

Below Charles Bartholomew in later life, from a hand-tinted photograph that once hung in the Blakesley Band Practice Room. *Author*

Right A 'momento', issued by the Wombwell Main Colliery Co on the eve of nationalisation in 1947, shows Charles, CW, James and Charles Edward Bartholomew. Also seen are their partners' family, the Roberts. *National Coal Mining Museum (YKSMM 2000656)*

82

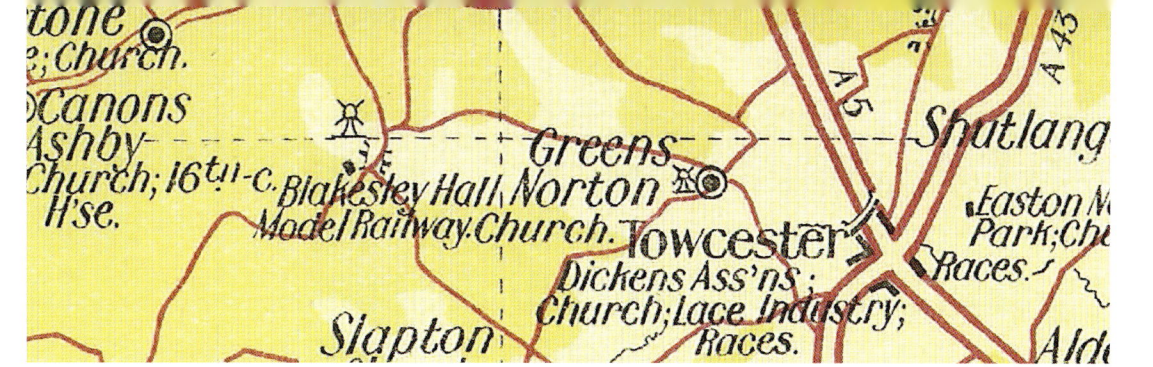

Above Even an early RAC road map identifies the 'Blakesley Hall Model Railway'.

Left CW as a young man, shown in a hand-tinted photograph that once hung in Blakesley Band Practice Room. *Author*

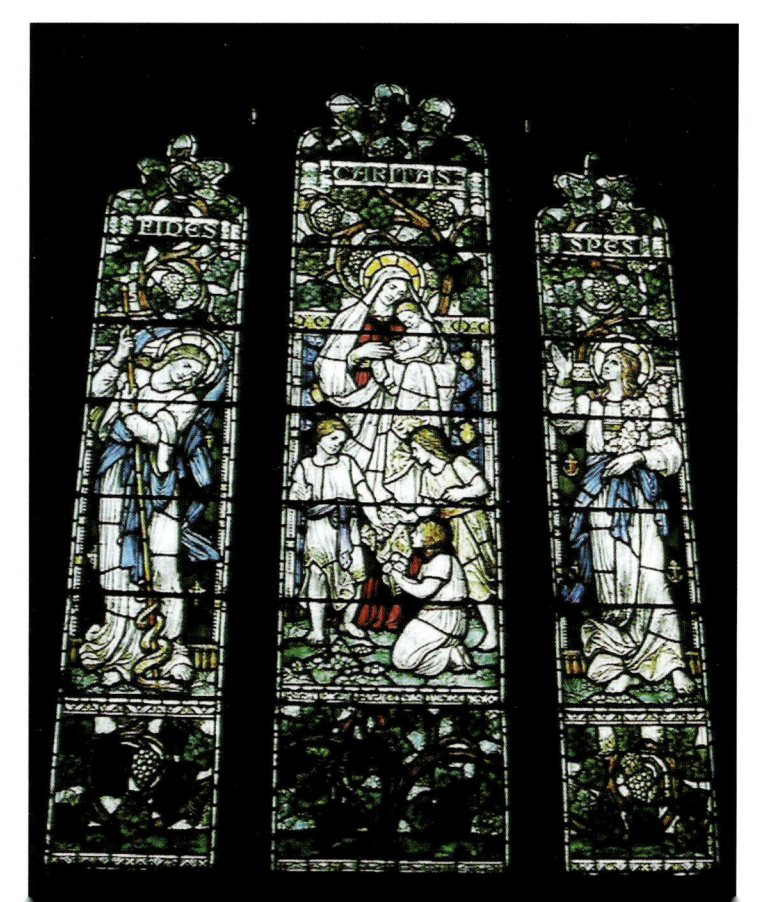

Right This stained glass window in the west wall of Blakesley church tower was erected by CW's family in his memory. *Author*

The Blakesley Hall Miniature Railway

Left A BMR 1 shilling adult ticket and a sixpenny child ticket (including admission to the Fete), issued only on annual Fete days; these were used probably only between 1903 and 1913, on the one day each year. *Dick Bodily and author's collections*

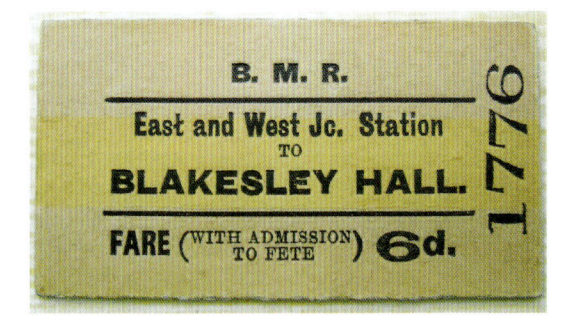

Below The Locomotive Publishing Company produced this coloured 'F. Moore' postcard of BLACOLVESLEY and a three-coach train on the main 15-inch bridge over the Black Ouse stream, heading towards the Hall. *LPC postcard, author's collection*

The Blakesley Hall Miniature Railway

Left A stained glass window relating to Charles Bartholomew in Blakesley Hall, showing the Bartholomew Arms. *Phil Kingston*

Above With their home colliery as a photographic backdrop, these OO scale models give the flavour of its wagons. *Author*

Below The 'heraldry' on the restored 'tank' side of BLACOLVESLEY. *Author*

85

The Blakesley Hall Miniature Railway

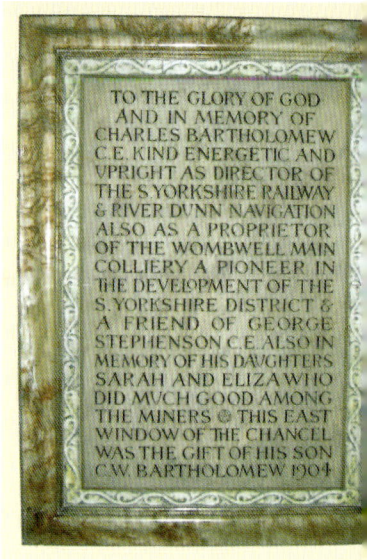

Above The east window and memorial tablet in St Mary's Church, Wombwell, gifted by CW for the new chancel in 1904 in memory of his father Charles and his sisters Sarah and Eliza. *Author*

Left The east window and memorial tablet in All Saints Church, Darfield, gifted by CW in 1915 in memory of his father. *Author*

Below The relatively simple stained glass window in St Mary's Church, Wombwell, funded by Dorothy Elliott in memory of her parents. *Author*

The Blakesley Hall Miniature Railway

Although no good colour photographs of the amazing Coronation livery of *ELIZABETH* have yet been traced, the extension 'streamline' panel to the right-hand tank side has survived in full 'war paint'. *Author*

Right BLACOLVESLEY in green livery with 'North Eastern' on the tank sides, outside the engine shed at Tom Tate's 15-inch North Eastern Railway at Haswell, County Durham. *Dr Mike Taylor*

Below The livery for the loco's display at Darlington in 1975, as part of the Stockton & Darlington 150th anniversary celebrations, was black with 'NER' on the tank sides. *Neville Knight*

Below right Yet another livery change: BLACOLVESLEY masquerades in pseudo-LNER livery as No 1326. The loco is standing outside the fine 15-inch loco shed at Lightwater Valley theme park. *Neville Knight*

Below A somewhat careworn clockwork Gauge O model of the L&NWR 'Precursor tank' made by Bing for Bassett-Lowke in about 1914, factory-painted in Great Northern Railway livery and bearing a remarkable resemblance to *BLACOLVESLEY*; the model is posed on the restored loco. *Author*

Below BLACOLVESLEY left Ravenglass for a lengthy proving run on 20 July 2000, posed here on Barrow Marsh; it continued to beyond Muncaster Mill, before returning non-stop to Ravenglass. *Author*

The Blakesley Hall Miniature Railway

Above The design of the proposed new Blakesley Hall, intended to be built on the footprint of the earlier Hall, as planned by Philip Burt. *Blakesley Hall Estate Sale Brochure, 2004*

Right 'Gateway to Paradise': these wrought-iron gates in the north wall of the Hall gardens mark the entry by which guests reached Blakesley Hall by 15-inch-gauge railway. In 2004 the broken concrete raft in the gateway still retained evidence of grooves 15 inches apart. *Author*

Below A view of BLACOLVESLEY, showing its stylish outline to best advantage, seen here at Saltburn in 2007. *Author*

7 Blakesley sows a miniature seed

W. J. Bassett-Lowke & Co

The Blakesley Miniature Railway was thus in full-scale passenger operation by the early part of 1904, and – for those not appreciating CW's dynamism – could be regarded as a completed system with its newly created bogie carriages hauled by the Cagney 4-4-0, giving pleasure rides between the East & West Junction Railway station and the Hall, as well as similarly collecting and delivering guests of the Bartholomew household.

Blakesley is only some 12 miles south-west of the county town of Northampton, where the famous model engineering firm of W. J. Bassett-Lowke & Co had been established in 1898, building and supplying model railway equipment in a wide range of scales and gauges (including to Blakesley in late 1901). Having already supplied this model railway to CW, Bassett-Lowke's entrepreneurial proprietor Wenman 'Whynne' Joseph Bassett-Lowke and its emerging and strong-willed engineer and designer Henry Greenly were thus well acquainted with the innovative Blakesley Miniature Railway virtually on the doorstep. Its operation of the scale miniature locomotives and open passenger-carrying carriages as an estate operation previously promoted by the Cagneys as amusement lines suggested to Bassett-Lowke that similar business opportunities must exist in Britain for providing equipment for miniature passenger-carrying railways for both estate and passenger purposes.

There is little doubt therefore that it was CW who, by example, started Bassett-Lowke and Greenly on the trail of 15-inch-gauge locomotive and carriage construction. The latter were not, however, to be satisfied with simply building and supplying locomotives and rolling stock – they decided that the claims in the Cagney catalogues of the huge profits to be made from operating such

A cast model of Wenman 'Whynne' ('Whynde') Bassett-Lowke by his firm, showing him in a smart blue suit with Homburg hat, and a suitcase lettered 'WJBL'. He is modelled in a hurry, as was frequently the case! *Courtesy of P. van Zeller*

89

railways in public parks and at exhibitions meant that they should combine both activities in a single company, just as the Cagneys had done.

This is confirmed by W. J. Bassett-Lowke himself, who recorded that 'With earlier experiments in view, [my] firm came to the conclusion that much might be done in this gauge by combining utility with realism...' Thus Heywood and his concepts played little or no part in instigating what Bassett-Lowke and Greenly would soon develop.

Roland Fuller, who was with the Bassett-Lowke organisation from 1917 virtually throughout his working life, neatly summed up the synergy and energy between these individuals: 'Whynne was the impatient and persistent entrepreneur while Greenly was the quick-thinking man of practical ideas who could undertake any new project with almost impetuous fervour.'

They had possibly seen one or more of the Cagney-equipped temporary exhibition lines in the early years of the century, as well as having close contact with the effectiveness of the same equipment in regular estate railway use at Blakesley. They first 'tested the waters' by acquiring the existing Greenly-designed 10¼-inch-gauge 0-4-4T *NIPPER* and running it in 1904 adjacent to a public park in Northampton. One suspects that Greenly more than Bassett-Lowke drove this evolution; after all, without the former's engineering prowess, there was no one to turn these ideas into practice.

Accordingly, in December 1904 'Miniature Railways of Great Britain Limited' was founded, with '...the object of acquiring ... develop and ... carry on the business of Model Engineers, Manufacturers of Miniature and Model Railway Engines, Carriages and Trains, and other articles and things used in connection with the business of Exhibitors of Miniature Railways, Trains and other things...'.

(This date for the formation of the new company is, intriguingly, almost exactly coincident with the falling-out between the Cagney and McGarigle families, leading to the virtually simultaneous demise of the Miniature Railway Co in America – though not, of course, to train production there, which continued apace.)

It was natural that, as the inspiration and catalyst for this idea, among the business partners holding shares in the new venture would be CW, with 20 of the 680 allotted ordinary shares; it is of note that he is described in the list of allottees as 'Gentleman', rather than 'Engineer'. The new company decided to adopt the Cagney supply philosophy almost exactly, but with a model of the latest of British express locomotives.

What is strange here, however, is that Bassett-Lowke now took a totally different approach to procuring locomotives and equipment for resale as his own product range in these larger scales from what he had adopted for the 'indoor' model railways. With the latter, Bassett-Lowke had sought out existing production-line overseas manufacturers (such as Bing and Carette), as found on James's model railway.

The parallel route for the 'outdoor' scales would have been for him to get the Cagney equipment manufacturers to produce somewhat 'anglicised' versions of their standard range. This did not happen – perhaps such an approach was made, but failed because of the confusion arising from the virtually simultaneous demise of the Miniature Railway Co in the USA.

Thus locomotive and carriage construction was undertaken in a new 'large gauge workshop', established in the J. T. Lowke works in Northampton. Not only was this concern 'within the family', but it was already a supplier of boilers – this therefore copied rather than employed the initial Cagney/McGarigle structure set up in America.

However, Bassett-Lowke was a supplier of quality – and thus relatively expensive – model railway equipment, mainly for a well-to-do market, and he seems to have failed totally to appreciate that the Cagneys achieved their success through quantity mass production from outside suppliers, allowing cheap, simple and basic, but still attractive, products and a high turnover to achieve profit; the indigenous Bassett-Lowke products would in no way be describable as cheap, simple and basic (though they were certainly attractive)!

Thus Bassett-Lowke misread the circumstances of the Blakesley railway, where a (very) rich 'playboy' Squire had lavished significant monies in buying from outside sources miniature railway equipment as a 'toy', initially for his children, for his medium-sized estate. Surely, therefore, there were others among his, now large, number of similarly affluent model railway 'gentlemen' customers who would indulge in such railways for their own estates?

Sadly, the resulting high costs meant that such people were not to emerge for many years (and even then precious few of them). However, this misunderstanding led indirectly to Bassett-Lowke having to adjust to fewer – and different – market opportunities for his 15-inch products, most of which did not really justify such quality items. Thus the entire subsequent evolution of the 15-inch miniature railway in Britain perhaps became an unintentional by-product of CW and his railway!

The 'Little Giant'

Bassett-Lowke's views on quality were carried through to the locomotive design adopted. By now the most important and modern express locomotives of the era, both nationally and internationally, were of the 4-4-2 'Atlantic' arrangement. R. A. S. Hennessey, in his monograph *Atlantic: The Well Beloved Engine*, considers that:

> 'The early years of the private, steam-operated, miniature railway coincided with the "Atlantic" fashion; the "Atlantic" form was well-suited to small railways laid along level ground ... these were ideal for miniature railway purposes as well as being de rigueur in public perception as the latest, raciest of steam engines. The large firebox ensured steam production in generous quantities; the short rigid wheelbase enabled the locomotive to adjust to the sharp curvature of many lines, and its general sprightliness kept traffic on the move.'

It is no surprise therefore that the first large-scale locomotive built by W. J. Bassett-Lowke & Co in the early part of 1905 was a 15-inch quarter-scale 'Atlantic'; designed by Henry Greenly, it was named *LITTLE GIANT* and was for a MRGB line in Blackpool. This was followed by a second 15-inch-gauge line at Sutton in 1908 (replacing a 10¼-inch one), using another Bassett-Lowke 4-4-2, *MIGHTY ATOM*.

Although Greenly produced 'scale model' designs in a variety of gauges, he chose to adopt the '...strange and wonderful combination of several types of engine...' in designing *LITTLE GIANT*; this may have significantly depressed the potential market for these 15-inch locomotives – and thus 15-inch miniature railways in general – over the coming years.

The 'Little Giant' was the British equivalent of the American express 'eight-wheeler' in its own timeframe but, despite their close examination of the Blakesley loco, neither Greenly nor Bassett-Lowke seem to have appreciated that Thomas McGarigle had based his design not on the famous (or infamous in British eyes) high-wheeled express

A new MRGB line at a zoo at Chevinedge near Halifax in May 1910. *LITTLE ELEPHANT* (the original *LITTLE GIANT*) heads a train of former White City coaches. *Author's collection*

loco No 999, but on a goods (or at best mixed-traffic) version of the standard American 4-4-0 with small wheels (on the Cagney version they came just two-thirds of the way up to the running plate). To find an American design mirroring what Greenly was trying to achieve with 'Little Giant' one needed to look, not to Cagney, but to the scale Olney & Warren design mentioned earlier – which also mirrored Greenly's own policies in making available detailed scale drawings and castings in a variety of scales.

Thus, although this major design difference was clearly visible from the Cagney at Blakesley, the 'Little Giant', with its scale large-diameter driving wheels, was really far too fast and low-powered for its intended purpose. According to the early 20th-century catalogues, the 15-inch-gauge Class D Cagney had driving wheels of only 10¼ inches diameter, whereas those on 'Little Giant' were no less than 18 inches.

The 'Atlantic' design, although featuring quite a flexible wheelbase, was also not sufficiently flexible to cope with the sharp curves likely to be needed at many sites – a serious design flaw. A minimum radius of 100 feet was quoted in advertisements, and even Blakesley's early curves and turnouts were really too tight for such a loco to operate, as was evidenced later when a 'Little Giant' derivative was built for there. The original design of six-wheeled tender was changed to a bogie version after this too was found unsuited to tight-radius curves.

Rather strangely, given that the later Cagney-operated lines in Britain used bogie carriages, and Blakesley had found it necessary immediately to convert its four-wheelers to bogie vehicles, Bassett-Lowke effectively reversed this process, initially obtaining three-compartment bogie carriages for Blackpool, before offering two-compartment long-wheelbase four-wheelers. While this improved, as Blakesley had done by the opposite process, the equivalent seating capacity per wheel-set, it made the new Bassett-Lowke carriages wholly unsuitable for sharp curves, such as would be expected to be found on estate lines.

The business seemingly took off in 1909, and between then and 1912 commissions involved exhibition lines, locomotives and stock at Nancy, London's White City, Brussels, Roubaix and Geneva. Although apparently popular, if the accounts in the Bassett-Lowke-influenced model railway press are to be believed, the return on these lines was small and MRGB Ltd was dissolved in 1912; overall the whole episode must be considered a dismal commercial failure. (Wealthy estate owners such as Heywood and Bartholomew, of course, had no need to achieve any return on either the capital outlays or the running costs of their lines.)

Nevertheless Bassett-Lowke seems to have concluded that the more profitable part of this business lay not in building large-scale locos and carriages, but in the long-term operation of 'permanent' 15-inch railways – in the public operation of Blakesley-type lines. MRGB Ltd was thus superseded by a new company, with these rather different objectives, Narrow Gauge Railways Ltd, and direct loco and carriage construction was soon to cease.

Despite the closeness of Blakesley to Northampton, and the obvious business contact between CW and W. J. Bassett-Lowke himself, it is surprising that no steam locos or carriages were ever loaned, tested or supplied to Blakesley by Bassett-Lowke. Only the one (non-steam) loco – albeit a remarkable one – was supplied, while another received 're-modelling', but that – and 'Master Jamie's' earlier model railway – strangely, was pretty well the sum total of direct business involvement.

The pioneering No10 *LITTLE GIANT*, for example, was taken straight to the Duke of Westminster's line at Eaton for its proving trials in 1905, rather than the virtually adjacent Blakesley. However, in early 1905 the Blakesley line still did not have a transhipment siding alongside the standard-gauge siding in Blakesley goods yard, and transferring *LITTLE GIANT* from a railway wagon onto the 15-inch line would have been difficult, so this missed opportunity is perhaps understandable. (Although the sharp curves at Blakesley would have prevented its negotiation of the 'circle' lines, it would have been operable on the 'main line' between Hall and station.)

That there may also have been some strain in the relationship between the two men could be suggested by various events described above, as well as by the apparent failure of W. J. Bassett-Lowke to give any written credit to CW for being the catalyst in developing his own ideas, despite the innumerable opportunities presented to the former in his many publications.

There is a photograph apparently showing W. J. Bassett-Lowke around 1905 standing somewhat pensively (perhaps both fascinated and frustrated) with CW's next – and far more revolutionary idea – completely eclipsing everything that the former had just put into developing MRGB Ltd!

8 Delivering the goods

The 'trolley'

The carriage conversions had, as noted, also 'liberated' a further eight Cagney carriage wheel-sets and axleboxes (the remaining four-wheel carriage body was simply scrapped). Four of these 'spare' wheel-sets were used to make two more bogies, with significantly more massive wooden side beams than were used for the carriage bogies. These were used to construct a so-called 'double bogie trolley or truck' (*The Model Engineer*) or 'light trolley' (*The Locomotive Magazine*) bogie wagon, with a rectangular 'flat-bed' body for service, rather than 'commercial', use at Blakesley.

The remaining four wheel-sets were soon to be made into two more bogies (but of the same design as for the carriages) for a revolutionary use to be described in due course. In the light of these additional two items of rolling stock, part-equipped with these spare wheel-sets, the original purchase of the four-wheel carriages seems, with hindsight, perhaps not such a bad buy after all!

The trolley was in reality a substantial general purpose bogie flat wagon, able to carry a variety of loads and equipment, including large pieces of estate-sawn timber as well as permanent way materials for the railway; it was not really envisaged as a wagon for goods traffic.

It does appear to have been somewhat misleadingly named by *The Locomotive Magazine*, for it is recorded that on '…the arrival of a new electric light plant, weighing 8 tons, the whole was taken from under the crane in the Railway Co's goods yard to the engine house on the trolley, including an 18 horsepower gas engine weighing 5 tons', continuing, with a masterpiece of understatement, 'This was considered to be a fair test for the road and the trolley too'!

The tip wagons

Now that CW had his own railway connecting his Hall with the local main-line railway station, to the goods yard of which Wombwell Main Colliery Co 'family' coal was delivered, he decided that his line should have a further practical function. Ignoring virtually all of Heywood's ideas regarding loco and rolling stock design, CW would, for the first (and only) time, adopt one of the former's basic 'minimum gauge' principles – that of goods as well as passenger carrying – but to do it in more of a 'miniature' style, in so doing even pre-empting the late-20th-century 'merry-go-round' coal trains of the 'big railway'!

In the light of this decision, CW needed to create a means of carrying the coal and similar materials between the main-line railway and the Hall, with its outbuildings. To achieve this he would need suitable wagons – and a suitable locomotive to pull them, as it was quite clear that the haulage power of the existing Cagney would be quite inadequate for this purpose. He also needed to remodel his railway to access the goods yard at Blakesley station to allow coal transhipment.

CW's choice of goods vehicle fell on a version of the industrial 'V'-bodied tip wagon. Soon to be an industrial narrow-gauge 'standard', these were still relatively rare in Britain at this time, although common in, inter alia, Germany. He obtained six of these in 1905 for his railway. (Had this idea arisen in 1903 or 1904, the carriage conversions could simply have used such wagon chassis as bogies.) Although Heywood used the term 'tip wagons' to describe vehicles of this type, they would today be more usually called 'skips' or 'skip wagons'. As the contemporary Blakesley references simply call them 'wagons', the Heywood term will be used here.

Once again, CW was demonstrating that there

were alternatives to at least some of Heywood's ideas. These tip wagons were the antithesis of everything Heywood recommended for wagons (which he believed should be adaptable to as many differing loads as possible); he had reluctantly supplied six such (of his own design of course!) to Eaton, but had managed to remove all but two within a short space of time.

Heywood had, rather grudgingly, written in his 1894 promotional booklet that 'For short distances, where the emptying bears a greater proportional relation to the running time, or where the load must be got rid of in a particularly short space of time, tip-wagons may answer...', but his real view was, as stated elsewhere in the same document, that 'I have always felt that the greater dead-weight of ... [tip] wagons in proportion to the load carried, and also their increased cost, heavily discounted their only advantage: celerity in unloading...'.

Clearly CW not only had a '...short distance...', but favoured '...celerity in unloading...' – and of course, unlike Heywood, he was catering primarily for one specific type of traffic on his line: coal. Yet they could hardly be considered to be in keeping with the Cagney 'miniature' tradition either! CW was developing his own distinctive 15-inch-gauge estate railway, drawing in both new ideas and the most appropriate 'best practice' from around the world – what he was quietly designing at Blakesley to haul these wagons would be part of the start of a revolution for the world's railways!

CW's godson, the railway enthusiast Charles Simpson, noted many years later that 'Some of the wagons were built in Germany...' (the 'light trolley' was, of course, not German but Blakesley-American), and this leads to intriguing possibilities.

Research has identified that, in about 1900, the Birkenhead tramcar-and-carriage-building firm of G. F. Milnes & Co entered into a financial partnership with Waggon und Maschinenfabrik AG vorm Busch of Bautzen, Saxony. Indeed, the latter provided most of the finance and management for the former's new Hadley works in Shropshire – although this arrangement collapsed financially in 1905, including the closure of the Hadley works! (It is known, for example, that certain turn-of-the-century British tramcars supplied from the Hadley factory are to metric dimensions, many of the components at least coming from Bautzen.) Of potential relevance to our story, Busch also supplied the usual complete range of German narrow-gauge industrial railway equipment.

In his 'Little Giant' monograph researches, Robin Butterell identified a new batch of bogie carriages for the Blackpool 15-inch line in 1908 as being supplied to Bassett-Lowke by the family-associated firm of Milnes Voss. These bogie carriages closely resembled simple industrial bogie flat cars with end aprons (as could be offered by several German suppliers such as Busch), on which were fixed swing-over 'toast rack' seating. A little later, a Bassett-Lowke 'Little Giant' loco operated with similar carriages at Breslau, not far from Bautzen, then also in Saxony.

However, 400mm-gauge wagons of this type were indeed also offered by several other German manufacturers in their standard catalogues, and the actual supplier to Blakesley is uncertain, although the Busch/Milnes connection seems likely, fitting neatly with their 1905 date. Busch records are scarce, but the 1899 catalogue of Koppel of Berlin, for example, features an approximately 300-litre outside-framed model of 400mm gauge and 450mm wheelbase with an overall length of 1530mm, a width of 1160mm and a height of 1010mm; the wheel diameter was 300mm. These are visually virtually identical to those at Blakesley. One early photograph featuring the Blakesley wagons shows an astronomically high number (apparently 28999) painted on the end of one hopper, suggesting a second-hand origin (presumably thereby also minimising Heywood's '...increased cost...' – possibly even 'free' if from one of CW's collieries!).

The Blakesley wagons may have been supplied as 15-inch gauge or had their wheels pressed in on their axles from 400mm to 15 inches (381mm), but the catalogues hint that (if nominally 400mm) no such change may have been necessary since the wheel gauge for such wagons was already well within the rail gauge (the centreline of the wide wheels corresponding with the railhead centreline), and thus closer to 15 inches anyway. The Blakesley tip wagons had conventional axleboxes, although several manufacturers were offering roller-bearing axleboxes for carriages and wagons as early as 1899.

In reporting the results of haulage trials with a new locomotive on the line in 1909, it is implied that each wagon weighed around a quarter of a ton empty. An approximately 300-litre standard 400mm-gauge tip wagon would take some quarter

The style of tip wagon probably used at Blakesley. *Arthur Koppel Catalogue, 1899*

of a ton of coal as the normal payload. In cold weather, it would thus require some 48 wagon-loads on the 15-inch to empty a single standard 12-ton main-line coal wagon – or some eight to ten round trips with the six-wagon miniature 'merry-go-round' train. These figures do rather confirm Heywood's negative views about such wagons in normal commercial terms; fortunately CW had no need to worry about such considerations on his railway!

The coal arrived in the goods yard at Blakesley in the family's own wagons, of course (something Heywood never achieved – although the Duke of Westminster did at Eaton)! These were standard 12-ton-capacity 'Railway Clearing House'-style seven-plank wooden wagons, weighing just over 7 tons unladen. By placing the new 15-inch siding directly alongside the yard's single standard-gauge siding, both at ground level, it was an easy job to move coal from the larger to the smaller gauge.

Although contemporary descriptions refer only to coal movement, the tip wagons were also used to transport estate-sawn brushwood and logs, and probably also to dispose of the ash residue from the burned coal, as well as moving incoming and outgoing farm-related produce – particularly when the line was extended up to the estate farm buildings. Certain photographs show them carrying wooden sleepers and other track materials.

One Cagney train set or two?

The article in *The Locomotive Magazine* for 15 May 1906 is quite clear that there was only one 'home' locomotive, there being two separate references therein to '…the steam locomotive…' together with, even more positively, that the passenger rolling stock '…is composed of one steam locomotive…'. However, this article does contain a number of obvious minor errors, so these statements must be treated with caution – particularly as the last quotation continues with '…and four bogie carriages…', which was untrue, there being only three!

To complicate matters, *The Model Engineer & Electrician*' for 5 July 1906 unintentionally created immense confusion for future historians of the Blakesley scene by, uniquely, publishing two photographs that show two Cagney locos and trains together at Blakesley. (Fortuitously these two views are also valuable in illustrating otherwise unphotographed parts of the railway.) One train, consisting of a loco and the three established Blakesley bogie carriages, as converted from the four-wheeled Cagney cars, is clearly the 'home' train, while the other has a near-identical loco, but this time with a full three-car train of bogie 'Adjustable Canopy Top' cars.

The latter loco differs visually from the 'home' one in the location of its whistle relative to its safety valve and the 'normal' lack of extra-wide tender footboards. It would appear otherwise identical in components (and thus date of building) to the 'home' Cagney, while both it and its carriages appear virtually identical to those operated at Alexandra Palace from March 1903 to April 1904. The likelihood is that it was this loco and carriages that visited Blakesley. However,

The Blakesley Hall Miniature Railway

FIG. 5.—PASSENGER TRAINS ON THE B.H.M.R.

FIG. 6.—"A DOUBLE-HEADED" EXPRESS.
VIEWS ON THE BLAKESLEY HALL MINIATURE RAILWAY.

Above The *Model Engineer* page showing two complete Cagney trains at Blakesley: one (a visitor) has Cagney bogie cars, the other (the 'home' train) has Blakesley-built bogie carriages. *The Model Engineer & Electrician, 5 July 1906, courtesy of West Riding Small Locomotive Society*

Below The 'Adjustable Canopy Top' bogie cars. *Cagney Catalogue, 1902/3*

CLASS D, 15 INCH GAUGE, GOLD MEDAL SPECIAL, ADJUSTABLE CANOPY TOP CAR.

WITH CANOPY TOP ON.
Dimensions of the above Class D, 15 inch gauge, Gold Medal Special, Adjustable Canopy Top Car, are 9 feet long, 3 feet wide, and with top on can be placed to any height desired up to 7½ feet, from track to top of Canopy. Finely upholstered Seats and Back and recommended for practical purposes. Capacity 8 Adults or 12 Children to each car 3 cars to a train Total 24 Adults 36 Children. Weight 370 lbs., complete with the Finest of Chilled Steel Ball Bearing, Swivelled Trucks, Springs, Journals, Coupling Links and Pins.

Class D, 15 inch gauge, Gold Medal Special, Adjustable Canopy Top Car.

WITH CANOPY TOP OFF.

Above A Class D Cagney with three 'Adjustable Canopy Top' bogie cars ran at Alexandra Palace in 1903/04, operated by Captain Boyton. It is probable that not only was this the Class D set for England ordered in his letter reproduced in Cagney's 1902/3 catalogue, but also the set that visited Blakesley in 1904 or 1905. *Tony Harden collection*

Below The 'visiting' train featured a standard Class D Cagney with three Cagney 'Adjustable Canopy Top' bogie cars, seen here on the 'wandering' link line approaching turnout T10. Angle House is in the background, beyond the E&WJR line. *Charles Simpson collection, courtesy of Sir William McAlpine*

similar stock did also operate at White City, Manchester (at least as recorded in some of the photographs of that line) from 1907 to 1911, at Edge Lane, Liverpool, in 1913, and at Earls Court, London, in 1914.

These dates would fit perfectly with a nomadic exhibition train 'resting' at Blakesley in 1904 or 1905. Even with this plausible explanation there are problems, however. The *Model Engineer* photographs suggest rectangular, possibly brass,

97

plates on the middle panel of each of the 'visiting' carriages at Blakesley – no such plaques appear on any of the exhibition lines' carriages, either before or after the date of the Blakesley visit!

There is one other, published but unillustrated, implicit reference to more than one Cagney at Blakesley. Henry Greenly, writing in *Model Railways & Locomotives* for September 1909, states: 'The steam engines are of the "American" type...' – note the plural. However, as he had almost certainly also written the 1906 *Model Engineer & Electrician* article when two probably were present, this idea of 'engines' could well have remained from that visit.

(The letter written by CW's godson Charles Simpson to Greenly's daughter and son-in-law in 1973 also makes reference, as previously noted, to two Cagneys at Blakesley, but as he was not born until 1906 he could only record what he had understood from some years later; for this reason he also reports what are today now obvious errors in relation to their origins and claimed building date(s). Thus, although the source appears impeccable, it is still only hearsay in relation to these particular events. The idea here probably arises from Simpson's personal collection of pictures of the railway, which include parts of those *Model Engineer & Electrician* photographs showing the two Cagneys together at Blakesley.)

Models, Railways & Locomotives for June 1911 carried a 'Trade Advertisement' that offered:

'FOR SALE – One 15-inch Gauge American 440 [sic] MINIATURE RAILWAY LOCOMOTIVE in good working condition. Can be seen by appointment at Blakesley Hall, near Towcester. Price £100 or offers – Bassett Lowke, Northampton.'

This could possibly refer to yet another Cagney as a temporary visitor at Blakesley, but as there is no mention of any accompanying carriages, it is more likely that CW was merely thinking of disposing of the now old-fashioned (to him) 'home' steam loco since he now had two petrol steam-outline miniature locomotives in his fleet.

Photographs prove that the 'home' Cagney was certainly still at Blakesley in mid-1912, so, if this advert did refer to the one-and-only home loco, it clearly had no takers at that time. (It will be seen later that it might just possibly have been 'borrowed' to help build another 15-inch line around this time.) As with the 1904-05 visiting Cagney engine and train, the 1911 advert also fits with clear spaces between the dates for the various exhibition operations mentioned above, so it too could, just possibly, have referred to a visitor.

There is, however, a perfectly rational explanation (but one that has never previously been suggested) for a 1904 visit by a second Class D Cagney train 'set', rather than it being purely a 'resting' exercise.

Options for hauling the goods

Having got his 'miniature' passenger train into satisfactory operation by early 1904 and determined now to introduce goods trains, particularly for coal, between the main line and the Hall, CW would have needed to consider carefully the motive power options available to him. The practical evidence of the limited haulage and non-existent braking power of his single Class D Cagney at Blakesley suggested that this would not be suitable for the new, more onerous, task.

Considering how restricted the options had been just one year earlier, by 1904 he now had quite a range open to him. Which ones he may actually have considered, or how seriously, is not known, but there are some pointers available that could logically explain previously puzzling happenings at Blakesley and elsewhere.

He could have obtained another Class D Cagney 4-4-0 (inevitably plus train), the design now more strongly built but no more powerful than his existing one, or maybe one of Sir Arthur Heywood's locos, or perhaps the first 15-inch design by Henry Greenly, or instead be revolutionary in the extreme.

The first possibility could well be the reason for that well-known visit by the second Cagney (of the same basic dimensions as the 'home' loco), complete with the newer type of carriages. If it was the 'set' from the Alexandra Palace line, it could have been at Blakesley as early as May 1904. With this, CW could assess the suitability of two Cagneys for double-heading these trains, as well as the value of more – bogie – passenger cars.

Presumably he felt the disadvantages associated with the need to run two small locos coupled outweighed any haulage advantages to be found. Had the larger and far more powerful Class E Cagney 4-4-0, newly introduced in 1904, been available for the 15-inch gauge (rather than just the 22-inch), the story might have been different, but the 4-4-0 design could not accommodate the larger features in this gauge.

Two Class D Cagneys double-head a train on the circuit at Blakesley, during the brief appearance of the 'visiting' train. The 'home' loco is at the front, with James Bartholomew and Percy Wyatt on the footplate. *Charles Simpson collection, courtesy of Sir William McAlpine*

In 1904 Heywood had produced the first example of his final design of steam loco to his 'standard' pattern. For some reason never previously satisfactorily explained, he had started to build two of them simultaneously, but while one (SHELAGH) was completed relatively quickly for the Eaton line, the other, though started at more or less the same time and speed, was suddenly left in abeyance for very many years, only being completed, for Eaton, in 1916 (where it became URSULA).

This finally allowed Eaton's original four-wheeled Heywood loco KATIE to be disposed of (to the Ravenglass & Eskdale line of Narrow Gauge Railways). It is an intriguing possibility that Sir Arthur had started this matching pair of locos for Eaton in 1904 in the (unduly optimistic) anticipation that his former student colleague CW might then take one of his existing locos, probably KATIE, since, after all, CW had at last adopted one of Heywood's 'minimum gauge' ideas – that of goods transport.

In 1904 this loco had recently had a long spell under repair back at Duffield Bank, being joined there by four of Heywood's six tip wagons, also from Eaton – thereby creating a complete train eminently suitable for CW's coal traffic. KATIE had not been very satisfactory at Eaton, being disliked for poor adhesion on 'leafy' rails, and renowned for punishing the track in view of the speeds adopted on this quite lengthy line.

The Railway Magazine had been somewhat unimpressed by the appearance of KATIE; in 1898 it commented that '...the funnel is hardly of an aesthetic type, and the appearance of the engine would undoubtedly be improved by a shortening of this elongated tube...', a sentiment likely to be shared by the modernist CW.

It is clear that Heywood was also somewhat embarrassed, to say the least, by KATIE; as early as 1898 he was saying, 'The long and short of my experience is that I should not again recommend a four-wheeler except for very short distances and low speeds', the latter features describing perfectly the conditions at Blakesley.

Such a transfer would in turn have allowed Eaton to have two identical and powerful new locos, but the lack of any interest by CW would have effectively ended any immediate need for continuing work on the second twin. Another

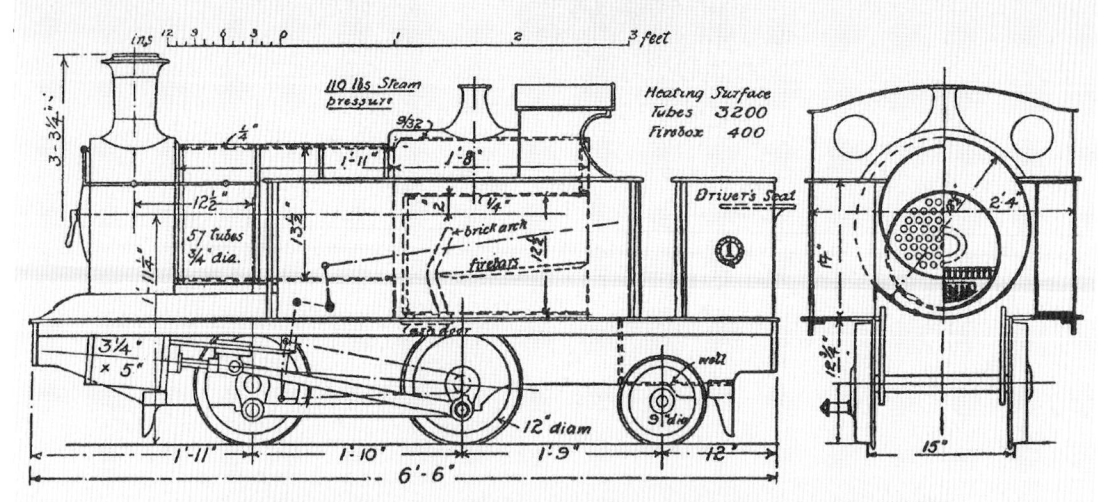

A DESIGN FOR A 15-IN. GAUGE ESTATE LOCOMOTIVE.

Coupled wheels, 12 in. diam.; cylinders, 3¼ × 5 in.; heating surface, 25 sq. ft.; tractive force, 450 lb.; coal bunker on left hand side; water tank on right hand side.

Greenly's first 15-inch design was specifically for a '15-inch-gauge estate' railway. *The Model Locomotive, 1904*

option for CW might have been Heywood's original, but now elderly and little-used, loco *EFFIE* (possibly in 1904 holding the fort at Dove Leys).

Also by 1904, the then rapidly emerging star in model railway design, Henry Greenly, had developed his first steam locomotive design for 15-inch lines. CW could not fail to have known of it, even if only because a detailed drawing of it featured in Greenly's first book *The Model Locomotive*, published by Percival Marshall in 1904; of great note was its description therein as being for a '15-inch-gauge estate railway'.

The entire section on 15-inch-gauge railways seems somewhat inconsistent with the remainder of the book's content, and it seems likely that this was all very much a last-minute addition. For example, the drawing of what is really the largest 'model' locomotive in the whole book is consigned to (indeed squeezed into) a ludicrously small part of the bottom right-hand corner of Plate VIII. Spurred on by CW's brand-new such railway at Blakesley, Greenly no doubt felt that he had to demonstrate to the world that his expertise covered the full range of current railway gauges.

Since only Blakesley and the two (or perhaps three, counting his Dove Leys line) Heywood 15-inch-gauge estate railways existed at that time (and for eight years thereafter), the first of these would have been its only existing market. The design, while eminently suitable for Blakesley – its overall design characteristics confirm that it was probably developed specifically with this line in mind – is, however, curious in a number of ways, and the published drawing and description display a level of carelessness, inconsistency and inaccuracy unusual in Greenly's work (again rather confirming this as something of a last-minute addition to the book).

It was to be an 0-4-2 steam side-tank locomotive, having 12-inch driving wheels, with outside cylinders 3¼ inches (on the drawing, or 3½ inches as quoted in the text) by 5 inches, and it would have had an unusual 'bullhead'-type boiler and firebox rather than one of conventional or Heywood style. The drawing shows 60 tubes in the boiler – but is annotated as only having 57 – and the quoted tractive effort of 450lb could only have been achieved if the boiler pressure had been 120lb per square inch rather than the 110lb per square inch shown!

The boiler and firebox arrangement had been chosen deliberately by Greenly as it '...renders the use of link motion a simple matter, and the motion may be protected from flying stones and grit [quite what speed Greenly envisaged on a 15-inch estate railway is hard to imagine!] by a plate fixed to the frames under the motion and parallel to the surface of the rails.' As an alternative, he suggested '…any of the radial valve gears commonly used for this class of engine…' could be used and thus '…the whole of the gear made get-at-able [sic] by being placed outside the frames and wheels.'

The trailing wheels were of 9-inch diameter (soon to become a Greenly 15-inch standard). These were to be in a radial truck, but there were no cut-outs in the main frames to allow for any side movement – such provision would have been impossible with the driver's footwell here extending down to the bottom of the frames. Its general design seems to have been evolved from his earlier 10¼-inch-gauge 0-4-4T *NIPPER*, which also had no provision for the trailing wheels to move laterally, and which started Bassett-Lowke on his 15-inch adventures.

It featured the driver riding actually in the loco (although he suggested it could be redesigned to avoid this), but in extremely cramped conditions (the only one he actually built on which the driver rode appeared five years later as a specific order for Blakesley, as we shall see). There was no hint as to who might be the intended builder of such a machine. This was his first steam design to such a large scale and, while the side view shows quite a well-balanced loco, freelance in style (but with some GWR features), the front view seems unnecessarily squat.

It is interesting to compare the relative tractive effort of each of these designs. For the Cagney Class D, it was a mere 287lb, the Greenly loco would have been 411lb, *EFFIE* was 658lb, and *KATIE* no less than 1,358lb. Accepting that the Cagney was known to be woefully underpowered, *KATIE* would seem to have been unnecessarily powerful for Blakesley's likely needs. Other, normally key, factors such as adhesive weights and the sustained steaming capability of boilers would be virtually irrelevant at Blakesley, given the short nature of the line as it then was.

Perhaps the last and most famous 15-inch design of all in 1904 (though not actually built until early 1905), Greenly's 'Little Giant' for Bassett-Lowke, would have been quite unsuitable for Blakesley at this time, given the all-too-apparent sharp curvature problems there, an issue that was to rear its head on at least two future occasions. (Given the crudity of his 0-4-2T design, rushed for publication earlier in the same year, there is a clear quantum leap in the quality and interpretation of 15-inch-gauge requirements in Greenly's designs between it and the 'Atlantic' design in such a short time.)

CW, of course, had the wealth to spare (as we have seen) to pursue any of these courses. However, none of these ideas was taken up by him (even assuming he investigated them all). Not having followed established practice before for his railway, it was unlikely that he would do so now! CW was an engineer of the 20th century; although interested in recording and preserving the past, as evidenced by his little museum at Blakesley Hall, he looked to the technological future.

Having both an estate workshop and a keen interest in road motor vehicles (with a large motor car garage and the first in the locality to own a motor car – several, in fact), it is hardly surprising that the Squire's thoughts had turned instead by the end of 1904 to the rejection of steam in favour of petrol power for his rapidly evolving railway.

Once again, CW was about to demonstrate that yet another of Arthur Heywood's original key principles had been overturned by developments elsewhere. Heywood had pronounced in *The Engineer* in 1881 that 'It is often not a question of whether steam is the cheapest form of transport, but whether there is any alternative…', and, at that time, he was perhaps right.

However, this short-sightedness on the part of Heywood was not replicated by the probable instigator of this comment, Sir Frederick Bramwell, who in that same year of 1881 had said to a meeting of the British Association that '…the steam engine … would become a thing of the past in about fifty years' time…'. As noted above, even by the early 1900s the options for mechanical traction had changed, and there was now a real alternative. Heywood, however, resolutely stuck with steam to the bitter end.

This seems unfortunate, as his 'minimum gauge' maxims could have directly and easily incorporated the internal-combustion locomotive; even his 'all wheels coupled with an equal overhang at each end' formula was, in essence, adopted for the most successful of such machines in the narrower gauges for half a century – the Motor Rail 'Simplex' design. (One of these did finally appear at Eaton in 1922, after Sir Arthur's death, immediately supplanting the steam locos, itself replaced there by a later model in 1938.)

In one of those magnificently ironic coincidences that sometimes emerge to brighten up mundane history, it somehow seems appropriate

Heywood's 0-6-0 *ELLA* of 1881 had all his distinctive design features, including all wheels driven and an equal overhang at each end. *R&ER Historical Series Postcard No 7*

today that the 15-inch-gauge Ravenglass & Eskdale Railway's 4-6-4 diesel-hydraulic locomotive *SHELAGH OF ESKDALE* (remembering that Heywood's 1904 loco happened to be named after a different *SHELAGH!*) contains significant running gear elements – such as the radiating gear axle sleeves, and five of the original six crank webs – from Heywood's steam 0-6-0 *ELLA* of 1881 (the year he made his fateful pronouncement). This surely makes them the oldest such active components in any internal-combustion railway locomotive in regular use anywhere in the world. Perhaps Heywood has the last word after all!

Anyway, by 1905 CW had applied his own engineering talent to the design, and his engineering staff and equipment at Blakesley to the production, of an innovative and pioneering petrol locomotive. It is truly amazing that such a landmark venture could be built 'in house' on this small estate in the rural depths of Northamptonshire, far from the country's manufacturing and engineering centres.

9 Enter internal combustion

Discovery of a new power

The basic principles of the internal-combustion engine were, like those of the steam engine before them, developed not by a single person or in a single country. British inventors were well to the fore, but have rarely been given the credit they deserve in this field. It is therefore perhaps fitting that the world's oldest surviving internal-combustion-engined railway locomotive of any gauge or type should be British-built to the order of a British Squire by a British model-engineering pioneer for a railway on a quintessential British country estate; not only this, but the remnants (at least) of an even earlier petrol locomotive from this self-same railway almost certainly also survive, moreover one actually built on this little estate.

Probably the first patent for such a machine was taken out by Robert Street of Christchurch, Hampshire, in 1794. Many others inevitably followed, including from Germany, France, Italy and the USA, as well as others in Britain. Nevertheless it was Gottlieb Daimler who, in 1883, patented the first high-speed petroleum engine and had sufficient faith in his principles that he soon had many examples – running at up to 900rpm – in service. Rudolph Diesel did not take out his first patent until 1892.

Daimler supplied his first internal-combustion locomotive in 1890; this was followed in England by the first oil-engined loco, equipped and built by Priestman Brothers of Hull, in 1894. Probably the main catalyst in Britain, however, was the firm of Richard Hornsby & Sons of Grantham, which supplied no fewer than six such locos, all commercially successful, between 1896 and 1903, and all fitted with the Hornsby-Akroyd patent oil engine.

By 1904 or 1905 a few other British manufacturers had followed, albeit generally with penny numbers of prototype and experimental locomotives, in these early years of the 20th century; despite their innovativeness, some of these did prove successful and reliable in their intended work. This brief historical diversion is important in placing in context just how pioneering CW was during 1904-05 (and later also in 1909) in the realm of internal-combustion railway development.

The building of *PETROLIA*

In 1905, therefore, the Blakesley Miniature Railway became one of the first in Britain to have a petrol locomotive in operation, and almost certainly the first to have built its own such locomotive. Although intended primarily for the coal trains, it was used at short notice for passenger work, and the line may well therefore have been the first in the world to haul passengers with a locomotive of this kind.

The North Eastern Railway had introduced two petrol-electric railcars – 'Electric Autocars' – in 1903 (the body of one of which – long used as a house and sadly long since shorn of all mechanical and running components – was, remarkably, recovered for preservation in 2003), and there were a number of earlier track inspection vehicles as well, in various countries. However, the Blakesley loco may have been the first internal-combustion rail vehicle in the world to have driving axles fixed to the body frame combined with unpowered pivoting bogies to help carry the weight and guide it around corners. Bartholomew was certainly pushing the existing technology to new limits; his loco was of a narrower gauge than any previously built, a small number for 18-inch gauge having been supplied by Hornsby for Woolwich Arsenal.

CW's locomotive was a 4-4-4 (or 2-B-2 in

103

The Blakesley Hall Miniature Railway

A new era dawns for the world's railways! Blakesley's home-built PETROLIA poses with a train comprising the entire goods stock (six tip wagons led by the bogie 'trolley'), conveying estate timber en route to the standard-gauge station. The train is astride (and hiding) turnout T5, having come from the Hall or estate workshops. 'BHMR' and 'PETROLIA' are stencilled on the dash panel. *Charles Simpson collection, courtesy of Sir William McAlpine*

today's non-steam nomenclature) of somewhat strange appearance (but exactly what was a petrol locomotive supposed to look like at that stage of design development?). The highly flexible wheel arrangement was a clever solution for coping with Blakesley's sharp, industrial-pattern pointwork. As befitted a 'home-grown' product, the bogies themselves were 'standard' interchangeable Blakesley-built wooden-framed 'carriage' bogies, using four spare Cagney carriage wheel-sets and axleboxes.

The name PETROLIA was painted on its front bodywork dash panel in a somewhat crude 'stencil' style of lettering (together with the similarly applied 'BHMR' – the only time these particular initials seem to have been used 'officially' for the railway). The name is clearly visible in a photograph (*not* spelled PETROLEA, as has been all too frequently quoted in more recent years) – the loco's livery may have been a 'works grey' rather than a substantive 'livery' for the loco, but no view is known of it painted otherwise. This 'stencil' style of lettering seems to have been in quite common use at this period – Pitmaston Moor stock used a similar style.

PETROLIA had a radiator at one end, followed by a neatly boxed engine compartment above the pair of driven axles, then the driving position, and finally a semicircular dash panel, its outer shape resembling that fitted to contemporary electric tramcars, containing the silencer and topped by a remarkably tall chimney with polished cap, which would actually not have looked out of place on a Heywood railway.

With this arrangement, the 2-B-2 layout was entirely logical, the main weight (of the engine) being carried on the driving wheels, with the lighter ancillary equipment over the bogies. A horizontal wheel on a vertical spindle in the cab area is suggestive of PETROLIA having brakes on its driving wheels, a highly desirable, but previously unknown, feature at Blakesley – its importance increased by the inability, unlike with steam, to reverse such a loco while running as a means of braking!

The above description is really 'back to front' in operational terms, but one would expect the radiator at the front in practical engineering terms! When hauling the tip wagons on the

The radiator end of **PETROLIA** is leading as the loco heads west towards the Hall with the tip wagons. It is astride turnout T6 and about to cross the Black Ouse stream by bridge B1. *Andy Thompson collection*

industrial-derived trackwork of the BMR, the complete ensemble looked as far removed from either a Heywood or a 'scale' miniature railway as could be. Certainly Heywood's principle of 'steam with all axles powered' had been countered by CW in his new loco.

Although bearing no resemblance to a miniature railway or steam locomotive, the layout of *PETROLIA* did suggest some similarity to motor cars of the period; CW of course moved regularly in such circles, and knew those in the forefront of these designs. Indeed – and not for the first time – the layout could have been developed in discussions within the hallowed portals of the Automobile Club. It is likely that the three-speed gearbox unit (and perhaps also the chain drive) came from such automotive suppliers – or perhaps were cannibalised from an early model in his existing fleet of cars.

The driving wheels, axleboxes, reversing gearbox and brake gear would have to have come from a railway engineering source – either locally or from a supplier of light railway equipment (most likely the one supplying the contemporary German tip wagons – thus perhaps Busch of Bautzen via Milnes). If the latter, perhaps the driving wheels were not really 16 inches in diameter (see below) but 400mm. Locally, the firm of Groom & Tattershall in Towcester is believed to have built or rebuilt several steam locomotives, and is just one example of a company that could have provided what was needed.

Once again, to obtain contemporary descriptions of this pioneering loco we need to refer to those same two articles of 1906. *The Locomotive Magazine* for 15th May records:

'The goods trains are worked by the *PETROLIA* motor engine having a single cylinder 4 in. in diameter by 8-in. stroke, built at Blakesley Hall from the designs and under the entire supervision of the owner. It is very powerful considering its size, and can take a full load of six wagons laden with coal or coke from the East and West Jn Railway sidings to the Hall coal cellars. This engine is also used for passenger trips, Blakesley Hall to the railway station, and vice versa, being more readily available than the steam locomotive, and sometimes has reached a speed of 30 miles per hour.'

105

Further information is provided in *The Model Engineer & Electrician* for 5 July 1906:

> 'For goods work and during "seasons" of heavy traffic a locomotive, built at Blakesley Hall, employing petrol for its motive power is used. This is fitted with a twin cylinder motor of about 9 h-p, having mechanically operated valves and lying in a horizontal position in the body of the vehicle. It is a water-cooled motor, with three speeds both forward and reverse. The exhaust, after passing through a silencer, is conducted to the funnel. The wheel arrangement is of the 4-4-4 class, the leading and trailing sets being on bogies. The driving wheels are 16 ins diameter, and are coupled with a chain inside the frames. This locomotive will haul a load of five or six trucks fully laden with coal, and will attain speeds of sixteen to eighteen miles an hour with lighter trains. Being more readily available than a steam locomotive, it is also used for emergency trips to the station.'

Clearly *The Locomotive Magazine* was impressed by speed, while *The Model Engineer & Electrician* was more impressed with its haulage capability at moderate speed! It is both fortuitous and amazing that the two reporters concentrated on different aspects of this loco's design and performance, thereby leaving us a better picture of this remarkable machine. Sadly, no firm date for its building seems to be known, although 1905 seems most likely as the date for its entry into service.

Unfortunately, the magazines were unable to agree on the number of cylinders the engine had, although the two suggested by *The Model Engineer* reporter (probably Greenly) seems more likely, particularly as we know that *The Locomotive Magazine* reporter was inaccurate about the line's steel sleepers (and also about the number of carriages on the railway). It is of course just possible that both are right – the discrepancies in the descriptions could relate to a rebuilding between the visits by the two reporters; certainly the 8-inch stroke quoted (and its 1,500cc capacity) in one seems more attuned to a small industrial stationary engine, while the 'flat twin' would fit better with the emergent motor car evolution.

A curious feature of the design, not copied from the Cagney, was the fitting, at the chimney end only, of an oil headlamp with not only a front lens, but two side lenses angled at 45 degrees. The reason for this desire for an internal-combustion loco to see round corners (the Cagney had a conventional single-lens lamp) is not known!

Once again we find a design definitely not to Greenly's taste. Although almost certainly the author of the 1906 *Model Engineer* piece, by 1909 he was saying '...the present petrol engine, although it has done good service, is an experimental machine entirely, and is simply a carriage containing the petrol motor mechanism, with no pretensions to external design' – the kind of opinion frequently vented 50 years later in respect of the early British Railways 'Modernisation Plan' diesel locos!

Nevertheless PETROLIA had worked most of the traffic on the railway for around four years by 1909, with the Cagney used only on special occasions; it must be regarded therefore as a considerable success and a true credit to CW and his estate staff.

The events of 1909

In 1909 the relatively stable world of the BMR was changed dramatically. It is usually claimed that this was mainly as an indirect result of the phenomenal, if transient, success of MRGB Ltd in establishing its exhibition lines in continental Europe. One such line, opened in Nancy in 1909, was, apparently, so successful that an additional locomotive became needed at short notice to handle the traffic on offer.

MRGB Ltd had no spare locomotives and Bassett-Lowke could not supply a new one in time (being fully committed with other 15-inch-gauge locomotive orders), so the only option was to 'borrow' an existing loco from an existing line somewhere. The choice, inevitably, fell on No 11 *MIGHTY ATOM* at Sutton, which, if borrowed for Nancy, would then leave the short Sutton line bereft of motive power – unless perhaps, on a personal basis, Bassett-Lowke could persuade CW to loan Sutton his Cagney from Blakesley for the summer season.

As we shall see, Bassett-Lowke unusually had, at this time, a business 'hold' over CW and, with his small financial stake also in MRGB Ltd, CW had little option but to agree to such a loan. No 11 *MIGHTY ATOM* was thus able to be returned to Northampton for repainting and also rebranding as No 13 *VILLE DE NANCY*, before rushing off to join its sister No 12 *ENTENTE CORDIALE*. The

The Blakesley Cagney in use on the Sutton Miniature Railway during its loan there in 1909/10. The train comprises two early Bassett-Lowke bogie carriages. John Tidmarsh collection

Cagney duly went to Sutton from Blakesley in June 1909 and photographs of it there show that it was clearly labelled 'BMR' on its tender and became in somewhat care-worn condition. The tender's side footboards confirm that it was the 'home' Blakesley Cagney.

At this time the Sutton line was in its original 15-inch-gauge form, consisting of an out-and-back line around 400 yards long with loops at each end provided with spring-loaded points to speed up running round. The line had three Bassett-Lowke 12-seater bogie coaches, which may have come from the original 1905 line at Blackpool. However, the Cagney was unable normally to handle the line's three coaches (just as at Blakesley), and its usual load was only two, thus reducing the line's capacity by around a third.

The MRGB Ltd Directors' Report for 5 May 1910 noted somewhat ruefully that 'The line at Sutton Coldfield does not show so large a profit as last year ... at the height of the season the Sutton Coldfield engine ... was transferred to Nancy... An engine was hired to do the work ... but being of a smaller type than the "Mighty Atom", the full complement of passengers could not be carried.' CW's generosity was damned with faint praise indeed!

The generally quoted version of events continues with the idea that, as compensation for this loan to Sutton, Bassett-Lowke agreed to build CW a new petrol-engined version of the 'Little Giant' design, ultimately to be known as *BLACOLVESLEY*. Close study of contemporary documents and the detailed design of this new locomotive for Blakesley do, however, suggest that this story does not represent the true course of events.

The concept of a steam-outline petrol locomotive seems to have been CW's own idea as he '...made the point that a smart-looking steam locomotive design always attracted attention, irrespective of what went on inside to make the wheels go round.' We also know of course of CW's commitment to the internal-combustion engine – both for cars and 15-inch-gauge railways.

Bassett-Lowke was the obvious – and most logical – choice of commercial manufacturer for such a locomotive, and its chief designer, Henry Greenly, the obvious man to translate CW's concept into practicality. Greenly himself, a reluctant 'convert' away from steam, commented that it '…may be deemed a new conception entirely'.

The July 1909 issue of *Model Railways & Locomotives* reported that this new petrol locomotive was being built for CW and '…is now nearing completion at Northampton'. Even more significantly, that same reference continues, 'By the time the next issue appears the trials will no doubt be over, and we shall make a point of fully describing this interesting engine.' Thus we know that, by late June, *BLACOLVESLEY* was thought to be within days of completion and scheduled to go to Blakesley for its operational trials during early July.

However, the Nancy line did not commence operation until May – and then poor weather resulted in equally poor patronage initially – and the Cagney did not go to Sutton until June. The new loco was thus clearly planned, ordered and largely completed before the need for an additional locomotive at Nancy was appreciated; indeed, it was part of the already committed Bassett-Lowke factory's work for, inter alia, the White City (London), which would prevent a further new engine being built there for Nancy!

Henry Greenly himself, writing in *The Model Engineer & Electrician* for 13 January 1910, records how the White City contract, let only just before Easter that year, required delivery of its two locomotives within 36 and 48 working days respectively or a penalty of £1 per day late would be payable. Thus all other work, including that on *BLACOLVESLEY*, would have had to be deferred to ensure that these deadlines were met.

A further significant, physical, piece of evidence exists by virtue of the diameter of the 'boiler' of *BLACOLVESLEY* (which affects the shape of the cab-front spectacle plate). The first loco for Nancy, No 12 *ENTENTE CORDIALE*, which was ordered in February 1909, had boiler cladding the same diameter as the dummy boiler of *BLACOLVESLEY*, while the two locos ordered that Easter for White City, Nos 15 and 16, had barrels three-quarters of an inch larger in diameter – as did the subsequent Class 10 locos, Nos 18 and 19.

Nos 15 and 16 were certainly delivered before *BLACOLVESLEY*; the number 17 seems never to have been positively identified in the Class 10 steam loco series and it has been suggested that, although it never carried the number, *BLACOLVESLEY* was regarded as Bassett-Lowke No 17. However, this is considered unlikely since a photograph in the June 1910 issue of *Model Railways & Locomotives* clearly shows *ENTENTE CORDIALE* working at the Brussels exhibition of that year.

If standard practice was being followed, this would simply have been renumbered (and perhaps renamed), thereby creating it as No 17 for this event. It does appear that *BLACOLVESLEY* was the last 15-inch-gauge locomotive to be supplied by W. J. Bassett-Lowke & Co, as all subsequent ones were from the incorporated firm of Bassett-Lowke Ltd.

With the delivery of the new engine due in July, this would mean that borrowing the Cagney from Blakesley to replace *MIGHTY ATOM* at Sutton in June would be expected to leave the BMR short of motive power for only a few short weeks at most. As it was, the various delays caused by problems with the new design, and the rush order for White City, resulted in *PETROLIA* having to soldier on alone for rather longer than expected, the new loco arriving only just in time for the late-September Show!

It would also appear that, if CW did not agree to the loan of his Cagney, the building of his own new engine might thus be delayed even further and so miss the 1909 Annual Show entirely! It was also reported that 'During the past summer Mr Bartholomew has had the line overhauled and the sharper curves and turnouts eliminated' in order to accommodate the significantly longer and less flexible wheelbase of the new locomotive.

This also suggests that these works had been planned well before June in anticipation of the different characteristics of the new engine, which would have become apparent at the design stage. This reconstruction work seems to have resulted in the abandonment of one part at least of the circle, although some of this was still useable as late as 1914.

What matters most, however, is that the result of these machinations led CW and Blakesley to give the world the dawn of yet another new age in miniature railways, and not just at Blakesley – that of the steam-outline internal-combustion-engined locomotive. Furthermore a new breed of 'engineman' was required, with much simpler and yet significantly different training and skills – a 'chauffeur' rather than an 'engine driver'.

To the modern world, this difference is perhaps seen as trivial; to that Edwardian era the issue was all too real. As Henry Forbes, General Manager of the County Donegal Railways, said later in connection with Ireland's first petrol railcar of 1906/07 (which still nominally exists, at least in small part, after a multitude of major rebuildings over half a century of service), following a disastrous gearbox incident with a long-time steam driver: '…the experience confirms the opinion of all motor experts, that steam drivers or firemen should not be allowed to handle or have anything to do with motor vehicles.'

Model, 'free-style' or progeny?

Despite the theoretical 'new era' advantages of a chauffeur, it is curious that BLACOLVESLEY was destined to remain as the only internal-combustion locomotive ever built by Bassett-Lowke – although there was quite heavy promotion of the concept by the company – and the world's only steam-outline internal-combustion locomotive for many a year to come.

BLACOLVESLEY was also the one and only Greenly-designed locomotive of any gauge or type actually to be built whereby the driver rode in it rather than in or on a tender or following truck. As we have already seen, Greenly had proposed this idea for Blakesley as far back as 1904. The end product of all this was the beautifully balanced design of a 4-4-4 tank locomotive, using many 'Little Giant' Class 10 components, but with its own distinctive features.

A 'tradition' had obviously developed on the Blakesley line that petrol locos should be of the 4-4-4 type (presumably because of the success of the original PETROLIA), a layout rare in Britain but quite common for steam tender locos in North America, where the term 'Jubilee' was applied to this wheel arrangement. The only full-size British examples of the steam inside-cylinder 4-4-4T were three supplied to the Wirral Railway (one in 1896 and two in 1903), with two to the Midland & South Western Junction Railway in 1897.

Although this innovative Blakesley concept of steam-outline internal-combustion locos was to be copied widely in future years, the logical use of unpowered bogies at either end of a powered chassis proved nearly as rare a precedent for miniature machines in all gauges as it did for non-steam-outline designs. Among the very few to follow were the impressive and massive 'Baltic' 4-6-4T diesel-hydraulics built by Hudswell Clarke for the 20'-inch and 21-inch gauges. These, intriguingly, were themselves developed as a freelance design from the company's corresponding 4-6-2 diesel tender design (based on the LNER 'A3' 'Pacifics') for the North Bay Railway, Scarborough – almost exactly the way in which BLACOLVESLEY itself developed.

W. J. Bassett-Lowke himself was later to acknowledge, concerning BLACOLVESLEY, that 'This engine may be regarded as the forerunner of a number of similar models that have been built in recent years, based on steam prototypes externally, but driven by internal combustion engines, chiefly of the Diesel type. The 15-inch [sic] gauge LNER Pacifics in the Peasholm Park [sic] at Scarborough are good examples.'

It is perhaps dangerous to try to suggest a full-size locomotive as the basis of this design for Blakesley, as Greenly developed very much his own style in all his miniature, as distinct from model, work; his 'Little Giant' design, from which BLACOLVESLEY was developed, did not really resemble any particular full-size 'Atlantic'.

Nevertheless, this new machine did, for a number of reasons, actually have a very strong visual affinity to a 'real' loco, albeit one with a slightly different wheel arrangement. CW was a modernist – and he would expect his new loco to be designed to mirror (but not necessarily copy exactly) the latest and finest full-size ones.

In May 1906 the LNWR's Crewe Works had turned out No 528, the first of 50 'Precursor tank' 4-4-2T side-tank locos designed by George Whale, and the overall similarity of BLACOLVESLEY to these is remarkable. They were designed for high-speed suburban service, as evidenced by their 6ft 3in driving wheels. In the fashion of 1909, the tender locos of this 'family' were seen as pre-eminent nationally – the noted author and train recorder Cecil J. Allen wrote challengingly in the February 1909 issue of Model Railways & Locomotives that 'As to external appearance it is doubtful whether more handsome machines could be found in the country than these neat and yet powerful…giants'.

That same February 1909 issue of Model Railways & Locomotives also records that:

'…Messrs W. J. Bassett-Lowke & Co's catalogue … the 1909 issue … published the second week in December [1908] … forms a precedent… The most important feature … is the numerous new models that the firm have introduced this season… First, in the clockwork department, there is an important

Above The first 'Precursor tank' 4-4-2T, built by the LNWR at Crewe in 1906. This view appeared in *The Locomotive Magazine* just three months after it carried the article on Blakesley. *LNWR postcard, author's collection*

Below An early drawing by Greenly of *BLACOLVESLEY*, before the petrol engine had been finally selected. The one eventually chosen required considerable internal (though little external) design changes. *Model Railways & Locomotives, September 1909*

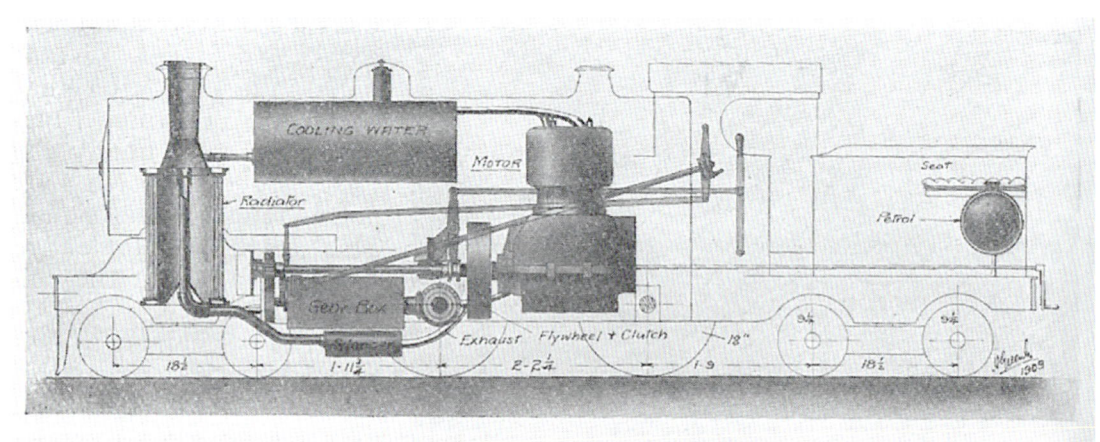

SKELETON DIAGRAM SHOWING INTERNAL ARRANGEMENTS OF MR. C. W. BARTHOLOMEW'S 3" SCALE PETROL TANK LOCOMOTIVE.

introduction of the scale model L&NWR tank locomotive No 528 in both gauges No 0 and No 1... This model has been much admired ... and it looks like having a record sale. In addition to fast and slow movement, the 1¾-inch-gauge model is fitted with a special device which enables it to be reversed from the track '

This date for the model's introduction is important. It is highly likely that one of these technically innovative and modernistic models was already the principal, and newest, motive power on the Blakesley model railway by early 1909. Greenly would have prepared all the detailed drawings for these models during 1908 and thus be completely familiar with the design characteristics at the start of 1909. What would be more natural now than for CW to want Greenly to design his latest 15-inch locomotive to resemble this, currently the 'last word' in both prototype and model form?

Enter internal combustion

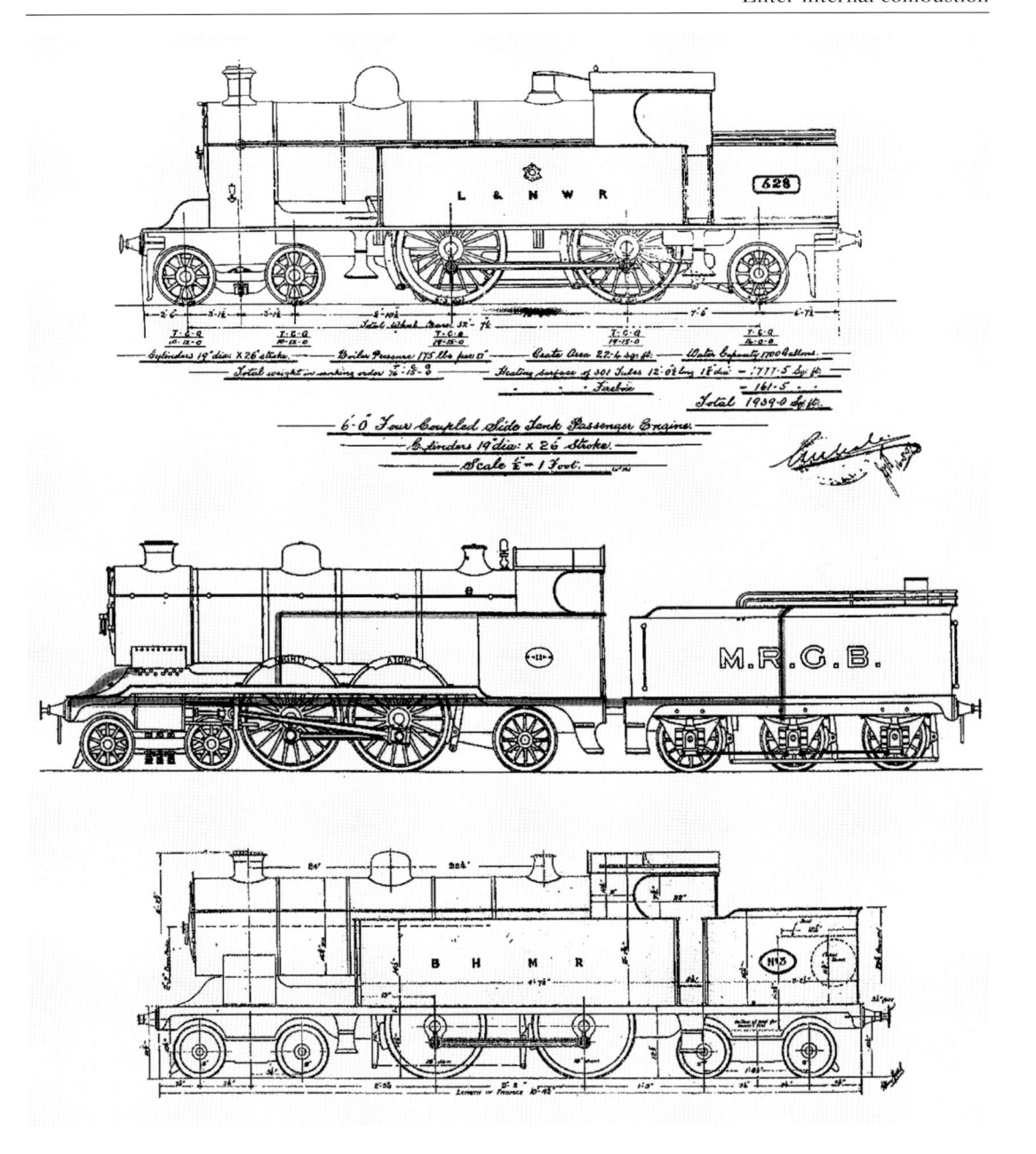

Interestingly, the 'Little Giant'-pattern 'extended' smokebox of BLACOLVESLEY is perhaps more akin to that of the contemporary LB&SCR 4-4-2T pioneering superheated locos of Class '13' built by D. Earle Marsh from 1907. These locos were the subject of an intriguing comparative month-long locomotive trial, also in this same year of 1909, whereby the through 'Sunny South Express' between Brighton and Rugby was alternately worked throughout by a

A comparison of the LNWR 'Precursor tank' No 528 and BLACOLVESLEY as finally designed, showing how the Class 10 'Little Giant' design (centre) was adapted to create BLACOLVESLEY, yet closely resembled the 'Precursor tank'.

'Precursor' and one of these tank locos. With Blakesley being close to the LNWR main line south of Rugby, CW may well have witnessed these trials directly.

111

The superheated tank proved superior to the 'Precursor' both in coal and water consumption, as well as being easily able to maintain schedule, leading to a more general adoption of the idea. Bassett-Lowke was soon also to offer models of this LB&SCR design from Greenly's drawing board. A model design combining the best visual features of both of these 'state-of-the-art' full-size locos could suit CW's modernistic aspirations perfectly.

That the new steam-outline design was certainly perceived at the time by outsiders as being derived from the 'Precursor' family is evident from the description in Strauss's *Liliputbahnen*, where he records it as '…eine 2B2- London & South Western Tenderlokomotive…', which translates directly as '…a 4-4-4 London & South Western Railway tank locomotive…', 'South' here being logically a simple misunderstanding by Strauss for 'North', as no LSWR design features are evident anywhere. (The text of the 1988 English translation of the book omits this comparison entirely.)

However much these full-size resemblances might have been used to 'sell' the design concept to CW, he does not seem to have sought an exact copy of any full-size locomotive; indeed, he perhaps wanted his 'own' design for his own railway. Many of the detail features were anyway in practice simply copied by Greenly from his 'toolbox' of such details used for previous model designs developed over many years (including obviously those of the 'Little Giant').

After extensive research and comparative measurement, the author believes that the above perceived origins of the design can be substantiated. Superimposing the plans of the full-size 4-4-2T 'Precursor tank' on those of the 15-inch Class 10 'Atlantic' design, as first built with six-wheel tender, shows that the basic dimensions and configuration of the two are amazingly similar. All Greenly had to do was to make the simplest of amendments to the latter to replicate the basic structure of the former. The similarity was coincidental, but nonetheless fortuitous.

Thus the new design could retain even the cab doorway width and the 'boiler' length, similarly the bunker sides and top flares, of the Class 10 from the (otherwise necessarily foreshortened) tender body! The few main bodywork differences from the 15-inch design are the straight, rather than partly raised, running plate from bufferbeam to cab, and the side tanks (these being basically forward extensions of the cab lower side panels of the 'Atlantic'). The widths and heights follow the same principles as the Class 10 design.

By adopting the existing Class 10 smokebox layout, rather than that of the 'Precursor', standard Class 10 components could be used here too. This effectively created a unique design while apparently modernising the 'Precursor' smokebox area through the adoption of the LB&SCR 'I3' 'superheater' extended layout.

The distinctive 'Precursor' S-shaped sweep of the mainframes between front bufferbeam and smokebox saddle remained unique to this one 'Little Giant' derivative; this seems to confirm the idea of the design being 'customised' by Greenly to CW's 'modernist' expectations.

Below the running plate, however, bigger concessions had to be made. The 'Precursor tank', to allow the firebox to depend between the two axles, had the extraordinarily long driving wheelbase of 10 feet (Greenly himself acknowledged that this was too long for many contemporary model railways). In contrast, the 15-inch Class 10 'Atlantic' had an excessively short driving wheelbase to allow its firebox to depend behind these.

With no firebox to worry about, but a combination of potentially heavy human driver, tight curves and a newfangled petrol engine to consider, Greenly adopted a middle course in regard to the position of the second driving axle. This, with the slightly elongated bunker, meant that a trailing truck was no longer appropriate, and a bogie was needed. Hence the 4-4-4T design emerged naturally.

The cab panels were of sheet metal (as in No 12 *ENTENTE CORDIALE* of early 1909), rather than castings (as used in Nos 10 *LITTLE GIANT* and 11 *MIGHTY ATOM*), while the 'smokebox' itself displays a curious difference from all other 'Little Giant' locos, as discussed later.

In his book *The Model Locomotive* of 1904, which featured the proposed 15-inch estate railway 0-4-2T for Blakesley, there are drawings (on Plate III) for a three-quarter-inch scale (3¼-inch gauge) spirit-fired 0-4-4T locomotive, which, despite the difference in size and wheel arrangement, has the cosmetic and detail characteristics of the 1909 *BLACOLVESLEY* (particularly in its front elevation), showing how adaptable – and long-lived – was Greenly's design 'toolbox'.

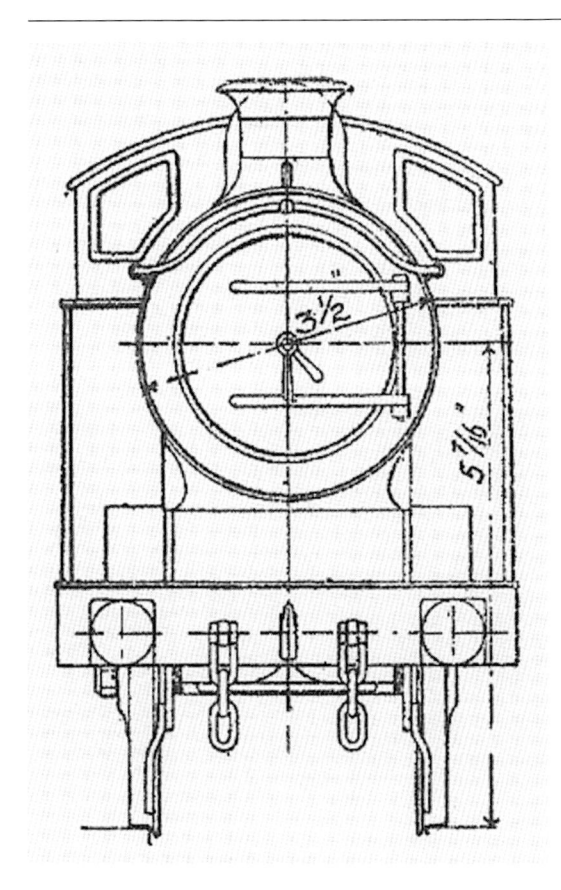

Enter internal combustion

FIG. 5.—VIEW DURING BUILDING, SHOWING MOTOR BEING LOWERED INTO PLACE.

Above The state-of-the-art 1502cc NAG engine is squeezed between the frames of BLACOLVESLEY at the Bassett-Lowke works. Model Railways & Locomotives, September 1909

Below The cheapest-bodied NAG 'Puck' car was this 'Doppel-Phaëton', priced in 1908 at 4,800 Marks ('without Soft-top, Lights, and Horn'). NAG Puck brochure 1908, author's collection

The front elevation of a 3¼-inch-gauge spirit-fired 0-4-4T design by Greenly in 1904, visually similar to BLACOLVESLEY as built to the 15-inch gauge in 1909. The Model Locomotive, 1904

Engine, gearboxes and cooling system

The major technical task, which would ultimately govern the whole of the remainder of the design, was to locate a suitable petrol engine that was both adequately powerful and yet had a sufficiently narrow crankcase to fit between the frames of a 15-inch-gauge inside-framed locomotive. It must be appreciated that in 1909 petrol engines – and the motor car – were still in their infancy and there was little experience of what could be made to work reliably. Most engines of this period were relatively large for their limited power output, even the Model T Ford, still in its earliest development stage in 1909, being of no less than 2,894cc for only about 20bhp.

Eventually, and certainly not Greenly's first thought, as is evidenced by the early general layout drawing of his (which shows a quite different one), a German NAG (Neue Automobil Gesellschaft mbH) engine was chosen. He described it as '…a 12-14 HP four-cylinder…' unit (although in Greenly's biography by his daughter and son-in-law they refer to it as two-cylinder). It had a narrow crankcase able to fit between the 15-inch frames, this last being a particular design feature from this manufacturer. Yet again, German

113

technical progress was about to be demonstrated at Blakesley!

However, accounts of NAG products show no engine quite meeting Greenly's rather bare description, the nearest being a 12hp (13/14bhp) 1502cc monobloc four-cylinder L-head unit, as used in the company's 'Puck' car. This engine was truly 'state of the art', as this car design had only appeared in 1908-09, being advertised as a revolutionary 'neuer kleiner Viercylinder Gebrauchswagen' ('new, small, four-cylinder 'runabout' car'). Each of the four cylinders was of 75mm bore by 85mm stroke. This may seem a physically large engine to squeeze into BLACOLVESLEY, but the NAG range featured really large units – of up to 8.5 litres. This particular engine was later upgraded to 15hp for NAG's 'Darling' model.

CW himself must have recommended to Greenly such an innovative, practical and 'sporty' unit, noted for its ability to run at up to unusually high speeds for the period (up to 3,000rpm, when 1,500 was 'normal' and 'anything over 2,000rpm exceptional'). The outcome of his active knowledge of, and contacts with, the contemporary motor car scene, no doubt as a result of discussions within the portals of the Royal Automobile Club ('Royal' was added in 1907), was well demonstrated during its initial performance trials at Blakesley. Although NAG was based in Berlin, the firm had a London Sales Agency, The Connaught Motor & Carriage Coy Ltd, of 28/29 Long Acre, WC.

A standard steam-loco-pattern regulator handle in the upper middle of the 'boiler' backhead formed the throttle control. In order to accommodate the lower part of the engine and the bevel-geared drive between the frames, the standard-size 'Little Giant' driving wheels of 18-inch diameter and of one-piece cast steel had to be spaced 26 inches apart compared to less than 20 inches in the steam design. This was the first, but by no means the last, element enforcing an increase in the overall effective fixed wheelbase.

This layout also required a slight elongation forward of the original design of the side 'tanks' to allow room for the exhaust system. The framework for these tanks was of wrought-iron angle, with the detachable side sheets held in place by wing nuts; this allowed for their speedy removal to access the engine and clutch.

The choice of gearbox would also be critical. Surprising as it might seem today, when one thinks of 'old-fashioned' cars having 'crash' gearboxes, there were many proprietary easy-change boxes on the market in the early years of the 20th century. Many small manufacturers bought in gearboxes and the like, rather than producing their own.

Thus Greenly had quite a selection open to him; no doubt he was influenced once again by CW and the choice fell on the Wicksteed Patent Change-Speed-Gear Box. This had been introduced to the motoring public at the Crystal Palace Show of 1907, and was given a full-page description in *The Automotor Journal* for 9 February of that year.

This gearbox had been designed by Charles Wicksteed, who, like CW, was Yorkshire born and bred with a Nonconformist church background. He spent time at locomotive builder Kitson's in Leeds before starting his own businesses. In 1876 he founded Charles Wicksteed & Co in Kettering (reasonably close to Northampton), and by 1912 he employed 200 people involved in a variety of engineering activities (including making bicycles).

He hoped to interest a number of manufacturers (including Humber) in fitting his patented gearbox to their cars, but it seems there were few if any takers. The one fitted to BLACOLVESLEY has the serial number 58, but no others are known to survive. This lack of outside interest is

The selector disc for the Wicksteed gearbox of BLACOLVESLEY. The 'Reverse' position was used here purely as a neutral. Author.

regrettable as the one in the loco has successfully survived a century of fairly continuous use and misuse!

Later in life Wicksteed established the Wicksteed Park in Kettering, and designed a 2-foot-gauge railway to be operated therein by steam-outline petrol locos built by E. E. Baguley Ltd. Today Wicksteed remains in the forefront of the manufacture of playground equipment.

The design basically featured a three-speed box, with a separate metal cone clutch for each speed, selection of which was by means of a crankshaft connected to a wheel at the driving position. Of particular interest in this 1909 unit fitted to the loco is that the operating handwheel is coated with a form of black plastic material; this is original and must be one of the earliest – as well as one of the longest-serving – operational pieces of plastic in existence.

In rotating this handwheel from one position to the next, the first clutch was disengaged as the second clutch was being engaged and so on, so this was a true semi-automatic gearbox. By careful adjustment of the positions of the cones for each clutch, it was theoretically possible to slip-engage the next position before slip-disengaging the first, thus keeping power applied through the change!

Although, for cars, there was also a low-speed reverse gear position, Greenly dispensed with this, relying on a simple reversing dog-box so that similar speeds and performance were available in each direction. The position on the gear selector was, however, retained as a neutral.

The engine and Wicksteed box were not joined directly. First came the normal engine clutch, which was operated by a clutch lever on the left side of the cab, designed to look like a reversing lever. A long shaft ran forwards from this clutch across the top of the Wicksteed box to a Greenly-designed reducing and reversing gearbox sited directly in front of it. This was a very simple dog-box and could only be engaged or disengaged with the loco stationary and the engine clutch disengaged. This too was operated by a lever, on the right side of the cab, also resembling an ordinary steam loco reverser lever.

Unfortunately this reversing gearbox had to be somewhat larger than originally envisaged, with the result that, during construction, the 'Little Giant'-pattern front bogie had to be modified in a somewhat curious manner as the already long overall wheelbase could not be further elongated. While the normal bogie frame swept over each axlebox hornway in a gentle curve, the left rear hornway was supported instead from underneath with the same gentle frame curvature but apparently upside down! This gearbox projection further reduced the flexibility of the wheelbase and thus the ability of the loco to negotiate tight curves.

For a petrol loco, the 4-4-4 arrangement should have permitted a perfectly symmetrical wheelbase, but in practice the gap between front bogie and front driving wheels is slightly longer than that between rear drivers and rear bogie. This too may have been forced on the designer by the size of the reversing gearbox, although this same asymmetry was also a feature of every one of those few 'full-size' steam 4-4-4T locos in Britain.

The rear bogie was, however, a standard Class 10 front bogie; all bogie wheels were of the same diameter, but two Greenly drawings on successive opposite pages of the September 1909 issue of *Model Railways & Locomotives* once again display some carelessness on his part as they offer both 9¼ and 9 inches as their diameter (the former is more likely to be correct as this was standard for Class 10 bogie wheels).

Neither of the bogies was braked, a brake pedal in the cab applying shoes to all four coupled wheels only. This meant that, wherever there was a 'dip' in the track, braking (as well as traction) could be lost. However, this arrangement seems to have been copied directly from *PETROLIA*, which was presumably regarded as satisfactory for the Blakesley conditions.

The output from the dog-box went straight into the Wicksteed box. This was of a nominal 20hp and was thus more than adequate to deal with the output of the 12-14hp NAG engine. In turn the output from the Wicksteed box drove to the bevel pinion and crown wheel on the driving axle (which was the front one of the two 'driving' axles). This driving axle had to be unsprung – or the bevel gear and pinion could disengage when passing over track inequalities.

The design of the water cooling system was also interesting. An obvious radiator was out of the question in an elegant steam-outline design, and Greenly overcame this problem by introducing two unusual elements. The first was an enormous cylindrical water tank contained within the front half of the 'boiler'; a filler cap for the water system was provided via the dome, as this was the highest point (exactly as in a steam loco!) – a standard Class 10 cast-iron dome cover was provided.

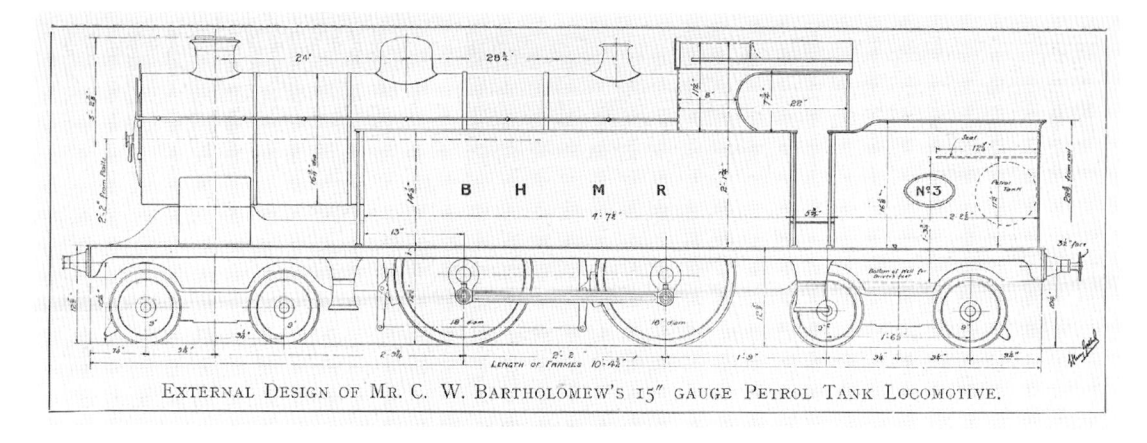

EXTERNAL DESIGN OF MR. C. W. BARTHOLOMEW'S 15" GAUGE PETROL TANK LOCOMOTIVE.

Greenly's second drawing of BLACOLVESLEY; the actual build differed mainly in cab-roof detail and the length of the side tanks. Model Railways & Locomotives, September 1909

Some good steam traction theory was used for the radiator. It was contained within the 'smokebox' and consisted of a cylindrical arrangement of vertical cooling tubes running from immediately above the front bogie to half way up the inside of the smokebox. The exhaust piping, having passed via a silencer box mounted laterally beneath the frames and ahead of the driving wheels, passed up the centre of the ring of radiator tubes to the bottom of the chimney.

A removable louvred panel between the frames in the front of the smokebox saddle beneath the door allowed fresh air to reach the radiator. The

The cab layout of BLACOLVESLEY as seen during its sojourn at Haswell. The electric meters were fitted at the time of the re-engining in the 1940s, but the rest is basically as first built. Dr Mike Taylor

exhaust, though hot, acted like a 'blower' in a steam loco (and in the same location!). Thus the harder the loco was working the stronger was the exhaust draught up the chimney and so the stronger the pull of cool fresh air through the radiator. Once again a standard Class 10 chimney was used, with a polished gunmetal outer top rim shrunk over the cast-iron core.

Excellent and imaginative in theory, this radiator/exhaust combination proved less clever in practice and Greenly admitted that a very early modification before it even left the factory was yet another cooling water tank, this time beneath the driver's seat in the bunker, under the petrol tank, together with a belt-driven 'Albany' circulating pump.

In something of a simplistic reversion to established Cagney practice, the 'smokebox' of BLACOLVESLEY was merely a forward extension of the 'boiler' barrel, and thus of the same diameter as the latter; this feature remains from the first Greenly drawing of the loco. As the barrel was in more than one piece anyway (and formed of heavier-gauge plate than usual in order to be self-supporting), it would have been easy enough to make a larger-diameter ring comparable with that on the steam locos, but this was not done.

This is all the more surprising given that 'Little Giant' locos Nos 15 and 16, built more or less concurrently with BLACOLVESLEY, had larger-diameter boilers and cladding anyway than either it or the earlier 'Atlantic's – which would have provided the necessary larger-diameter rolling pattern for such a smokebox ring.

10 The world's first 'steam outline' loco emerges

Building *BLACOLVESLEY*

All 15-inch-gauge Bassett-Lowke locomotives were built in a specialised 'large gauge workshop', which was actually sited within the J. T. Lowke works in Kingswell Street, Northampton. The shop manager was Fred Green and the basic staff consisted of four people.

One of these was a William Vaughan, who gave a graphic description of the laborious techniques required in the building of the locomotives. One of his principal tasks had been to cut out the quarter-inch plate main frames for the various 15-inch-gauge locos, which meant 'a month's hard labour for one man' for *BLACOLVESLEY* (once again demonstrating how the design must pre-date the Nancy exhibition moves).

The workshop had facilities for running the steam locos in a raised rig with their driving wheels supported just above rail level, and it is presumed that *BLACOLVESLEY* was similarly 'run in' and tested here. This is how the overheating problem mentioned earlier was discovered, and an additional under-seat water tank added in the bunker before the loco left for Blakesley.

However long the gestation period for its building had been, the final completion was necessarily somewhat rushed in order for it to be tested 'live' at Blakesley and any defects – or incompatibility with the revised track layout – to be remedied in time for the Show in late September.

Changes to the railway

Irrespective of its design ancestry, the detailed layout of the new locomotive confirmed that significant parts of the existing Blakesley railway would be unsuitable for its operation. Besides easing some curves and replacing the sharper turnouts, the rebuilding work during the summer on the BMR also included an extension of the main line '…up a steep rise past the Hall towards the farm buildings' (as described by Greenly).

His description is accurate but somewhat misleading. This 1909 extension only went as far as the then farm manager's bungalow, certainly 'towards', but a fair way short of, the farm buildings themselves. Some of the pointwork was renewed, and a 'desirable minimum' radius of 100 feet adopted, although the diverging route at certain pointwork was allowed to be of 80-feet radius, presumably for sidings intended primarily for tip wagon movements.

The author can confirm that a turnout of 80-feet radius is only just tolerated by *BLACOLVESLEY* today, and even here any slight vertical convex curvature through such pointwork will sometimes result in derailment of the front bogie as a result of the rigidity of its wheelbase and the lack of significant movement in the suspension.

The works almost certainly included the abandonment (though not necessarily removal) of much of the circle, and also the 'wandering' line between T5 and T11 (via T10). The new extension commenced with a new turnout (T12) from the engine shed line, sited alongside the eastern end of the gas producer plant.

The remaining part of the circle track, now without the associated connections forming a triangular layout able to turn locos and stock, would still not be useable by *BLACOLVESLEY* because of the sharp curvature; however, the Cagney and *PETROLIA* (in its original form) could still use these remnants. The provision of a new turntable outside the engine shed now allowed the locos to be turned here.

Henry Greenly's survey recorded that the main line was at this time some 1,503 feet long, with the

The Blakesley Hall Miniature Railway

Above Looking east in 2004, on the course of the 1909 extension to the farm manager's bungalow, to the right are the workshops and (nearest the camera) the motor garage. The grassy area to the left is where the engine shed and gas plant once stood. *Author*

Above right These combined electricity and telephone poles, which carried those services to the farm buildings, were still intact in 2004; their tapered, sectional, galvanised steel-tube construction was yet another of CW's innovations. *Author*

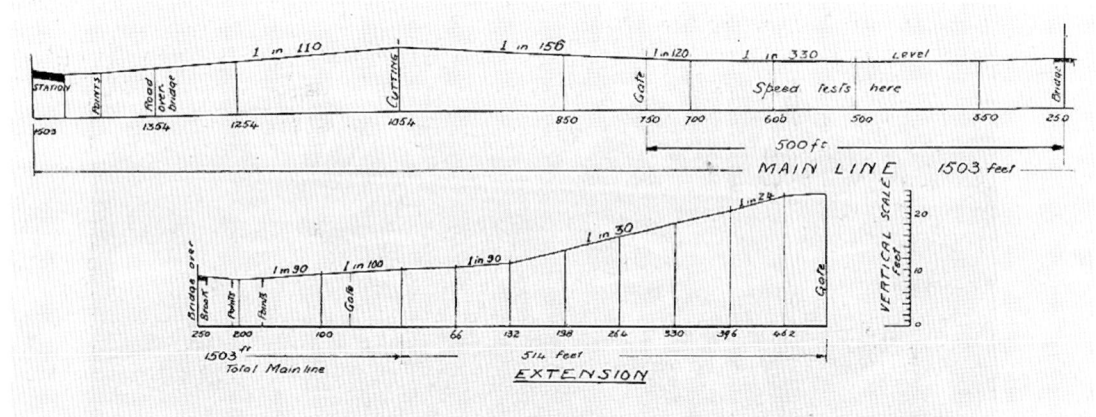

FIG. 3.—THE GRADIENTS OF THE BLAKESLEY HALL MINIATURE RAILWAY.

Henry Greenly undertook a detailed gradient survey of the line in 1909, ready for the trials of the new loco. This is the only contemporary definitive plan of the railway in any form.
Model Railways & Locomotives, October 1909

first part of the new extension forming an additional section of some 514 feet; the last few feet crossed the artificial feeder water course for the canal (or 'Moat' as it is shown on the Ordnance Survey plan), possibly by a bridge (B4), but more likely by a culvert (as found latterly). It terminated at a gate (G5) leading into the pasture containing the farm buildings.

While the original line had nothing steeper than a short length at 1 in 90, the 1909 extension was severely graded, with over half of it, 264 feet, at 1 in 30 and 66 feet at a vicious 1 in 24, before the last short level section over the feeder water course to the gate.

This extension was itself extended in 1910 by

The world's first 'steam outline' loco emerges

up to a further 400 feet or so by continuing it through the field gate G5, past the bungalow and the Hall's tennis court (the Duffield Bank line also linked House and tennis court – though at Blakesley it would probably have been quicker to walk!), and diagonally across the pasture to the farm buildings themselves on similarly steep gradients all the way; it probably ended at or just beyond a gateway (G6) in the fence enclosing the yard to the buildings. Perhaps taken from one of the abandoned sections, a Sykes banner signal was erected at the new blind corner by gate G5.

Fortunately this last steep section was virtually dead straight and in open field, clear of any trees. No previous written reference to this later extension exists in any report or article, but fortunately – and rather curiously – it is better illustrated than many longer-established parts of the railway (including the 1909 extension itself)!

BLACOLVESLEY arrives

CW, with his family, and W. J. Bassett-Lowke ('Mr Whynde') had been on one of the latter's intensive continental tours, which included a visit to the Nancy exhibition at which two Class 10 locos were now working. They arrived back at Blakesley just in time for the running trials of the new petrol locomotive on Saturday 11 September 1909. This tour perhaps indicates something of a reconciliation at last between the two men.

The Cagney and BLACOLVESLEY top-and-tail a trainload of visiting members of The Railway Club in 1912, on the 1910 extension from the bungalow to the farm buildings. The photograph is looking west, the fence marking the estate boundary. John Alsop collection

The loco had been hurried to completion because of the forthcoming Blakesley Show (the 35th such event) at the end of the month and was delivered painted only in 'light lead' primer. It carried a simple oval works plate on the bunker with just the number '3' thereon, presumably on the basis of it being the third 'home' loco to enter service on the BMR.

The trials were highly successful. No doubt aided by the wide speed range offered by the NAG engine, a top speed of 32mph was attained running light, and the loco proved able to haul 5¼ tons. Three different loads were simulated – light, ordinary and heavy. With the medium load of two bogie carriages, the full end-to-end 2,017 feet of the then line were covered in 1 minute 20 seconds, taking just 16 seconds to cover the 'measured 500 feet' across the flood plain; these speeds were equivalent to 17½mph over the full line and 21⅓mph over the measured section.

When the load was increased to around 5¼ tons the loco could still manage the 1 in 30 on the farm bungalow extension, but was unable to climb the last 1 in 24 section and two wagons had to be detached, reducing the total train weight to 4¾

The Blakesley Hall Miniature Railway

Left In plain 'works grey' lead paint, the brand-new *BLACOLVESLEY* poses on bridge B1 over the Black Ouse stream during its first trials on Saturday 11 September 1909. *Author's collection*

Below The commissioning team pose for the local newspaper during the 11 September 1909 trials. *Model Railways & Locomotives, from The Northampton Independent*

Reproduced by permission] [*Northampton Independent.*

AN INTERESTING GROUP AT BLAKESLEY.
C. W. Bartholomew, Esq, Mr. W. J. Bassett-Lowke, Mr. F. Green, Mr. H. Greenly, Mr. James Bartholomew.

tons. With this reduced load, the end-to-end journey time was just under 2 minutes, giving an average speed of 11½mph.

At the 'speed test', with the load reduced to one carriage (with five passengers), the end-to-end time was reduced to only 1 minute 10 seconds, or 19mph. Over the 500 feet measured length the '...flying speed was no less than thirty-two miles per hour, which we suppose is the highest yet attained on a 15-inch-gauge railway'. Truly BLACOLVESLEY was a perfect 'Gentleman's Light Sporting Locomotive' (in the motor vehicle idiom of the time), as well as a beast of burden (although comparison with the 1906 descriptions of the line suggest that the original PETROLIA was equally capable of around 30mph)!

The new loco went straight into daily service, pausing briefly from its activities only to 'show it off' (still unpainted) to the Bassett-Lowke works staff the following Saturday, 18 September, and then to ensure that it was painted and lined in readiness for the Show.

Development of the livery and numbering

To meet the Show date this therefore meant yet another rush. The article by Henry Greenly in the October 1909 issue of *Model Railways & Locomotives* records that '...at the time of writing [it] is being painted in Great Northern standard colours in readiness for the Flower Show to be held on Sept 30th'. It has been suggested in more than one reference that this was Squire Bartholomew's favourite railway, but evidence elsewhere suggests that he was far more attuned to the Great Central.

As Bassett-Lowke was building large-scale model Great Northern 'Atlantics' in a variety of scales at that time, there would have been no problem in ensuring paint of virtually the perfect hue for BLACOLVESLEY. Also, the 'Little Giant' 'Atlantic' MIGHTY ATOM, when re-branded for its expedition to Nancy, had reportedly been painted at the Northampton factory in Great Northern colours only a few weeks earlier.

Bassett-Lowke had realised the difficulties for modellers in matching the paint shades of mainline railways. In the June 1909 issue of *Model Railways & Locomotives* it was described how it had arranged with '...two well-known manufacturers of locomotive and coach paints (Messrs Gay & Sons, London, and Messrs R. Kearsley & Co, Ripon)' to supply enamel paints through them in '...colours in 1/- tins of a uniform size. The colours are exact to railway companies' shades...'.

In perfect time for both MIGHTY ATOM and BLACOLVESLEY, among colours initially available that June were 'Great Northern Railway green' and 'Great Northern Railway border green', but of course these paints were enamels, not coach paints, and were also probably 'scaled' to look right on small models rather than on quarter-size locomotives. As will be discussed later, there is some uncertainty as to how close a match was actually achieved to the green used by the GNR at that time.

Because it was derived from the 'Little Giant' and 'Precursor tank' designs, the general body shape had little in common with Great Northern practice of the time, which thus affected the livery details. This was particularly true of the cab, where GNR locos had the roof as merely a curved-over continuation of the sides – until, that is, the coming of the Gresley 'Pacifics' in 1922 (and even these had also originally been intended to have this style).

The bodywork, 'boiler' and cab panelling was therefore painted in the two shades of Bassett-Lowke GNR green, with wheels also in green, all with appropriate black lining edged in white. The conventional, curved, separate cab roof was also in lined green, as the 'wrap-over' GNR cabs of this period were thus painted. It does not, however, appear that the chocolate brown colour normally used for GNR framing at this time was applied (black being used instead).

A contemporary coloured postcard issued by the Locomotive Publishing Company showed BLACOLVESLEY in a deep green, similar in shade to that used for GNR locomotives in other LPC postcards of this period; it also shows red lining on the black framing (which is not evident on monochrome views of the locomotive – although photographic emulsions of this period could not differentiate clearly between red and black).

During restoration in the mid-1990s it was discovered that, such had been the rush to get the loco to Blakesley from Northampton, that no paint at all had been applied to the cab roof beneath the sliding plate thereon. Photographic evidence suggests that BLACOLVESLEY was fully painted and lined in time for the fete, but that there was still insufficient time to apply name banners and family crests to the tank sides. The

Left Fully painted and lined, but still with the number '3' and devoid of name banner and crest, BLACOLVESLEY takes a party in their 'Sunday best' to the 1909 Blakesley Show. Fred Green from Bassett-Lowke is driving. *The Model Railway Handbook*

Below Now fully painted and with suitable tank-side adornments, No 1 BLACOLVESLEY poses near gate G2 on the 15-inch 'main line'. *Author's collection*

temporary works number plates hurriedly applied for the initial trials were replaced by more conventional brass ones recording 'W. J. BASSETT-LOWKE & Co. MAKERS 1909 NORTHAMPTON' and the number '3', all in hand-chiselled characters.

Subsequently the name BLACOLVESLEY was applied to each tank side on a curved banner with a shield above, on which was the head of a grey goat, taken from the crest at the top of the Bartholomew coat of arms. These distinctive tank-side banner embellishments are somewhat out of scale and out of keeping with normal railway practice.

A significant clue to CW's derivation and use of such an obscure and rather unpronounceable version of the Blakesley name may be found, somewhat surprisingly perhaps, in a 1920 issue of the *Mexborough Times* newspaper: '…Councillor John Robinson, Wombwell's "grand old man", gave a very interesting account of old Wombwell, based on the Doomsday [sic] book, a copy of which Mr Robinson has himself seen at Blakesborough [sic] Hall, the home of the Wombwell Main Bartholomews…'.

This demonstrated CW's commitment to delving into village history. Thus 'Blacolvesle' – in which form the village name was shown in the Curia Regis Rolls of 1203 – or the variations in the original Domesday Book ('Baculveslea', 'Blacheslewe', 'Blaculveslea', 'Blaculveslei') appeared on the tank sides as BLACOLVESLEY, this being the form to which it had evolved by 1460. Court of Chancery archives for that time record 'Blacolvesley' as the exact village spelling given in connection with the then vicar John

The world's first 'steam outline' loco emerges

Grene! It is certainly the case that over the years few writers or printers have managed to spell the name correctly in published accounts!

The stylish new shape of BLACOLVESLEY made the utilitarian appearance of PETROLIA unacceptable to CW. Although it had served the BMR well for around four years, it now looked dated in comparison – and, perhaps more importantly, did not look like a miniature present-day main-line railway locomotive. Also, the 1909 internal-combustion engineering of BLACOLVESLEY had progressed somewhat beyond that used in the creation of the original PETROLIA.

Having established that the often-quoted story of BLACOLVESLEY being in part a 'reward' by Bassett-Lowke to CW for his help in the 1909 crisis is false, there is some probable substance to this story – but the reward was the rebuilding of PETROLIA, not the building of BLACOLVESLEY! Accordingly CW arranged in late 1909 for PETROLIA to go to Northampton, which meant that the unproven BLACOLVESLEY became the sole motive power on the line for nearly six months, as the Cagney was still away at Sutton.

Either coincidentally with or relatively shortly after this, the works plates were replaced by new ones, otherwise identical but now carrying the number '1' instead of '3'; at the same time the inscription 'No 1' was applied to the front bufferbeam. With BLACOLVESLEY being alone on the railway at this time, giving the third locomotive the number '1' was actually quite justifiable!

PETROLIA is rebuilt

Bassett-Lowke (no longer 'W. J. Bassett-Lowke & Co' by the time it emerged, but now 'Messrs Bassett-Lowke Ltd') rebuilt PETROLIA somewhat in the fashion of a further steam-outline locomotive. The editorial in the April 1910 edition of Model Railways & Locomotives recorded that 'At the moment of going to press, Mr C. W. Bartholomew's rebuilt locomotive PETROLIA is undergoing tests at Blakesley Hall. The engine has been re-modelled into a 0-4-4 type tank engine and is to be used for goods work almost entirely.' Blakesley's railway was thus, once again, a true 'miniature railway', with all three locos now conforming to this philosophy.

Suddenly, however, silence descends on all aspects of Blakesley, and no further references appear to the railway or its locomotives in this magazine (even the attempted sale, mentioned earlier, by Bassett-Lowke themselves, of a Cagney at Blakesley in 1911 was consigned merely to the 'trade advertisement' page!).

Henry Greenly was at this time the editor of Model Railways & Locomotives, as well as Bassett-Lowke's chief designer, and it is probable that he redesigned PETROLIA in its new guise. Modesty was not a Greenly strong point and, had the rebuilding been a success, it would undoubtedly have featured in effusive descriptions in the magazine within a couple of issues.

There is a strong clue to the existence of a problem in an anecdote by CW's godson, Charles Simpson, a very young visitor to Blakesley Hall at that time. He quotes CW as telling him that '…if that man Greenly came to Blakesley again he could dine in the servants' quarters!'

The comment was thought by Simpson to refer to a problem with BLACOLVESLEY, but in view of this loco's long-term success, evident from the way it remained in service at Blakesley until the line closed in the early 1940s, and elsewhere thereafter, it seems more likely to have arisen because of PETROLIA not performing to expectations – and perhaps even being inferior to its previous abilities.

However, Greenly was a rather tetchy individual and the argument between the two men could have been a simple irresistible force meeting an immovable object! This schism between them receives further confirmation from the fact that the June 1910 issue of Model Railways & Locomotives records the return of MIGHTY ATOM to Sutton, but conveniently ignores the consequent return of the gratefully borrowed Cagney thereby to Blakesley.

PETROLIA now looked somewhat awkward and unbalanced inside its new pseudo-steam outline; it certainly lacked the elegance either of BLACOLVESLEY or other Greenly or Bassett-Lowke 15-inch products. It hints of being done 'on the cheap' (particularly likely if little or no payment was envisaged). It does seem probable

The Blakesley Hall Miniature Railway

The rebuilt PETROLIA, in 'works grey', stands on the station spur. This is the only known view of the loco after rebuilding by Bassett-Lowke in 1910 into a steam-outline 0-4-4T. The overall impression is of an awkward, low-cost adaptation of the original. Author's collection

that the 'remodelling' was mainly cosmetic and concerned with putting a steam-outline body over existing mechanical parts, with relatively little new internal work, apart from some rearrangement (and perhaps a contemporary engine and framing).

The long side tanks and pseudo-boiler, for example, appear of similar overall dimensions and location to the original box-like engine compartment and arrangement of PETROLIA. The original chimney seems to have been re-used (if somewhat shortened), while the original radiator above one of the bogies (at the opposite end to the driving position), and the former exhaust box above the other bogie, would have been relocated to enable a relatively simple transition from 4-4-4 to 0-4-4.

The appearance of PETROLIA at 'events' was rare – it was treated as the 'goods' loco, or perhaps even the 'loco of last resort'. The only known satisfactory photograph of it in its new guise is a front view, where its somewhat ungainly stance is all too apparent. The cab has circular spectacle windows and the roof profile is of much smaller radius than for a 'Little Giant'. The only visible items in this photograph that might be of 'Little Giant' pattern are the buffers. The arrangement of the coupled and bogie wheels is (infuriatingly in the light of future research needs) quite invisible.

The original driving wheels were almost certainly retained, with outside axleboxes and chain-drive between frames and wheels, rather than being of steam loco pattern. There is a subsequent implication that a new bogie based on Bassett-Lowke carriage bogie wheel-sets (possibly a complete such carriage bogie) may have been used as its new rear bogie; it seems unlikely that Bassett-Lowke would have retained one of the two crude wooden-framed Blakesley-built bogies in such a rebuilding (which could have been returned to Blakesley as spares for the carriages) or used one of the substantial 'Little Giant' pattern bogies.

11 An Indian summer

CW hosts railwaymen and enthusiasts

According to the June 1910 issue of *Model Railways & Locomotives*, 'The track at Sutton Coldfield Park, near Birmingham, has been laid with a heavier section of rail, and the engine "Mighty Atom" has now returned to its duties.' This allowed the Blakesley Cagney to be returned, although contemporary photographs show that it had got into quite a poor state while at Sutton, presumably being worked hard day in and day out in comparison to its usual peaceful and cosseted career at Blakesley.

Photographs of the Cagney at Blakesley after its return home show it in fine fettle, both mechanically and cosmetically, and it is presumed that Bassett-Lowke undertook at least a light overhaul and repaint of it en route from Sutton to Blakesley, which may have delayed its return until July or even August 1910. Combined with the re-working of *PETROLIA*, this suggests that Bassett-Lowke ultimately paid dearly for its loan to Sutton!

Although the plain black livery of the

On 20 June 1914 the Blakesley Cagney stands on the engine shed approach spur, outside the corrugated-iron gas producer plant, after its return from Sutton; it has been refurbished en route by Bassett-Lowke. *Charles Simpson collection, courtesy of Sir William McAlpine*

locomotive remained unchanged, still without name or number, the tender acquired full lining with scalloped corners, somewhat in the style of the tank sides on *BLACOLVESLEY*, and the lettering 'B. M. R.' in elongated block sans-serif lettering (complete with full stops).

This work suggests that CW had no immediate intention of parting company with his steam loco, even though he now had two petrol locomotives available. For the first time, therefore, the railway now had a full complement of three locomotives (the Cagney, the rebuilt *PETROLIA* and *BLACOLVESLEY*), and all were now of 'miniature' format.

At this time CW appears to have 'got his second wind' and, from then until the Great War, Blakesley, its estate and its little railway achieved quite a prominent position in amateur and professional railway circles alike. An example of this significance is given by the Locomotive Publishing Company producing a coloured postcard of *BLACOLVESLEY* and train on the main bridge (B1).

Perhaps because of all the earlier publicity associated with the rapid changes to the line's motive power in 1909 and 1910 in such periodicals as *Model Railways & Locomotives*, visiting parties of interested professional and amateur railwaymen became quite common. This was undoubtedly encouraged also by CW's membership of The Railway Club, which he joined in February 1911, at which time its membership stood at around 125.

He was also made an honorary Vice President in the same year. He remained a member until his death and, though not apparently a Vice-President in 1912, was so again in 1913 and 1914. (After this date, Vice-Presidencies were only granted to senior active Club Members.) It is believed that the Club visited Blakesley for the first time on 10 September 1910, which may account not only for him joining but also for his near-immediate Vice-Presidency.

The survival of an S&MJR 'Excursion Ticket' for 30 adults from Blisworth (connecting from the LNWR main line) to Blakesley dated 17 August 1912 (the ticket being illustrated in *Railway World* for February 1961) demonstrates that the Hall had a substantial visit on that day, believed to have again consisted of members of The Railway Club. They were, however, on this occasion unusually favoured not just with a trip along the line hauled by *BLACOLVESLEY*, but with it and the Cagney apparently 'topping and tailing' their special train (see the photograph on the title page). As CW had been indisposed the previous Saturday for an ambulance competition, he may have been unable to welcome these guests either.

Perhaps because of this absence in 1912, The Railway Club visited the line again on 20 June 1914 – and was also honoured by a trip behind *BLACOLVESLEY*. This time the Cagney was displayed outside the engine shed for them and even seems to have been taken for a run along at least the surviving – western – part of the circle (as usual, *PETROLIA* seems to have remained hidden away). Despite CW's recent antagonism to Greenly, he was apparently in the party for this last visit! (The frequently illustrated 'top-and-tail' trip has been attributed to this occasion, but this is an error – only the 1912 visit was so favoured.)

It is likely that E. W. Twining would also have become a regular visitor to Blakesley following his move to Northampton in 1912, as both he and CW shared passionate interests not just in small-gauge railways, but more significantly as avid early motorists, and in stained glass (Twining as a maker and CW as a long-term patron of such windows in several churches, as well as in Blakesley Hall itself – see the colour plates).

Twining ultimately developed quite a phobia about the '…two fundamental errors…' of the 15-inch gauge, it being '…too narrow…' and in the '…adoption of scale models for the locomotive stock'. One wonders if this derived from too close an acquaintance with the small-scale nature of the Blakesley locos and wagons.

Perhaps the most famous traveller (and even driver) on the little railway around this time would have been George Bernard Shaw. Knowing of his interest in motor vehicles from the earliest days, a chance to drive the pioneering *PETROLIA* or sporty *BLACOLVESLEY* during (one of) his visits to Blakesley would have been irresistible. Though a keen motorist, he did travel by train frequently – and might have arrived thus at Blakesley S&MJR station, requiring a 15-inch journey thence to the Hall.

It was around this time that the NAG company reached a pinnacle in motor sport circles, its 'Puck' and 'Darling' cars, fitted with engines very similar to that in *BLACOLVESLEY*, winning the Gothenberg Cup at the Swedish Winter Trials in 1912, 1913 and 1914. Shaw's involvement in the RAC would have ensured his knowledge of these successes.

The Great Central Ambulance Cup

CW's interest in the St John Ambulance activities has been described earlier, and in 1909 he instituted an annual competition among ambulance teams from the Great Central Railway. He was a diabetic and photographs of him from about 1909 onwards do not show a well man; one wonders if this increased his interest in these activities. In 1909 it was merely '…a little friendly competition…', the first 'proper' one taking place on Saturday 20 August 1910.

At a luncheon accompanying one of these events it was recorded that 'Mr Bartholomew was a good friend to the ambulance men of the GCR. He was, as a matter of fact, deeply interested in the GCR long before most of them there that day were born.' Virtually all the railway and canal interests in which Charles Bartholomew had been involved passed ultimately into the hands of the Great Central Railway, and CW no doubt retained personal contacts from that era.

The magnificent Cup was a '…very fine piece of Sheffield plate which came into his [CW's] possession some little while ago', with the inscription 'The Bartholomew Challenge Bowl, to be competed for annually by the Ambulance Corps of the Great Central Railway Co. Blakesley Hall, Northants'. The *Great Central Railway Journal* for October 1910 records that 'Mr Bartholomew met his guests at Blakesley Station, and they were conveyed on his miniature railway to the Hall…'

The July 1911 issue of the same *Journal* announced the forthcoming 'Ambulance Competition for the "Bartholomew" Invitation Cup, presented by C. W. Bartholomew, Esq, to promote "First Aid" work on the Great Central Railway', and the same issue also notes that 'The generosity of Mr Bartholomew is well known amongst railwaymen…'

It had been intended to hold the competition that year on 19 August, but a railway strike caused its postponement until Saturday 30 September. The announcement of the postponement includes a quote from CW himself: 'It is with great regret that I shall not be able to see you tomorrow, but with all good faith let us see your faces in the work that makes the world wonderous [sic] kind – that is, the great work of helping and giving those assistances to the relief of the body and saving of life', this indicating as it did his deep commitment to this cause.

The November 1911 issue of the *Journal* was able to report that 'For the third successive year Mr C. W. Bartholomew has entertained a large number of Great Central Railway Ambulance men at Blakesley Hall for the purpose of competing for his handsome massive silver bowl.' It continued, 'The model light railway was used to convey a good many from the Station to the Hall.' The number of visitors to the event exceeded 80 and must have put quite a strain on the 18-seat-capacity train, connecting as it did with '…a special train [on the S&MJR that] left Woodford for Blakesley at eleven o'clock'.

A photograph of some of this number, with CW, and showing the truly mammoth bowl, appears in the same issue, although strangely it features not the winning team (which was from Lincoln), but the runners-up, the local Woodford team, with their District Committee.

An interesting part of the description of that day's events covers the inevitable cricket match involving the Blakesley team, the latter '…captained by Mr J. Bartholomew'. It continued with how the visitors '…wished the young Squire every success, who was that day starting out in life to make a name for himself… The day finished with a grand display of fireworks and illumination of the grounds; also a visit to the Squire's valuable museum.' James was, of course, actually 'starting out in life' in a way quite different from his father – or, subsequently, his own son – by returning to the family roots, deep in traditional Great Central territory, to study Mining Engineering at the new University of Sheffield.

The 1912 competition was held on Saturday 10 August, but it was '…with great regret … that the genial Squire was unable to leave his bed, and was unable to see anyone…' James acted as host on this occasion, but the 'Luncheon and tea' were provided unusually at the Red Lion hotel in the village rather than at the Hall, conveniently requiring further round trips on the miniature railway!

CW also missed the 1913 competition, but this time because he '…was away at Norwich'. James again acted as host and, as he had just celebrated his 21st birthday, was presented with a cigarette case inscribed 'Presented to Mr James Bartholomew by the Great Central Railway ambulance teams as a mark of esteem upon his attaining his majority in June 1913'.

In a rare display of sexual equality in this era, 'The Cup was handed to the winning team by Miss

ph by]   *[Mr. J. Settle*
BACK ROW—Dr. Hope, — Butcher, T. Liddell, J. J. Eaton.
SECOND ROW—R. Hayes, T. Cave, J. Coulson, A. J. Floyd, H. Minshaw, W. E. Hobbs.
THIRD ROW—H. C. Higson, F. Patman, C. W. Bartholomew, Dr. Stewart-Murray, Dr. Black.
FRONT—G. Askew.

Photograph by]   *[The Northampton Independent.*
MR. W. E. HOBBS, *Sec.*   MR. J. BARTHOLOMEW.   MISS BARTHOLOMEW.   THE WINNING TEAM.

Left The magnificent Bartholomew Invitation Cup with CW, members of the local Woodford GCR team, and the Doctors who judged the 1911 Ambulance Competition. It is possible that A. J. Floyd was a relative of CW's partner, Sarah. The steps on which they are standing survived into the 21st Century. *The Great Central Railway Journal, November 1911*

Below left CW was away for the 1913 GCR Ambulance Competition, so son James presided at the event, with daughter Ivy presenting the Cup. *The Great Central Railway Journal*

Bartholomew' – and she was even photographed, somewhat self-consciously, with Cup and winners by *The Northampton Independent*. There is no record of further events in subsequent GCR *Journals*, and it is presumed that the Great War brought an end to the competition.

The regular reports in the *Journal* refer to a Mr A. J. Floyd of the GCR at nearby Woodford as being involved in organising each year's event, and one wonders if he was related to Sarah (Woodford being the next village to Byfield); such a relationship could have been the original catalyst for these competitions at Blakesley.

Photographs and loco usage

There was a very clear hierarchy in the way the locos were normally seen on the railway, at least when visitors were present. The Cagney is seen in photographs only ever hauling carriages, while the original *PETROLIA* (despite being the only loco through the summer of 1909) is only seen with the wagons.

BLACOLVESLEY, though alone on the line from the autumn of 1909 to March 1910, is similarly only ever photographed with the passenger carriages – yet it must have hauled the tip wagons of coal to the Hall during this time, while *PETROLIA*, upon rebuilding, was intended to resume its career with the wagons!

That single clear photograph of *PETROLIA* as rebuilt is the well-known view of it beneath the S&MJR bridge at Blakesley station, alongside and in front of, but not coupled to, several tip wagons. This is presumed to have been during its trials, and supports the question whether it worked sufficiently well after rebuilding to bother with it at all.

There is a local story that, in due course, its engine was taken out and used to power some farm machinery in the Blakesley area. It was,

A variation on the 'classic' view of **BLACOLVESLEY** with train: a group of visitors poses on bridge B1, with Alec Wyatt in attendance. How many of these young men, one wonders, failed to survive the Great War? *Charles Simpson collection, courtesy of Sir William McAlpine*

129

The Blakesley Hall Miniature Railway

BLACOLVESLEY heads a special for The Railway Club on 20 June 1914; it is on the 1910 extension, with the farm manager's bungalow in the background. Note the open-jaw socket and pin coupling. John Alsop collection

apparently, stored unloved and unused in the engine shed in the early 1930s, painted in a brown/prune colour, according to the recollections of granddaughter Doreen Birks.

One small physical change to BLACOLVESLEY that occurred in the latter part of the 1910-14 period lends further credence to the notion that PETROLIA was not a success. This loco had been delivered with standard Class 10 'Little Giant'-type buffers and draw-hooks, with an integral D-link on the latter, and this arrangement remained for some years. The description of its trials in 1909 demonstrates that in this form it could couple at Blakesley both to carriages and wagons.

However, its front draw-hook was eventually replaced by a rather home-spun open-jaw socket and pin coupling (this is well shown on The Railway Club visit photographs of 1914). If PETROLIA was proving a failure, it would make sense for BLACOLVESLEY to be modified in such a way that it could more easily work the tip wagons as well as the carriages.

While there are several photos of son James 'driving' BLACOLVESLEY, particularly on the occasion of its trials in 1909, and several pictures of Ivy and James, when much younger, on the footplate of the Cagney in 1904 or 1905, CW only ever appears alongside a train – never in a loco cab, or even in a carriage. The nearest we get is a view showing him sitting on the running-board of BLACOLVESLEY during its trials on 11 September 1909 (see page 6).

Whether he considered that, as local Squire, he should not descend to the level of being an engine driver is not clear, but perhaps Alec, and later Percy, Wyatt played the role of 'chauffeur' too well. Despite CW's renown as a pioneering motorist, most photographs showing one or more of his fleet of cars also show him alongside, rather than in, the driving seat!

However, it does seem to have been the convention at that time for 'gentry' to pose in this way beside, rather than on board, their vehicles. Even Sir Arthur Heywood is only formally photographed posing alongside his locomotives, although one chance family snapshot does show him (in the background) on the footplate and driving a train – reassuringly wearing a stout mackintosh!

The family children, however, had no reservations about actively being on the railway,

An Indian summer

The only known illustration of standard-gauge and 15-inch-gauge trains together; it is also the only known view of 15-inch passenger and goods stock together, and the barely visible loco could just be *PETROLIA*. The 0-6-0 is E&WJR No 4. *Charles Simpson collection, courtesy of Sir William McAlpine*

and recollect 'punting' wagons and carriages, and enjoying 'gravity' rides, presumably when grown-ups were not around to run a loco for them!

Strangely perhaps, there is only one set of photographs that shows more than one 'home' Blakesley loco in any one view, and that is during the party visit there in 1912 when both *BLACOLVESLEY* and the Cagney 'topped and tailed' the special train. Nor, amazingly, are there any satisfactory photographs showing 15-inch-gauge and standard-gauge locos together side by side under the bridge at Blakesley station – an obvious photo opportunity if ever there was one.

The one photograph that does feature both standard and miniature stock in the same view at the Blakesley stations is also unique in showing 15-inch-gauge passenger and wagon stock together. It is further unique in appearing to suggest that the rebuilt *PETROLIA* perhaps hauled at least one – albeit single-coach – passenger train!

Railway photographers seem always to have chosen similar standpoints for their pictures, and to have ignored locations such as the engine shed and goods yard. This has made identification of the layout far more difficult than it need have been.

As already indicated, the heyday of the line was just before the Great War. Although it was in use from 1903 to (probably) 1942, all known photographs are from the period up to 1914 – not one single view is known to the author showing any part of the railway after that date. Thus the entire later two-thirds of the line's life seem to be unrecorded.

Operations

The Duffield Bank Railway was very much a private family railway, open to invited guests on special occasions only. As Heywood recorded in 1898, '…my own experimental line … has been continually altered and only irregularly worked…' The Eaton Railway was a completely private line, not even being used when Eaton Hall and its grounds were open to the public.

In contrast CW made great efforts to ensure that the Blakesley Hall railway in its various forms, although equally a 'private' estate line, was well used and enjoyed by visitors on very many occasions – and was thus in practice well on the way to being considered a public recreational line

131

(at least by the locals). The autumn Annual Show was of course a key event but, as we have seen, CW (and subsequently Sarah) allowed the estate grounds – and the railway – to be used for all sorts of celebratory events, concerts and competitions, both locally and nationally, for some 35 years.

For example, *The Locomotive Magazine* article of 1906 recorded:

'Picnic parties are numerous during the season, and on one occasion about 40 visitors, all railway employees, from the District Manager downwards, from one of the large trunk lines, held their annual picnic in the park. The steam locomotive and coaches were placed at their disposal for the whole day, and the various trips were much enjoyed, several preferring the miniature train trips to cricket or other sports.'

It is the stranger therefore that we know almost nothing about how the line was operated. We do, of course, know that each of the locomotives could properly hold only its driver, that there were no brake vans or the like on the line, that there is no evidence of 'mixed' trains being run (except during loco testing), and that none of the carriages or wagons had any brakes!

As the Cagney loco had no brakes either, and the braking ability of *BLACOLVESLEY* is demonstrably limited, the gradients as steep as 1 in 24 on the line must have made for some exciting rides at times! We know that, at least in the early 'children's ride-on model railway' operating days, CW's children and village people were encouraged to run the railway, being equipped with suitably labelled hats and armbands (see page 7).

The trains were normally driven by Alec Wyatt (the estate engineer) or his son Percy (in either case often supervising CW's children in the early years), although photographs exist of Henry Greenly and Bassett-Lowke staff driving test and public service trains.

With only the three bogie carriages, there was little opportunity to run more than one passenger train at a time (except during the 1904-05 visit of the Cagney and its train), and the various changes to the track layout after 1904 would seemingly have made it difficult, if not impossible, for locos

This view shows the A-frame poles that carried the telephone and electricity services between the Hall and the station. A stencilled 'BEWARE OF TRAINS' sign is attached. *Charles Simpson collection, courtesy of Sir William McAlpine*

to run round their trains at either end of the line without recourse to hand-shunting. CW's eldest granddaughter Hermione confirms that, by the mid-1920s at least, trains were generally propelled in one direction.

From contemporary descriptions, there does seem to have been a private telephone link between the station building by the S&MJR station and the Hall, so that a train could be summoned to collect Hall guests or visitors. However, one suspects that, upon such a call being received for an unexpected guest, it would have taken longer to prepare a train and despatch it from the Hall than it would for the visitor to walk the quarter of a mile along the good path instead – or, even more easily, be collected by one of CW's motor cars!

Apart from the Sykes signals, few signs decorated the railway. The only one seen in any illustration is a wooden board attached to an electricity/telephone pole with 'BEWARE OF TRAINS' stencilled on. (In this respect it mirrors the stencilled lettering on the dash panel of the original *PETROLIA*.)

While the Cagney had a conventional American-style oil headlight, and *PETROLIA* (in its original guise) had its peculiar three-aspect lamp, there is no evidence that *BLACOLVESLEY* ever carried a lamp of any kind. It certainly had the standard Bassett-Lowke three lamp-irons (two above the bufferbeam and one at the top of the smokebox), but no views exist of a lamp being carried thereon.

At this time 'Little Giant' locos at overseas exhibitions carried a chromium-plated Lucas acetylene lamp on the top bracket. None of the Blakesley locos had a rear lamp or even provision for a rear lamp bracket, and it must be concluded that night running – if practised at all – was done entirely in the dark.

During the Great War the entertainment value of the line was perhaps taken too exuberantly. Godson Charles Simpson recorded many years later how the wounded 'Tommies' of CW's hospital, who had apparently been given virtually free use of the line, eventually had to be banned from their own direct operation of the railway, it being '… placed out-of-bounds to them following an accident – due to excessive speed – which resulted in a number of broken legs and arms…'

One wonders if such an incident – presumably a fairly significant derailment of a loco and a coach or coaches, probably on the tight-radii curves of the circuit – could have resulted in the final demise of *PETROLIA* as a working loco. As an unloved machine, it would anyway have been the obvious one to let the soldiers use (and any damage a good excuse to leave it derelict). This incident might also have marked the end of the use of the circuit entirely. There are later indirect hints that the accident might have damaged one carriage body beyond worthwhile repair, and also caused CW to lose interest in the railway.

We have been very fortunate that the recollections of John Butler were obtained during 2008 – a man who remembered the line (just) in CW's era. He has been able to confirm a number of obscure points in various areas – and, more importantly, to describe periods of hand-working of coal trucks. Apparently CW sought to provide employment for a couple of village youths with learning difficulties. In John's own words '…he [CW] didn't care how long it took them, he just wanted to give them something useful to do to earn a bit of cash as no one else would employ them. As long as they provided the producer plant with enough anthracite he was happy…' The youths would fill one tip wagon at a time and push it all the way up to the producer plant. This seems to have been an occasional rather than usual practice, probably during summer months when little fuel was needed, and was at the very end of CW's era – when the line had already fallen out of favour as a pleasure activity.

Tickets please!

Amazingly for what was essentially a private and very short estate railway, proper 'Edmondson' card tickets were produced and actually sold to passengers for a specific journey; however, this occurred on just one day each year, in connection with the village Annual Show or Fete each September.

It is notable that the charge is, quite precisely, described as a 'fare' for the railway journey, but including admission to the Fete, rather than being simply the Fete admission price with the train journey included as one of the Fete attractions. Versions are known for both 6d and 1/- (presumably child and adult – see the colour plates). Heywood had tickets on the Duffield Bank Railway, but these were never sold for travel.

The Blakesley railway thus earns itself another British 'first' – that of being the first 15-inch estate railway (and also the first 'permanent' 15-inch railway of any kind) apparently charging ordinary members of the public as passengers a real fare for a real, functional, point-to-point journey.

However, as the return Show-day 3rd Class excursion fare in 1907 on the E&WJR from Towcester to Blakesley was 6d for a journey of some 4¼ miles each way, the BMR 'fare' of 1/- for a journey of just a quarter of a mile each way would have been truly excessive. It seems probable that CW would simply have given the whole of the collected 'fares' to the Show proceeds – and that the Fete admission price (without using the BMR) would quite probably also have been 6d or 1/-!

Since the E&WJR, and later the S&MJR, offered these special excursion fares to Blakesley on Show days, and even ran special late-evening trains to get everyone back home afterwards, it is likely that stations along the standard-gauge line had stocks of the BMR tickets for sale as an 'inclusive package' – if so, yet another 'first' for the BMR.

Unless this did happen, the use of sequentially numbered tickets, reaching at least 9744, implies at least around 1,000 adult tickets sold each Fete day, in turn requiring more than 50 15-inch train round trips each day – not allowing for the child tickets sold! Such numbers are quite feasible – some 500 were expected each day by the special E&WJR trains, with the return specials not leaving until 9.15 or 9.30 each evening, well after the last ordinary passenger trains!

The 6d tickets were dark-buff-coloured with a yellow horizontal band across the centre, and a sequence number on the right. The example in the author's collection has 'SEP 10' impressed in small characters on the reverse; this is believed to imply 'September 1910' rather than the more normal meaning of '10 September', the year of issue being more important than the actual day in the month.

These tickets clearly date from the earliest days of the railway, with their reference to the E&WJR, which ceased to exist at the end of 1908, but are believed to have been available for Fete passengers (and possibly also given out as souvenirs to visiting railway enthusiasts) for somewhat longer – at least into the S&MJR era.

We know that The Railway Club visited the line on 10 September 1910 and the author's ticket could well be a survivor from that visit – on such a date either usage of the '10' would be appropriate if they were given out as souvenirs to the party.

The Fete had ceased by 1914 because of the Great War, and by the time it re-started in the mid-1920s CW had died and the tickets had probably been abandoned – this gives them an issue life of some 12 days in total! It is believed that no further versions were produced, and very few seem to have survived.

One-third scale beckons

A definitive monograph on Heywood railways has suggested that a range of 15-inch-gauge loco designs by Henry Greenly, published in *Models, Railways & Locomotives* in 1916, included a new one – to one-third scale – possibly intended for Blakesley. As this suggestion has been made in such circumstances, it is desirable to explore features of this design in more detail to test the validity of the idea.

This was to be an outside-framed 0-6-0, and the monograph's author suggested that it so closely resembled such locomotives on the adjacent Stratford-upon-Avon & Midland Junction Railway that Blakesley was the intended destination.

While the E&WJR, and its successor the S&MJR, did buy 0-6-0s with straight outside frames – the two largest examples as late as 1908-09 – these were actually double-framed (with very shallow outside frames), and had small boilers with tall chimneys and domes, the later ones with Belpaire fireboxes, quite unlike the (relatively speaking) massive-boilered Greenly proposal.

It also seems inconceivable that the by-now unwell, yet still modernistic in outlook, Squire would have seen any value whatsoever in buying new steam traction at this late stage (he was now in his 60s) – and with a design of somewhat antiquated appearance – after many years of successful internal-combustion operation. Indeed, in 1911 he had already advertised for sale his line's only steam loco.

Investigation of this 0-6-0 design does reveal some intriguing features. Sadly, the closer one looks, the less likely seems any possible role for Blakesley. For example, the 5-foot fixed wheelbase would have been uncomfortable on the Blakesley line's curvature, even after the 'easing' undertaken for *BLACOLVESLEY* in 1909.

The design actually dated from 1912, and Greenly had used it then to illustrate how a 15-inch estate railway train could look combining a fairly scale appearance with what was approaching narrow-gauge engineering. Its height from rail to chimney top of 4ft 7in shows that Greenly

An Indian summer

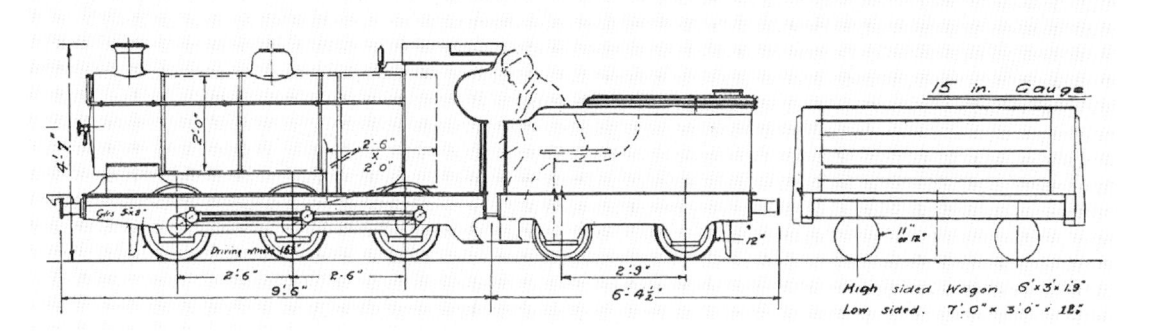

Above Greenly's 0-6-0 15-inch-gauge outside-framed tender locomotive design of 1912, not for Blakesley as has been suggested, but probably an illustration of how one could adapt Heywood's SHELAGH into a miniature outline for use at Eaton. *Models, Railways and Locomotives*

Below Heywood's 0-6-0 SHELAGH at work at Eaton; one of his tip wagons is to the rear of the train. *Author's collection*

The last double-framed 0-6-0 for the S&MJR was No 18, built in 1908. It is standing at Stratford S&MJR station, displaying its relatively small boiler and Belpaire firebox; the LMS classification was only 2F. *Real Photographs (46012), author's collection*

(though perhaps not on his own, as we shall see) had concluded by 1912 that quarter-scale models were inadequate for 15-inch-gauge load-hauling and that something larger was desirable.

The 0-6-0's huge boiler was pitched high over small wheels to provide power while accommodating the deepened firebox and ashpan (which Heywood avoided with his launch-type boiler). Its very traditional British arrangement as an outside-framed and inside-cylindered 0-6-0 tender loco was somewhat unusual for Greenly, who could generally be relied upon to adopt the latest ideas in loco design.

As might be expected, there was a very logical reason for this arrangement. The outside (not double) frames improved stability and provided more space between the wheels (even allowing an option of 'sealed' valve gear), while the inside cylinders not only aided that stability (by minimising 'nosing'), but also enabled the overall width to be kept at a 'scale' 3 feet.

Upon examination, the boiler diameter, cylinder diameter and stroke, wheel diameter and wheelbase of the 0-6-0 are actually found to be all the same, or within half an inch, of those for Heywood's final steam loco design *SHELAGH* of 1904 for Eaton. Perhaps the most significant 'give-away', as to the origin of this design, is the front coupling; the drawing shows it as a Heywood combined 'chopper' coupling and buffer, never used at Blakesley or by Bassett-Lowke, but standard at Eaton. Just to back this up, the wagon sketched behind it in the 1916 drawing has almost identical dimensions to the Eaton Heywood wagons.

CW's opinion of Greenly was, as we have seen, also at an all-time low in 1912, following the debacle with the re-working of *PETROLIA*. Put simply, this design was, sadly, not for Blakesley, but purely a demonstration of how the dimensions, strengths and abilities of Heywood's latest locomotive and wagon designs (for which Greenly had a very great respect) could be harnessed and adapted to a one-third scale 'miniature' outline design, able to do the same work as *SHELAGH* at Eaton, in a more modern and comfortable fashion.

In doing this, Greenly was only putting into practice a comment he had made in *The Model Engineer & Electrician* back in 1905 about Heywood's then new *SHELAGH*: '…personally, I think the outside appearance might easily have been improved…' If a real home was envisaged (and this is doubtful), it was Eaton rather than Blakesley.

Perhaps the only element of this particular design actually to appear was the unusual four-wheeled tender, which Greenly persuaded Roland Martens of Krauss in Munich to adopt, virtually identically, for his construction loco *THE BUG* (Krauss 8378) for the Romney line in 1926 – and the two other subsequent 15-inch locos of the same type.

It is regrettable that Greenly and CW were at odds just at this time, as the former was particularly active in 1912 in developing larger 15-inch designs, and Blakesley would have provided a good local testing ground. The Class 20 'Atlantic' design of this year for Bassett-Lowke was followed immediately by the quite different Class 30, with its near-one-third-scale boiler on a slightly-over-one-quarter-scale chassis.

As O. S. Nock records about the Class 30 in rather picturesque fashion, 'So far as putting outsize boilers on "Atlantics" of the generic Great Northern design went, Messrs Bassett-Lowke out-Ivatted Ivatt himself with the magnificent *SYNOLDA* built for the Sand Hutton Railway…'

Ernest W. Twining, who had become associated with Bassett-Lowke from 1912, was later to record that he did much of the design work for the Class 60 'Pacific' developed from the Class 30 and usually attributed to Greenly. One must wonder, given Twining's subsequent development of more-massive 15-inch designs, whether he had quite a large hand in the Class 30 also.

It would be another decade before one-third-scale locos such as *RIVER ESK* for Ravenglass and *GREEN GODDESS* for Romney would actually be built (both to beautifully balanced designs by Greenly). However, steam was by now already 'old hat' for the modernistic Blakesley line.

'Blessed Trinity'

By 1912 there was, at last, another 15-inch-gauge estate line in embryo, besides the Heywood and Bartholomew ones. This was the first Sand Hutton line, and it too was to be of miniature rather than minimum gauge style. Robert James Milo Walker, born in March 1890, had succeeded to the baronetcy as Sir Robert Walker at the age of 10, and had, in his teenage years, constructed an outdoor model railway on the Sand Hutton estate.

He claimed, in a 1924 article in *The Railway Magazine*, that he had started to experiment with a 15-inch-gauge line as early as 1910, although this is hard to substantiate, particularly as he went to Trinity College, Cambridge, in 1908, graduating there, with his MA, in 1911. (We thus find that this same small – and very appropriately named! – College in Cambridge produced the first three builders of 15-inch-gauge estate railways in Britain: Heywood, Bartholomew and Walker!)

The standard histories of the Sand Hutton line record that Sir Robert received advice from Sir Arthur Heywood. No doubt he did (the two men both being Eton scholars of similar 'social standing'), but it is clear that the former favoured the miniature railway approach of CW rather than the minimum gauge one of Sir Arthur. As initially built, the Sand Hutton line was purely for passenger-carrying pleasure and within the Hall grounds, just like Blakesley, and it thus seems likely that he would have consulted equally, if not more, closely with CW.

Although the Sand Hutton line is recorded as being built and opened in 1912, the timescale for the supply of its supposed first locomotive does not fit well with the few available facts. Sir Robert purchased the first Bassett-Lowke Class 30 'Atlantic', which he named SYNOLDA after his first wife, but this was not completed until December 1912 – see page 8. It was apparently originally commissioned not by him but by Narrow Gauge Railways Ltd for an exhibition line in Oslo (although they did not take delivery of it).

There is no indication of what locomotive Sir Robert had envisaged when he started the planning and construction of his line. Designing and building a new loco would take time – and Sir Robert was clearly a man of action – hence the need for a temporary loan to get his line built and operational ready for his own loco. Was the Blakesley Cagney perhaps loaned to Sand Hutton in 1911 to help with the line's construction and initial operation?

As his leaving university coincided, to the month, with the advertisement, in Bassett-Lowke's *Models, Railways & Locomotives*, of the Blakesley Cagney in June 1911, could this offer have been an attempt to interest Sir Robert in a loco well suited to starting up his 15-inch-gauge estate railway? This would have replicated almost exactly what had happened at Blakesley in 1909, W. J. Bassett-Lowke persuading CW to loan this same Cagney 4-4-0 to another 15-inch line in order to get the model-maker out of a short-term loco supply difficulty. With Sir Robert being a fellow Cambridge graduate of Trinity College, such a request to CW would hardly be refused – and CW had no real use for the Cagney by now.

In support of this Blakesley Cagney loan idea, it is notable that Sand Hutton had a most impressive home-built saloon carriage of unusually lightweight construction (as was revealed in later years on the Ravenglass & Eskdale, where it was hauled over that line's vicious gradients by even more lightweight and low-powered scooters). This otherwise unnecessary lightness would have made an ideal 'train' for a Cagney. It would have allowed passenger trains to be operated prior to the arrival of the altogether heavier standard Bassett-Lowke four-wheeled open carriages, and a suitable loco to haul them. However, it is believed that the Cagney was at Blakesley on 17 August 1912, so if it had been borrowed for Sand Hutton it had been returned at least four months before the arrival of SYNOLDA.

An alternative scenario might have been the loan of black sheep PETROLIA (in its inept-performance new guise). This could have stayed beyond August 1912, as it is not known to have featured in The Railway Club visit to Blakesley of that time. Such a loan would have required the retention of the Cagney at Blakesley as spare loco, thereby preventing its sale.

If the Cagney had been borrowed, its return to Blakesley was perhaps prompted by the hasty repatriation of the Class 10 'Little Giant' BERTWHYNNE [sic] from Geneva, coupled with a desire to make it (and perhaps its train of standard Bassett-Lowke four-wheeled carriages) 'disappear' for a time to avoid legal problems; their transfer to rural Yorkshire for the second half of 1912 could have 'lost' them quite conveniently.

Another clue that there might be some substance to the loan of equipment from Blakesley arises from the Sand Hutton line's goods stock – one tip wagon! Although Blakesley certainly had six such wagons at the start of goods trains around 1905, photographs post-1911 do not show more than five. Could the sixth have gone to Sand Hutton with the Cagney or PETROLIA, but not returned as it was still needed, with the line's construction not yet finished?

Once SYNOLDA was ready, PETROLIA would be able to be returned to Blakesley (or BERTWHYNNE returned to Northampton to metamorphose into HUNGARIA). The various 'visits' postulated above to Sand Hutton are, however, pure circumstantial speculation on the author's part, there being no photographic or written evidence to support them, so these ideas should be treated with due caution.

Just as happened with CW and his line, Sir Robert quickly decided to develop his ride-on 'toy' into a useful estate line for goods and passengers and, even though much further away from a mainline railway than was Blakesley, to establish a connection thereto. He needed – and secured – a Light Railway Order, as its course crossed several roads.

One of the larger Greenly designs from the previously mentioned 1916 article is known to have been seriously developed further with Sand Hutton in mind. Sadly, although this more extensive 15-inch line was partly built, it was quickly replaced and completed by one of 18-inch gauge using available second-hand industrial equipment.

Last of the 'summer wine'

The Edwardian era is often perceived as an 'Indian summer' of British life, before the cataclysms of two World Wars separated (or perhaps linked) by the Depression changed the world for ever. This perception is equally valid for Blakesley and its little railway. The years from 1903 to 1914 are full of happy events and historic developments. There even seems to have been a reconciliation at the very end of this period between CW and Greenly.

As indicated at the start of the book, the Great War had a relatively light impact on the Blakesley locality, though of course a number of local personal family tragedies occurred. CW's son James and son-in-law Douglas served as Army officers. His own contribution to the war effort by providing hospitality for recuperating soldiers has already been recorded, and the BMR was used extensively for entertaining the patients between the Hall and the local S&MJR station and village – to the line's detriment, as has been noted.

This was perhaps the war to make maximum use of narrow-gauge railways, although something larger than 15 inches was chosen. The 60cm-gauge railways of the Western Front, with their trains of bogie flat wagons and skip wagons hauled by Simplex petrol-mechanical locomotives, looked remarkably like the 'light trolley', 'tip wagons' and original PETROLIA respectively, as developed and introduced to Britain by the pioneering CW in 1905 when converting the Blakesley railway to a useful goods function. Far more so than did the products of Sir Arthur Heywood, despite all his years of trying to persuade the War Department of the advantages of his brand of minimum gauge.

We must regard 1914 as a 'watershed' year, not only for world politics, but also for 15-inch-gauge railways in general, as well as for the Blakesley Miniature Railway in particular. It marked the Squire's last 'public' operation at Blakesley – for The Railway Club visit on 20 June of that year – as war had broken out by the due dates of both the Annual Show and the GCR Ambulance Competition (neither of which is believed to have been held that year).

For 15-inch-gauge railways the old order was giving way to the new. The two 'elder statesmen', Sir Arthur Heywood and C. W. Bartholomew, were now in their mid-60s, and Sir Arthur was, somewhat reluctantly perhaps, re-boilering SHELAGH and re-starting long-delayed work on his last loco (its twin, which became URSULA at Eaton). His Duffield Bank line was no longer used for demonstration purposes, and the Dove Leys line was (quite literally) getting nowhere. CW, pragmatist and philanthropist as always, having already developed the BMR into an internal-combustion operation, then turned it into a military line in connection with his hospital for wounded soldiers in the village, while still maintaining coal deliveries.

The next generation (W. J. Bassett-Lowke and Henry Greenly, aided and abetted on occasion by Ernest Twining) were in full flow with their plans for larger locomotives and public, rather than just estate or exhibition, lines (the last continental exhibition line was at Oslo that year), via Narrow Gauge Railways Ltd. These plans manifested themselves in the Ravenglass & Eskdale Railway (from 1915) and the Fairbourne Railway (from 1916). The following generation had even grander plans, however.

By 1914, Sir Robert Walker had finished the first version of his estate line and had a scheme for its major development into a public goods and passenger one, while the Twining/Greenly Class 60 'Pacific' – which effectively marked the culmination of Bassett-Lowke building of 15-inch-gauge locomotives – was supplied to J. E. P. Howey for his Staughton Manor line at the beginning of that year, as JOHN ANTHONY (also known as COLOSSUS).

Howey was, after the war and with the aid of Greenly, to implement one-third-scale 15-inch gauge on a truly grand scale with the Romney, Hythe & Dymchurch Railway, while Twining was later to develop – almost as an art form – the 'half-scale colonial narrow gauge' style, entirely for his '…too narrow…' 15-inch gauge. However, Bassett-Lowke itself was no longer in the 15-inch manufacturing business.

While Bassett-Lowke Ltd did try to re-enter the 15-inch supply field in 1930, after so many years of abstinence, with a 15-inch-gauge bid for the proposed North Bay Railway at Scarborough, for which an updated and enlarged *BLACOLVESLEY* design would have been ideal, its proposal featured steam locos. The firm was almost certainly up to its old tricks by bidding on the basis of a *COLOSSUS*-type 'Pacific' loco (despite the one and only example being broken up three years earlier), but perhaps intending to use either or both of the pre-war existing 'Little Giant' locos, No 18 *GEORGE*

The only Class 60 'Pacific' JOHN ANTHONY (later COLOSSUS), owned by J. E. P. Howey and seen here undergoing trials at Eaton, makes a miniature-outline/minimum-gauge comparison with Heywood's 0-4-0T KATIE. Bassett-Lowke postcard, author's collection

THE FIFTH and No 30 *SYNOLDA*, quietly re-worked and re-branded.

This attempted re-flowering of the old pre-Great War one-quarter scale, relatively flimsy equipment failed, as a result of strong competition from Baguley and Hudswell Clarke, with internal-combustion proposals. The latter was successful with a beefy, two-fifths-scale, steam-outline design, leading in due course to a number of new lines of 20-inch and 21-inch gauge around the country; the two 'Little Giant' locos went to Southend.

Let us therefore salute 1914 not only as the 'beginning of the end' for the Blakesley line, but as the watershed for 15-inch railways in general, with all the main developers of its first century of progress – Heywood (1849-1916), Bartholomew (1850-1919), Twining (1875-1956), Greenly (1876-1947), Bassett-Lowke (1877-1953), Howey (1886-1963) and Walker (1890-1930) – simultaneously active in 15-inch-gauge railways, to greater or lesser degrees.

The like would never be seen again.

12 Closure and dispersal

The death of the Squire and after

That the Great War marked the end of an era for the railway was sadly all too firmly confirmed on 29 April 1919 with the death of CW. Not surprisingly, his funeral, on 5 May, was the most notable in the village for many a year and a large procession followed the hearse to Blakesley Church; the *Northampton Independent* claimed that it was the first burial there for 30 years!

The little railway did not feature in his last journey, although the route of the cortege crossed the line by the S&MJR station. CW had specified that '...I desire to be buried in a Vault at Blakesley and I desire my funeral to be as simple as possible'. Bearing in mind the ancient history of Blakesley Hall, it is notable that one of the wreaths was from the then Earl Spencer KG, great-grandfather of the late Princess Diana, Princess of Wales, with another from the Priory of St John.

Although his will of 1918 dealt in detail with such things as '...horses and carriages and all my motor cars and motor accessories ... agricultural stock ... all farming machinery and implements ... also my wines liquors and consumable stores...', there was, surprisingly, no mention of his railway or its equipment. The railway was by then presumably considered simply as part of the estate, which rather hints at his complete change of heart about the line, perhaps brought about by the 'Tommies' accident.

Following CW's death, Sarah continued to live at the Hall. The miniature railway did continue to function, even if on a rather more occasional basis and in a more restricted fashion; a greater proportion of supplies – and visitors – were inevitably coming by road as the years passed.

Progress and development ceased and what then existed had to survive thereafter with limited maintenance, no replacement and certainly no evolution. Outside interest in the railway seems to have ceased and virtually no further publicity about it appeared again. An unsuccessful (though anonymous) attempt may have been made to sell the Cagney in 1923, and Greenly is known to have brought a visitor to the line in 1936 with a view to purchasing disused stock, so some very limited contact with the 'outside' world of 15-inch-gauge railways was maintained.

The 1920s – and an enigma

This reduction in the line's utility and activity meant that there was no real requirement for more than one locomotive, and rolling stock needs would also be less. The Cagney had seen no use for many years (CW's eldest granddaughter Hermione – born in 1919 – remembers seeing it in the early 1930s, but never in steam) and *PETROLIA* was considered at best a white elephant. The Cagney may possibly even have paid a repeat visit to a revised version of the Sutton line around 1922-23; this re-opened briefly from mid-1922 until the end of the 1923 season, but no record of the loco or stock used on it has yet been traced.

This also coincides mid-period with a somewhat enigmatic sale advertisement in *The Locomotive Magazine* for 14 April 1923, which clearly illustrates the Blakesley Cagney (with a photograph taken in about 1903), inviting interested parties to contact the magazine publishers quoting 'Small Loco'. There is no specific reference to the railway it was on or came from and the Blakesley view may have simply been a 'file' shot (it is a well-known LPC card view) used to illustrate the offer of another Cagney from elsewhere.

It is described as a '15-inch Gauge Miniature Locomotive, American Type for Disposal...

Suitable for Private Railway', which 'May be seen by appointment'. The advert contains the statement, 'Has hauled sixty passenger [sic] at 12 miles per hour', a capacity fitting neither Blakesley nor Sutton, thereby increasing the uncertainty as to the actual identity of the offered loco.

One possibility dates back to the 'visiting' Cagney time, when the total child passenger capacity of the combined trains could indeed have been 60 (36 in the 'home' and 24 in the 'visiting' carriages). The loco offered in the advert could thus have been not the 'home' one, but the brief 1904-05 visitor – thereby partially justifying the use of a photo of a Cagney at Blakesley, albeit the wrong one. However, if this was the last known attributable reference to the 'home' Cagney, there appear to have been (once again) no long-term takers at that time.

In 1924 the family presented a magnificent stained glass window, in the west face of Blakesley Church tower, in CW's memory. This was by Powell's of Whitefriars, a leading exponent in the field. With CW's clear interest – and philanthropic expenditure – in such windows for some 20 years at least (including in this church), it is rather sad that this commission was just a couple of years too early to have been by E. W. Twining, now becoming as famous in this field for producing high-quality stained glass windows as he was in miniature railways.

Recognised as one of the foremost authorities on the subject, he supplied some to several Northampton area churches just a little later in this decade (it is tempting to speculate that both CW's and Twining's interest in this somewhat esoteric field was cultivated during visits to Blakesley, in view of the former's long-standing patronage of them).

The 1910 extension to the farm had become disused and removed (at any rate beyond gate G5 by the bungalow) by the end of the 1920s, if not earlier; by this time too the 'circle' lines had been abandoned (and perhaps even become buried under vegetation). The arrival of mains electricity to the area in 1931 spelled the end of the Hall's own power generation, significantly reducing the need for coal.

The 1930s

By the early 1930s all that remained useable of the railway was the 'main line' between the 'farm manager's bungalow' and the standard-gauge station, together with the spur to the engine shed. (By this time too this bungalow was, more prosaically, occupied by the cowman, Jack Jones, and his family, and the 'farm buildings' were known more simply and accurately as the 'cowstalls'.)

As indicated earlier, some coal did continue to arrive by rail from Wombwell Main Colliery and the railway even resumed its play function in due course as CW's grandchildren spent happy long summer holidays at the 'family seat' at Blakesley, being well entertained by the railway; this would have been in the late 1920s and early 1930s.

It is joyfully remembered by the perpetrators (CW's grandchildren and their friends) at this time that a wagon pushed up to what was by then the end of the railway – the top of the 1909 extension near the bungalow – could, with the aid of sticks used as 'punting' poles by the children, achieve a fair speed down the 1 in 24/30 towards the level ground by the Black Ouse stream!

The railway was still a key part of local events, including of course the Annual Show (while it lasted – a 'washed-out' event of 1932 being the last involving the railway). The Hall grounds were also still often opened on Sunday evenings in summer for concerts by the Blakesley Band. One wonders if the elite 'through' passengers on the bus-based LMS 'Ro-Railer' en route for Stratford and the Welcombe Hotel, during its brief period of operation on the ex-S&MJR line in 1932, ever encountered the strange juxtaposition of it and *BLACOLVESLEY* with its train of open carriages running alongside them by the station bridge.

The grounds – and the railway – were also opened for national celebrations; for example, local historian Philip Kingston's son Robert, as well as CW's granddaughter Doreen Birks, remember riding on the railway during festivities such as those for the Silver Jubilee of King George V in 1935 and King George VI's Coronation in 1937.

With all these changes, *BLACOLVESLEY* effectively chose itself to be the line's sole remaining locomotive (being not only the newest, but also the most convenient and reliable), and the others were disposed of. Quite 'how' remains a mystery, but at least 'where' and 'when' can now be answered, probably for both the other locos, together with a carriage – as well as the 'circuit' (and perhaps other) trackage!

Sarah Bartholomew presides over a splendid family group on the Hall terrace in the early 1930s. James Bartholomew, courtesy of 'The Bartholomew Arms'

1. 'Maisie'
2. Miss Hookey (Sarah's life-long companion)
3. Doreen Ann Birks
4. Sarah Ann (Floyd) Bartholomew
5. Heather Mary Birks
6. Cyril Douglas Birks
7. ?
8. Charlotte Hermione Bartholomew
9. Charlotte Mabel Bartholomew (née Hempson)
10. ?
11. Ivy (Birks)
12. Charles Edward Bartholomew

The fate of the Cagney

In 1936 a Cagney locomotive, sadly without its smokebox ring date, appeared as the motive power of a new miniature railway, on the Isle of Bute on the Firth of Clyde, associated with the Rothesay Tramways Co, which operated an electric tramway on the island between Rothesay and Ettrick Bay. The miniature railway opened on 1 June, a bare four months before the company's electric trams gave way to buses, its last tram running on 30 September. This loco had been in use at East Balgray Farm, Irvine, near Glasgow since at least 1932.

The locomotive and its carriages are believed to have been purchased for the son of Mr Sword, a director of the tramway concern, but its previous history is uncertain. Eventually, after many subsequent vicissitudes, it was placed on exhibition at Strumpshaw Hall. Many authors have claimed (without substantive evidence) that this was the Blakesley Cagney.

This story has now been told so often that it has become, quite unjustifiably, treated as fact. This is to some extent surprising as one of the first – and most authoritative – descriptions of this new line and its locomotive, which appeared in *The Model Engineer* for 3 June 1937, makes no such claim for its ancestry.

Though an historic genuine British-operated

The Strumpshaw (ex-Rothesay) Cagney visited the Cleethorpes Coast Light Railway in 1997; of the same design and date as the home Blakesley Cagney, it has often been (wrongly) claimed to be that locomotive, although it could be the c1904 visitor. Neville Knight

Cagney Class D loco, this was not the 'home' loco from Blakesley; it is, however, quite likely that it was the 1904-05 visitor, as only a handful of them were operated in Britain during the 20th century (and few of those had the same physical features as the visitor at Blakesley – as this one does). Its general features demonstrate that it is an early Cagney, almost certainly dating from exactly the same build period as the 'home' example, ie around 1902 to 1904. It might even have been the one advertised in the 1923 issue of *The Locomotive Magazine*.

An excellent example of the trail of confusion and unsubstantiated claims leading to, or derived from, oft-quoted 'evidence' is the lengthy, and apparently authoritative, description given about it in the catalogue issued by Christie's for its auction of 'Fine Historical Steam Engine Models and Ship Models' on 5 October 1966.

Lot 88 was the ex-Rothesay Cagney loco and tender, offered for sale here by Lord Bruce. The catalogue recorded it as:

'A 15in gauge model of an American type 4-4-0 locomotive and tender, made by Herschell Spillman & Co, of North Tonawanda, of New York, late 1890s, and delivered in 1905 to C. W. Bartholomew, of Blakesley Hall, Northants, where it was used between the main railway station at Sutton Park and the Hall until the 1920s…'

The description is clearly in error in so many respects, for example by confusing Sutton and Blakesley, but its quote of a delivery date of 1905 to Blakesley is an interesting coincidence in that such a date would just about fit with the *Model Engineer* photographs of two Cagneys together at Blakesley, if this loco was the visitor.

The catalogue claim must overall be treated with considerable caution; for example, the Cagney bogie carriages seen at Blakesley (which would have been expected to accompany their loco on whatever travels it undertook) certainly did not go to Rothesay (which used three four-wheeled carriages with running gear in no way resembling Cagney equipment).

As the subsequent history of the 'home' BMR

Above The Blakesley Cagney, with fully lined and lettered tender, poses on an unrebuilt bridge on the 'circuit' during The Railway Club visit of 20 June 1914. The S&MJR line is in the background. *LGRP photograph (8262), courtesy of National Railway Museum/SSPL*

Left This snapshot of the Cagney and coach of the Deans Mill Railway finally unlocked the mystery of what happened to the Blakesley Cagney (and probably one of its carriages). The tender lining and lettering, plus footboards, match exactly that of the Blakesley loco post-1910, except for the substitution of a 'D' (in a different font) for the 'B' on the tender. *Miss Agnes McBain, courtesy of Brian Gent*

Cagney is actually so different from those oft-quoted reports, it is worth exploring here in some detail the logic that leads to the present conclusion. It is based on simple and clear, if fortuitous, photographic evidence.

The last-known photographs of the Cagney (and of the railway) at Blakesley were taken during The Railway Club visit in June 1914. These clearly show the tender (with its unique side footboards) painted with a double-lining panel, the corners scalloped, in Great Northern or *BLACOLVESLEY* lining style, and 'B. M. R.' (complete with the full stops) in elongated block shaded lettering within the panel.

Close examination of this lettering shows it to be slightly unevenly spaced, with the 'M' nearer to the 'R' than to the 'B' (on the right-hand tender side at least) – this may sound trivial, but is critical evidence in identifying what really happened to the loco subsequently!

The other significant piece of evidence, by which the author finally unlocked the mystery, came in the form of a snapshot fortuitously unearthed by Brian Gent of a lady, Miss Agnes McBain, taken in 1937 sitting on the somewhat home-spun-looking open carriage (indeed the only carriage) on the then new 15-inch-gauge railway at Deans Mill, Lindfield, near Haywards Heath in Sussex. The tender and the top half of the cab of what is clearly an early Class D Cagney loco are also visible in the snapshot.

While one may regret that so little of the loco is visible in the photograph, it is the tender that is important here! The first item of interest relates to the wooden footboard along the side of the tender at running plate level – no British Cagney other than the one at Blakesley is known to have had this added feature, and the Rothesay Cagney's tender neither had, nor retained any evidence of ever having had, such footboards.

The second item is that the right-hand side of the tender is lined and lettered exactly as in those July 1914 views of the Blakesley Cagney, except that a 'D' appears instead of a 'B'. That this letter 'D' is a later change to an already existing livery is evident from its condensed font in contrast to that used for the 'M' and the 'R'. Equally importantly, close examination of the lettering spacing shows that the 'M' is too near the 'R', exactly as with the Blakesley Cagney.

The likelihood of there being two Cagney tenders painted in this way is so remote that one may conclude that the Deans Mill Cagney must have been the Blakesley 'home' loco. This evidence is pretty conclusive that Blakesley's Cagney did not go to Rothesay, though the visitor may indeed have done so in due course.

The BMR goes to Sussex

This single snapshot is, however, far more significant than in simply helping to trace what happened to the Cagney; it leads us to an understanding also of what probably happened to other Blakesley material, including one of the carriages, together with the rails, etc, of the old 'circuit' lines, and almost certainly also to *PETROLIA* – in other words, to virtually all of the Blakesley equipment disposed of prior to the line's closure.

The Deans Mill Railway was created following the acquisition of the then disused mill complex by George Horsefield and his family in May 1935; they had previously operated a similar establishment in Wales. Not only did they restore the mill to working order, but they also set up tea rooms there as well as a vegetarian restaurant in Haywards Heath. They organised boats for hire on the adjacent river (coincidentally also a River Ouse).

They seem to have got the railway operational in 1937, suggesting that it was constructed in or about 1936-37. We know from a recollection by Charles Simpson (who was present at the time) that Greenly came to Blakesley in 1936, bringing someone with him to look at the line's equipment; this could well have been George Horsefield searching for stock and equipment for his proposed line (the date fits perfectly).

The 15-inch-gauge Deans Mill Railway was some 300 yards in length consisting of an irregular circuit. As the Blakesley line's own circuit (of equally irregular course and of similar length) is known to have been abandoned by the time of this line's construction, it suggests that the track probably also came from Blakesley. (If this is true, these circuit lines had most likely remained in place, disused and invisible in the undergrowth for around a quarter of a century.)

The layout at Deans Mill was thus probably determined by what was then available from Blakesley. The rails appear from photographs to be of the same weight and deep-but-narrow cross-section as used at Blakesley. A low tunnel (apparently formed of all-too-contemporary 'Nissen' corrugated-iron segments) was provided for visitor access to the middle of the circuit.

The tracks to the combined loco and carriage shed close to the Mill itself were quite elaborate – far more so than the line's stock of two locos and one carriage would seem to justify. They included a turntable (again an unnecessary extravagance here). However, Blakesley's three-track engine shed layout, approached by a track fan (with an adjacent turntable) would have equally become an extravagance there once much of the stock and track went to Deans Mill, and it is concluded that all this material too came direct from Blakesley.

Obviously at Deans Mill by 1937, one story is that the Cagney had some problems in about 1942 or 1943 and was taken away for repair by a group of Canadian soldiers at that time based at Burgess Hill – but was never returned! If this is the case,

The Blakesley Hall Miniature Railway

With Deans Mill in the left background, the single-coach train makes a clockwise circuit of the railway towards the River Ouse, past the spur to the engine shed. Was this the Blakesley circle reincarnated? *Brian Gent collection*

the Cagney barely outlived the railway for which it was built. However, other sources claim that steam (presumably the Cagney) was still present – and occasionally operational – on the line well into the 1950s (probably throughout the Mill's ownership by Horsefield). Whether it was ultimately scrapped, or taken away by the Horsefields when they left – or even repatriated to the North American continent – is unknown.

A further steam loco was an 0-6-0 tank loco named *TRIXIE*, which came with its own 'tender' and four-wheeled carriage; this proved unsuccessful, and was quickly disposed of. Had *BLACOLVESLEY* been available from Blakesley at this time (which of course it was not), it could well have gone to Deans Mill with the Cagney.

It is also interesting, in the light of later events, that *BLACOLVESLEY* is known to have been accompanied by only two of the three Blakesley bogie carriages to its new locations after the 'home' line closed in 1942, and that Deans Mill had just one open bogie carriage of its own. While the latter's body in no way resembles a Blakesley one, parts of the bogies and the body underframe length do bear close similarities.

It is therefore highly probable that this was a (fairly substantial) body conversion of the third Blakesley carriage; it was of a fairly crude, but quite massive, nature, with six wooden swing-over 'toast rack'-style two-passenger benches on a plain rectangular wooden base. Coincidentally, almost identical conversions were eventually to be applied to the other two Blakesley carriages during their subsequent travels. This particular carriage may have been stored unserviceable at Blakesley for many years, perhaps having been damaged in the wartime accident mentioned by Charles Simpson, and thus needed rebuilding anyway.

Does *PETROLIA* survive?

There is yet a further – and most intriguing – Blakesley twist to the Deans Mill story. Besides the Cagney and the short-lived 0-6-0 steam loco,

146

The Deans Mill petrol loco as it first appeared in a simple representation of the streamlined era of the mid-1930s.
Brian Gent collection

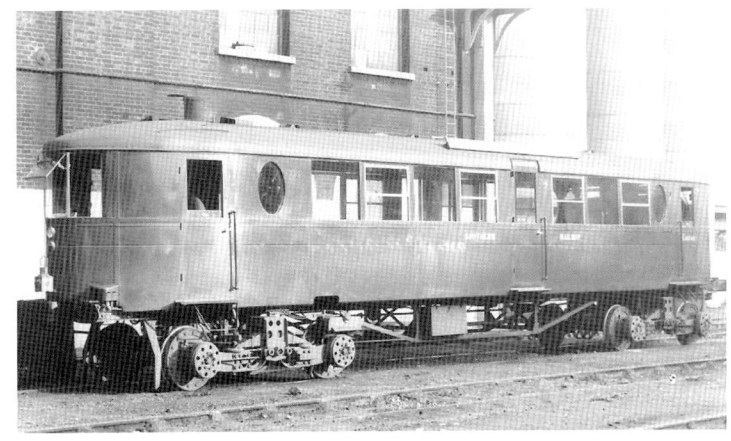

The state-of-the-art 'streamlining' era of the 1930s was well illustrated by this Sentinel steam railcar used on the SR's branch to The Dyke, terminating not far from Deans Mill; the Mill's petrol loco resembled (crudely!) this style.
Author's collection

there was a 4-4-0 petrol loco there, which appeared initially in partially built or rebuilt chassis form within a few months of the Cagney entering service.

This loco has long been thought to have been built for the line by R. H. Morse (it received his works number 82), but it is more likely to have been a very heavy rebuild, partially undertaken by Morse and partially by George Horsefield, of what was left of the moribund PETROLIA. The well-engineered plate-frame bogie of the loco at Deans Mill looked quite new and had definite Morse characteristics.

Certainly the Deans Mill petrol loco had chain drive inside the 'frames' (strictly inside the axleboxes) to its 'fixed' four-wheel chassis (as did the original PETROLIA). Its all-over body with deeply curved roof and bullet-shaped ends, though perhaps curious to today's eyes, reflected the strong but short-lived 'streamline' image of the time. It bore a close resemblance not only to an experimental Armstrong-Whitworth diesel-electric bogie railbus, but also to a unique Southern Railway Sentinel steam railcar built in 1933 specially for the nearby branch to The Dyke, terminating only a few miles from Deans Mill.

This, the last steam railcar built for Britain, was operating thereon until at least 1937 (and probably until the line closed at the end of 1938), and was thus contemporary with the building of the Deans Mill line and the (re)building of this loco. In this form the Deans Mill loco may well have been the first ride-inside miniature locomotive of 'modern' outline, contrasting with the steam-outline miniature concept of CW.

Although this will briefly take the Blakesley story rather out of chronological order, it is worth exploring here the subsequent history of this somewhat strange locomotive through to the present day, as it is only recently that its true

The Blakesley Hall Miniature Railway

The Deans Mill 4-4-0 petrol locomotive stands, with the line's single coach, outside the engine and stock shed.
National Railway Museum/SSPL (Rick Eyles R12/10)

pedigree has been suspected and the possible link to Blakesley discovered.

Unlike the Cagney, this Deans Mill loco has survived. The Mill complex was sold in 1957 and the 15-inch line closed; this may all have been precipitated by an accident that caused several injuries – possibly caused by passengers standing when passing through the line's low 'tunnel' (which was demolished).

The track, petrol loco and carriage remained derelict there for some time following the Mill's sale to another milling family (named Cooper),

The Dreamland Miniature Railway, Margate, with 4-4-0 petrol locomotive '359', rebuilt from the Deans Mill petrol loco, running round its train.
Robin Butterell

who clearly had no interest in 15-inch railways. Eventually all the remaining equipment, with one exception, is believed to have gone to a '...showman at Blackpool...'

In March 1959 the petrol loco went to the Greenly-designed Dreamland Miniature Railway at Margate, where it received yet another major rebuild. Its now unfashionable 'Sentinel' body was replaced by a much more shapely one and it received the number '359' (as it arrived in the third month of 1959). By 1962 it had been relegated to 'spare loco', and remained thus until 1980 when this line closed.

It then moved to the long-established line at Rhyl (also Greenly-designed), although in 1982 it was used at Flamingoland in Yorkshire for a spell. Re-engined at Rhyl with an Austin unit and renamed *RAILWAY QUEEN*, it was offered for auction in April 1986; despite all the work on it, it proved unable to haul more than a couple of carriages and spent most of its time stored in the back of the loco shed. No buyer was found and it eventually found its way into a Denbigh scrapyard by 1991.

In 1998 it was rescued by Alf Pilbeam for his Tal-y-Cafyn line at Llandudno, but went that same year to Brian Gent. He undertook some restorative work before it passed in turn to Austin Moss at Windmill Farm. He sold it to Jim and Helen Shackell, as they owned, inter alia, the Morse-built post-war 0-4-0 American-style 'Switcher'.

During his researches into Blakesley, the author had become increasingly suspicious about the origin of this machine. Close examination of 'No 359' at this time, while in temporary storage on the Markeaton Park Railway in Derby, revealed 16-inch-diameter driving wheels (precisely the same somewhat unusual diameter as those of *PETROLIA* as built), as well as the same rare and distinctive chain-drive layout inside the axlebox framing but outside the wheels on both sides of the loco.

These suspicions were reinforced by the subsequent discovery that its so-called Morse bogie appeared to feature standard Bassett-Lowke carriage wheel-sets, suggesting that the loco might, at some stage, have had Bassett-Lowke build or rebuild connections. The loco was moved to the Evesham Vale Railway for long-term restoration in October 2007.

The coincidence of a 4-4-0 petrol-mechanical loco chassis appearing at Deans Mill at roughly the same time as the Blakesley Cagney (and perhaps also a carriage) immediately increases the probability that this might logically have been based on something also coming from Blakesley.

PETROLIA, if it still existed at Blakesley, would then be in its 0-4-4 petrol-mechanical form by Bassett-Lowke, but would by then probably also be devoid of its engine and bodywork (if the story of its engine being taken out and used locally to drive farm machinery is true), in which state an 0-4-4 internal-combustion chassis could equally be described as a 4-4-0. It might even have been stored damaged and unserviceable following the wartime 'Tommies' accident.

What would be more natural than for a buyer, arriving at Blakesley to secure the Cagney (and also a carriage and some track) to provide the equipment for his emerging railway at Deans Mill, to decide also to take along the unwanted, half-dismantled and cannibalised discarded remnants

The running gear of the Deans Mill petrol loco. The wheel-sets and chain drive between wheels and axleboxes correspond to the arrangement originally used in *PETROLIA*, while the bogie wheel-sets are standard Bassett-Lowke carriage ones, as could have been fitted during the latter's 1910 rebuild by that company. *National Railway Museum/SSPL (Rick Eyles R14/16)*

of a latterly unsuccessful petrol loco that would otherwise be scrapped?

As yet no concrete evidence outwith that offered by the wheel diameter, with the chain-drive and its layout, together with its Bassett-Lowke carriage bogie wheel-sets, and its poor performance despite several rebuildings, has surfaced to prove or disprove the author's theory – the evidence is significant, though largely coincidental and circumstantial, but would seem at the very least to have a far better, and more logical, basis than the long-held, and erroneous, idea that the Blakesley Cagney went to Rothesay! Indeed, there seems no clear alternative, upon finding such a loco with all these features, than that it was a further adaptation of the 1910 Bassett-Lowke rebuild of *PETROLIA*.

It is still not clear as to the extent to which the 1910 *PETROLIA* contained components of the 1905 original; certainly the axleboxes, hornways and springing of the Deans Mill petrol loco chassis appear to be a little differently arranged from those of the original *PETROLIA*. If the original powered four-wheeled frame unit was simply incorporated in the re-working (albeit in a slightly different form), as seems probable, then the 1905 'four-coupled' chassis part of *PETROLIA* almost certainly survives to this day – achieving its centenary in 2005.

The author's assessment is that there is a strong possibility that the driving wheels, axles and associated chain-sprockets of 1905, together with the axleboxes, guides and springing of the 1910 re-modelling, as well as the bogie wheel-sets of the latter date, survive. It would thus be too much to claim that *PETROLIA* may exist as a 'true' 1905 locomotive in the way that the almost completely original 1909 *BLACOLVESLEY* does, but that driving part-chassis may well be the oldest surviving internal-combustion locomotive power chassis and drive unit in the world – unrecognised and unappreciated for more than 70 years, and using up more lives than a cat!

Of course it could just be that, while the basic historical evolution outlined above may be substantially correct, the multitudinous rebuildings and reconfigurations over so many years have resulted in a locomotive that today actually contains virtually no original parts whatsoever – the classic 'genuine George Washington axe' with five new handles and three new heads! The preserved 'original' County Donegal railcar No 1 of 1907 is more or less in such a position – as indeed is the world-famous *FLYING SCOTSMAN* with but a couple of minor genuinely attributable original components!

Collectively, the sum of all this evidence and interpretation is that virtually the whole of the Deans Mill line – track, layout, locomotives and carriage – was in practice simply a reincarnation in Sussex of much of the old, built-for-fun Blakesley line, while that line was still surviving and operational in its later, more utilitarian, form for a few more short years. There is no direct proof of any of the above, which is why the very considerable circumstantial evidence has been set out in such detail.

The personal accounts of CW's grandchildren using a wagon or carriage for 'gravity runs' on the steeper grades at Blakesley in the twilight of that line's existence seem to have been mirrored here too in the last years at Deans Mill. Peter Lemmey has recorded, from his own experience, that latterly here '... a group of energetic children could ... propel the bogie coach ... up through the orchard to the highest point of the line ... and then scramble aboard to come careering down round the curve under the apple trees ... ending up almost at [Ouse] river level...'

The Deans Mill Railway was truly in the Blakesley tradition!

The end of the railway

With the transfer of much of the permanent way, two of the locos and a carriage to Sussex around 1936, the Blakesley railway was now reduced to something like its original scale, albeit now catering primarily for the semi-serious business of coal trains hauled by steam-outline internal-combustion loco *BLACOLVESLEY*, rather than steam-hauled passenger trains as a 'for fun' ride-on model railway.

With improved road transport, and no supporting squire, even the value of the former was becoming increasingly dubious. Inevitably, therefore, the railway became a fairly pointless liability, and usage dropped away to nothing. The actual date of this is uncertain, but the probable year (and the latest possible for loco operation) is 1942, as this is when the surviving locomotive and carriages went to Yorkshire.

Surprisingly perhaps, it would appear that the periodic 'scrap drives' of that era did not result in the disposal of much of the remaining steel track, sleepers and wagons to help the war effort. The

Blakesley station is seen here after the Second World War, with a number of wooden-bodied mineral wagons visible in the standard-gauge transhipment siding. The 15-inch-gauge line, with its station, has gone, although the iron fence separating it from the main line remains. *LGRP photograph (25682), courtesy of National Railway Museum/SSPL*

track of the '1909 main line' between the station and the bungalow (by gate G5, near the start of the farm buildings extension) was observed still physically there but disused in 1945; perhaps the failure to dispose of the remaining five tip wagons made the railway look still operational and ensured that this did not happen. (Indeed, perhaps it was operational with the petrol shortages of that era – once again by hand power!)

The 4-4-4T steam-outline petrol locomotive *BLACOLVESLEY*, and the two remaining carriages, were 'acquired' by Miss Dorothy Elliott, the Secretary to the Wombwell Main Colliery Company, and transported by a Mr Albert Field to her residence 'Two Trees', near Wombwell, Yorkshire. While some of the track probably accompanied *BLACOLVESLEY* and the carriages, all the remaining material of the railway (including the tip wagons) seems to have gone for scrap around 1946, as the RAF aerial photographs taken at the beginning of 1947 show no obvious track anywhere.

After the track was lifted and the wagons scrapped, only a few parts of the course of the railway remained traceable. Photographs of Blakesley standard-gauge station, shortly before the end of its passenger train services in 1952, show the iron fencing separating it from the course of the miniature line still largely complete at the west end by and through the road bridge.

13 The 'Two Trees' saga

The story unfolds

In war-weary 1944 Britain, a picture of BLACOLVESLEY, with one of the Blakesley carriages, was deemed worthy of appearing in the Daily Express national newspaper!

This was remarkable on several counts; first because non-war news photographs of any kind were rare at that time, second because the loco had been gone from Blakesley for some months, third because the photo of it was taken in the garden of a house called 'Two Trees', 48 Hemingfield Road, Wombwell, near Barnsley, and fourth because its then 48-year-old lady 'owner', Miss Dorothy Elliott JP, had just been sentenced, on 24 March, at Leeds Assizes to six years penal servitude.

She had been found guilty on 66 counts of defrauding The Wombwell Main Colliery Company and The Wombwell Coke & By-products Company of no less than £91,630. The jury had rejected her plea of temporary insanity. To give an indication of the then value of the sum involved, as Company Secretary in 1943 she was paid £610 per annum including bonuses!

Because this fraud dramatically affected the future of BLACOLVESLEY and two of the carriages, as well as the Bartholomew family's financial situation, it is worth exploring the fascinating, if sorry, story in some detail. This fraud almost brought those businesses to their knees. It was spotted by pure good fortune by the companies' Chairman, Sir Samuel Roberts, himself.

He had been at a company board meeting where a healthy financial picture was presented; fortuitously he was also on the board of the companies' bankers, and shortly after that meeting he was at a bank meeting where those same Wombwell companies were identified as being seriously overdrawn.

In an effort to recover some liquidity, the colliery company even had to resort to selling many of the company houses in Wombwell, including those in Bartholomew Street. This took place around March 1944 (concurrently with the various proceedings against Dorothy and as soon as the scale of the fraud was appreciated), and things must have been desperate to be trying to sell strings of terraced houses in a high-risk industrial area in wartime.

She had been arrested on 14 December 1943 and was taken that day before Barnsley West Riding Police Court (in which she had served herself as a magistrate) where she was remanded for 21 days. The charge then was a relatively small one of defrauding £614 13s 10d (even so, this was still more than her annual salary!), but it was hinted that this was just a holding charge – and so it proved.

At a further hearing at the same court on 11 February 1944, the full extent of her fraud emerged, and she was sent for trial at the Leeds Assizes. There it was revealed that, between 1936 and 1943, she had kept a duplicate set of accounts and diverted the huge sum of money mentioned earlier.

She had built the large house 'Two Trees' (employing two maids and a cook therein), where she extended the garden enormously by buying three adjacent plots and having it all landscaped, the total garden size ultimately being more than 3 acres. She bought a farm (Smithley Farm, Wombwell), where she had lived as a young girl, and stocked it with rare and pedigree animals (very similar to what CW had done – legally – at Blakesley half a century earlier).

'Lady Bountiful'

Her father, Charles Henry Elliott JP, as the company's Agent and Manager, had lived latterly

The 'Two Trees' saga

at Wombwell Hall (sadly then merely a pleasant, but rather mundane, Victorian building, rather than the former rambling Elizabethan manor house of the Wombwell family). He had enjoyed a close relationship with the Bartholomews, being seen directly alongside James at his 21st birthday celebrations. James would have got to know him well from 1911, as he lodged with the family when at Sheffield University (with half his time being spent at Wombwell Main Colliery), and he even benefited from CW's will. Upon her father's death in 1926, Dorothy had inherited some £3,000 from his estate.

It did not therefore seem particularly strange to friends and outsiders that she was now, as Secretary to that same company, able to enjoy such a comfortable lifestyle. She did not keep all the money for herself as she undertook many 'good works' in the neighbourhood, being nicknamed locally 'Lady Bountiful'.

In March 1944, for example, the local Barnsley British Co-operative Society was able to buy at auction an 'Assembly Room' that she had originally had built at 'her' expense in 1939 in Wombwell for 'her' company of Rangers. The building became known as the 'Dorothy Elliott Hut', although the stone above the doorway, even today, reads simply 'THE HUT 1939'. At the same auction the hut contents, together with a hostel at Smithley, also owned by her, were also sold.

At the Leeds Assizes she pleaded not guilty, the defence claiming that she was insane at the time these various acts were committed. The learned Judge, Mr Justice Hallett, described her as 'this lady of magpie propensities', while Mr Fenwick, her own defence lawyer, actually said in court (this being Yorkshire) that she had '…gone daft'! One must have sympathised with the defence view when it was revealed in court that Dorothy also had in her back garden an air-conditioned underground air-raid shelter capable of holding 500 people, and an electrically lit underground tunnel linking the house and the shelter!

THE TWO TREES SPECIAL
6 years' prison for Lady Bountiful

Express Staff Reporter

LEEDS, Friday.—Dorothy Elliott, 48-year-old Wombwell magistrate, heard Mr. Justice Hallett sentence her to six years' penal servitude at Leeds Assizes tonight. Her only sign of emotion was a slight tightening of her thin lips.

And as she turned to go down the steps to the cells she smiled at the wardress who waited to follow her.

Miss Elliott, found guilty of robbing two companies, of which she was secretary, of £91,630, ended her four days' hearing on the hard, wooden seat in the dock.

When she first stepped into the dock on Tuesday morning, people in the gallery who had queued to hear the trial thought she was a prison wardress. The only touch of colour to her blue clothes was a small orange and green feather in her blue Girl Guide model hat.

Today there was no evidence, only speeches by the prosecution and defence and the judge's summing-up. Throughout the day Dorothy Elliott sat quite still, her hands folded in her lap.

Composure

She had heard with composure two psychiatrists tell the jury of five men and two women that she was insane. She saw friends and relatives go into the witness-box to give evidence about her mental state. She heard also how she had for seven years robbed Wombwell Main Colliery Company and its subsidiary, Wombwell Coking Company, of nearly £100,000. Throughout she sat bearing no notice, apparently taking no notice.

For the first time today Miss Elliott, greying haired, bespectacled and only just over five feet tall, appeared to take an interest in what was going on around her. She peered shortsightedly over the dock rail as the judge summed.

"This miniature steam locomotive lies in the grounds of Two Trees, Dorothy Elliott's home at... ...gave evidence at the trial that she had bought a model railway for 'sentimental reasons.' She had ridden on it as a child.—Daily Express picture.

Tonight, after the jury had been out over half an hour she heard Mr. Justice Hallett sentence her to six years' penal servitude for larceny, falsification of accounts and forgery of a cheque.

To this was added 2 months for libraries, bank certificates and balance sheets, the sentences to run concurrently.

Before sentence was passed she was asked if she wished to say anything. She replied in a quiet thin voice, "I have nothing to say."

Treatment

This is what she heard Mr. Justice Hallett say to her tonight:—

"In so far as there is anything in your mental condition which required treatment I have no doubt whatever it will be ascertained by the competent medical men who advise the authorities in such matters.

"I agree with the view of the jury that nothing has been established which would excuse your conduct in these respects on medical grounds.

"For nearly seven years under the guise of a faithful servant you have been robbing these two com-

Matthew Kerr collection

The 'Dorothy Elliott Hut' built in 1939 for her Rangers in Wombwell.
Author

This was legal point-scoring to some extent – 500 people could really only be accommodated if everyone was standing and in distinctly close proximity to each other. The long linking tunnel pursued a twisting course between house and shelter, with a second exit emerging at the side of the large greenhouse, just beyond the shelter itself. The original plot was acquired in 1931, and it is believed that the shelter dated from around 1936 when the grounds were extended and the relatively formal paths and gardens created (although the connecting tunnel dated only from 1940).

A strange, and apparently purely coincidental, fact that has only emerged recently concerns one of Dorothy's junior office clerks at Wombwell Main – a Miss Christine Barnes. In later years she became Mrs Barrett, and she and her husband in due course bought Lowdale Hall, which had once been owned by Charles Bartholomew, and was sold by CW as executor of his father's estate! Miss Barnes's uncle, Albert Silverwood Barnes, was Chief Cashier at Wombwell Main at the time of Dorothy's escapades, and while in no way involved in her activities, both were inevitably caught up in trying to sort out the resulting financial mess! Albert Barnes took Dorothy's place as Company Secretary, becoming the last such before nationalisation.

It would appear that Dorothy Elliott had had a great fondness not only for other people's money between 1936 and 1943, but also for the little railway throughout her life. Somehow she had persuaded the family to let her have BLACOLVESLEY and the two remaining carriages. They apparently reminded her of happy visits to Blakesley in her youth with her father, and it should also be remembered that she was only a little younger than James and was at home while he was lodging there during his studies at Sheffield University before the Great War, so she would have known him very well indeed.

Following the case it was noted that no offer of restitution had been made by Miss Elliott, but that '…it may now be expected that the colliery company will take steps to recover as much of their money as they can'. This proved to be the case and Miss Elliott's assets were auctioned in November 1944 to recover some of the stolen funds. The house and grounds went for £3,975 to Sir Lindsay Parkinson & Co, while the entire contents of house and garden were sold at auction by Messrs C. E. Smith & Son on Tuesday 7 and Wednesday 8 November, all '…being by order of the administrator for Miss Dorothy Elliott'.

Perhaps to add insult to injury, the auction of 400 lots of the smaller household items took place, now courtesy of Barnsley Co-op, in what had been the 'Dorothy Elliott Hut'! The sales raised in total around £21,000 – a long way short of the £91,630 taken. At long last some remorse was shown when Miss Elliott's solicitor said on 10 November that 'Miss Elliott was anxious to make restitution to the Company', but by then there was little more to be recovered.

The railway that (probably) never was!

Dorothy's efforts had come very close indeed to spawning yet another, complementary, reincarnation of the Blakesley railway, as far removed therefrom as was Deans Mill but to the north rather than the south – using most of the remaining equipment not at Deans Mill. In the process, this would have put it at the very doorstep of the source of the Bartholomew family income.

One problem remains. In the highly detailed newspaper reports (those of the sales even included details ranging from a 'Benares elephant bell' for 70 shillings to the wooden summer house in the garden for £61, exclusive of dismantling and carrying away) there is no mention whatsoever of locomotive, carriages or railway track. Where were they? When were they sold? There seems to be no record.

The photograph in the *Daily Express* shows the loco and one Blakesley 1904-style carriage crammed into a very small area close by the south-east corner of the house directly accessible at the end of the main drive; snow is visible in the background, indicating that the picture was contemporary with the verdict and sentencing, in late March 1944. We know (from later events) that there was a second carriage there also, and probably some track. (It is this photograph that proves that the rebuilding of the line's three carriages was not undertaken at Blakesley but subsequently, at two widely separated locations, to near-identical designs of relatively crude wooden 'toast racks'.)

A recently discovered rare original copy of the auctioneers' brochure for these sales has confirmed that no railway-related items featured as or in any of the lots. This, and the lack of any mention in the newspapers at this time, suggests that all such material was uplifted from 'Two Trees' between the date of the verdict and the auction. They, of course, had never been the property of the Wombwell Main Colliery Co, but of the Bartholomew family directly, and thus (strictly speaking) not directly relevant to the court fraud case at all.

It is thus likely that the Bartholomew family, presumably via James, simply reclaimed all this material as still being their own personal property, as one suspects no payment had been made to them by Dorothy (either with her or anyone else's money!). (It was, of course, the colliery company, as principal creditor, that was seeking recovery of its monies through these sales.)

The trial itself was reported in some detail in both local and national newspapers, with many references to a railway. The *Daily Mail* for 18 March 1944 recorded that 'The money she stole … commanded such things as … a small-gauge model railway which was to be the centre-piece of a pleasure park in her grounds…' This suggests, given the '…was to be…' quote, that the discovery of her fraudulent activities had prevented any significant progress with the intended railway, or resulted in any works already undertaken being abandoned.

The company's Assistant Secretary, Edward Irving Allen, was asked in court, 'Did you see in the garden a small gauge railway?'

'It was pointed out to me by Miss Elliott,' was the response.

He was then asked, 'Did you observe that this railway must have been very costly?' to which Allen replied, 'I do not know how much it cost.' Similarly, when questioned, 'Did you see in the garden parts of an 18-inch [sic] gauge railway?' Chief Detective Inspector Marston replied, 'Yes.'

Further questioning of a builder, Mr Albert Field, during the trial revealed that he '…went with her to Northampton in 1942 to buy the railway, which was put in her garden'. The *Yorkshire Post* newspaper in reporting the same exchange in court recorded that Mr Field said that '…he went with Miss Elliott to Northampton to buy the 18in [sic] gauge railway. She did not say what she wanted it for.'

A follow-up reference, also in the *Yorkshire Post*, says that 'she bought … a small gauge railway – a plaything that was never fixed', but it continues even more intriguingly, 'A second, complete with station, has never been unpacked.'

With the court evidence so obviously sloppy in regard to the wrong gauge and failing to distinguish between 'railway', 'locomotive' or 'train', it may well be questioned as to whether the above reference to 'Northampton' really meant Northampton (if so, presumably the Bassett-Lowke works) or, more likely, nearby Blakesley itself.

It is equally questionable as to the significance of the other 'never been unpacked' reference – was this perhaps the Blakesley model railway layout, particularly in view of the 'complete with station' comment, as we know that some model railway rolling stock – but not the layout – was sold in the Hall contents auction in 1947?

Thanks to the kindness of owner Terry Watford, the author was able to make a thorough examination of the former 'Two Trees' grounds in December 2003, almost 60 years to the day since Dorothy was arrested. The major parts of the garden remained just as in her time, except that obviously trees and plants had matured, but the edged crazy-paving pathways, large greenhouse, brick-built dog kennels (more like small stables for her two pedigree Sealyhams), etc, survived intact.

The air vents still showed clearly the tortuous course of the 1940-built underground passage between house and shelter. Some of the southern part of the garden had been lost in recent years through the construction of a new dual-carriageway, leaving an isolated and derelict remnant south of the new road, so large had been her garden.

Nevertheless there was no obvious sign of the course of a miniature railway even having been prepared; the most satisfactory route for any proposed railway would have been in a south-easterly direction (perhaps where the new road now cuts through), as this would have been nearly level.

The why and the wherefore

We must not forget, however, that without Dorothy's affection for *BLACOLVESLEY*, almost certainly neither it nor its carriages (or parts thereof!) would have survived to the present day in near-original condition to bask in their rightful place in history.

Thus a locomotive, originally ordered and bought with the legitimate earnings from the Wombwell Main Colliery Company, survives in part through her misuse of that same company's funds perhaps to 'buy' it from one of its own principal shareholders, and to give it sanctuary in a World War on a property also developed with those same misused funds within half a mile of their main business activity, before it was recovered and sold to make restitution of funds to the Bartholomew family!

It is perhaps appropriate that she is as well remembered in Wombwell for her support for her community as much as for her financial misdeeds! As the *Daily Mail* at the time reported, 'By a strange freak of her ego she coveted money for only two purposes – to give it away or buy things for other people.' Indeed, while the income of this side of the Bartholomew family was primarily derived from the Wombwell area, they did not appear to reinvest much of it in community projects there but, as has been seen, in deepest rural Northamptonshire and Bedfordshire.

In contrast, Dorothy did spend all 'her' monies locally, either directly with local shops or businesses, or by contributing in all sorts of ways to local 'good causes', which may well account for the seeming total lack of animosity in Wombwell even now, more than 60 years after her trial, about her activities – local folklore today considers her more a 'Robin Hood' figure than a 'Lady Bountiful'!

With the benefit of hindsight, and the opportunity to compare the interaction between the Bartholomew and Elliott families, Dorothy's actions are perhaps slightly less inexplicable, if not excusable. She was 22 when CW died and had visited Blakesley Hall in her formative years on quite a number of occasions. She would have seen the family's 'gentrified' living, the exotic animals on the estate farm, the charming personal large miniature railway of the Squire – and would no doubt be made aware of the various village 'amenities' that CW had provided.

It would be easy for her, as a daughter of the former Manager of the same company that the Bartholomews owned, to have 'delusions of grandeur' and acquire her own slightly more modest estate, with farm and exotic livestock, provide much-needed amenities for her local community, become a Justice of the Peace, commemorate her father and mother (who died in 1926 and 1913 respectively) in 1928 with a stained glass window by Jones & Willis of London in Wombwell Church, and establish a direct link with that world she so much cherished in memory by being able to secure the Blakesley train itself as a direct hands-on link for her estate.

A psychiatrist said of her during the court hearing, 'To the girl's mind the colliery belonged to her father, the colliery money was her father's money. She belonged to her father and saw nothing wrong in taking what was her father's. When he died she lost his affection and she retaliated for that by taking it out of the colliery.'

Following her eventual release, she returned to live close to her sister and brother-in-law, who had started a motor car garage and dealership, J. C. Snell Ltd, on Doncaster Road, Barnsley, in 1934.

Sale stirs up past of house built with stolen colliery money

IT was built in the 1930s with money Dorothy Elliott stole from Wombwell Main Colliery where she worked as company secretary. Now the most famous house in Wombwell is up for grabs. **Carla George** found out more.

THE defence at her trial claimed insanity but Dorothy Elliott was shrewd enough to build a £600 air raid shelter and tunnel in the garden of her home in the years leading up to the Second World War.

This was just one of many unique features the former company secretary added to 'Two Trees', the luxurious property she had built on Hemingfield Road – a house with an eccentric financier and intriguing history.

In 1944, Miss Elliott was con-

Robes, chairman of the two companies and director of the firm's bank, attended a meeting in London and happened to see a list of companies which had been granted overdrafts – including his own – that an investigation was launched and Miss Elliott was found out. She was sentenced to six years in prison.

At her trial in 1944, it was reported that the former company secretary had spent heavily on refurbishments on her home but would scrap them after six months in

with all the other possessions bought with her fraudulent money – and some of the internal features have also been changed but the house remains a hidden gem in Wombwell.

Owner Terry Watford says it has been an absolute delight living in the house and as a family home it has provided him and his wife with many a happy memory.

The house was the perfect Valentine's Day present for the couple who moved in on

Stalagmites and stalactites have grown out of the lime in the concrete. It is unique to say the least. Not many houses can boast such history.

"About four or five years ago, a gentleman came to the house and said he had got the train which used to be in the garden. Apparently, when Dorothy was a little girl she had rode on the train and enjoyed it so much that when she had the money she bought it. It is a shame it has gone

Just before this book went to press, 'Two Trees' came on the market again, and the local *Barnsley Chronicle* reopened the story of 'Lady Bountiful' and the proposed railway – and even mentioned the author's researches for this book. *Courtesy of Barnsley Chronicle*

14 A nomadic period for *BLACOLVESLEY*

A visit to Tyneside

However *BLACOLVESLEY* came to leave Wombwell, it was now about to enter into a truly nomadic existence as it wandered around North East England. For much of this period the two ex-Blakesley bogie carriages (or parts thereof), which had accompanied it to Wombwell, travelled around with it. Circumstantial evidence suggests that a quantity of ex-Blakesley track – perhaps as much as 400 feet in total – also accompanied them.

The equipment was secured (probably directly from the Bartholomews) by Mr E. Younger, the owner of E. W. Younger & Co Ltd, a haulage and distribution business based on the Quayside in Newcastle-upon-Tyne, who lived at 'Redlands', Woolsington, near Ponteland. Here it was used on his private Redlands Railway, which was essentially a single line alongside his drive leading from the Newcastle-Ponteland road to his house; it featured such things as signal gantries and a bridge over a stream.

It was at this stage of its career that its original – and by now antique – NAG engine was stripped out, the frames were rather savagely and crudely butchered, and a replacement, commonplace, petrol engine fitted of the type designed for the Austin 8 car (but possibly in this case taken from a former War Department or Air Raid Precautions fire pump unit).

To provide room for the carburettor, a small opening had to be cut in the right-hand side of the 'firebox' upper wrapper plate – although this spoiled the appearance slightly, it provides a perfect identification as to which engine is fitted internally! Although this was no doubt an easily and cheaply available unit, for which spare parts would be no problem for years to come (and are still not a major problem today!), the engine was poorly matched to the loco's gearboxes and drive-train.

Compared to the flexibility of the NAG engine, the Austin 8 unit, though still of reasonable power at its designed operating speed, had little power at very low speeds and was in any case designed to run normally somewhat faster. Having an 'RAC' horsepower rating of 7.99 (hence the name 'Austin 8'), it was only of 900cc capacity, with a brake horsepower rating of 27bhp at 4,400rpm; this was an uprated version of the engine in the short-lived 'Big 7' car. This car appeared in 1939, though production was halted during 1941-44; the engine may thus be regarded as 'state of the art' for that period, in the same manner as the NAG unit had been a quarter of a century earlier.

Unfortunately the degree of cutting of the main frames severely weakened them, over half of their depth being removed in critical places. The cutting was achieved by the traditional method of drilling a succession of closely spaced holes, before chiselling or sawing through along the hole lines, but without then smoothing out the remnants of the drilled holes.

This led to the right-hand frame suffering a fracture above the hornway for the rear right-hand driving wheel in due course, leaving barely an inch of complete frame surviving there. (It is a credit to Greenly's design, the quality of the steel plate used, and Bassett-Lowke's – and William Vaughan's – workmanship, that the small section beyond the crack itself held firm until it was welded and strengthening finally added in the year 2000!)

This rebuilding with an engine unit only operating satisfactorily at much higher speeds unfortunately initiated the recurrence of a half-century of overheating problems, which resulted in the early removal of the smokebox door.

BLACOLVESLEY was painted in a green livery with complex lining, re-christened *YVONNE* and

The Austin 8 engine, replacing the original NAG unit, was a tight squeeze in the 'boiler' of BLACOLVESLEY, requiring savage cutting of the main frames. *Robin Butterell*

given the number 2, with new brass bunker-side works plates reading 'Redlands Railway No 2', No 1 being a post-1903 Herschell-Spillman (or possibly Cagney Brothers) 4-4-0 with wagon-top boiler, previously on the Southend Kursaal line.

For a period of some eight weeks (from mid-June to mid-August) in the summer of 1945 it was used in Exhibition Park (still more commonly known by its original name of Bull Park), at the south-eastern corner of the Town Moor, Newcastle-upon-Tyne, on a short line constructed there in connection with the wartime regular annual 'Holidays at Home' programme. This temporary line, probably comprised of the recently arrived ex-Blakesley rail, was laid on the Moor side of the main pathway through the Park between Claremont Road and the Boating Lake; the Herschell Spillman 4-4-0 was on static display here at this time.

Here YVONNE pushed and pulled a train of two 'toast rack' carriages, which were actually the two original Blakesley bogie carriages with new bodies built by Younger on their existing underframes and bogies. One carriage had seven reversible high-backed 'toast rack' benches, while the other appears to have had its underframe extended slightly so that eight such benches could be mounted. (The similarly rebuilt carriage at Deans Mill, with its cruder and more massive reversible seats, only had six such benches.)

Together these two carriages therefore now provided a capacity for around 30 adults. As with the rebuild at Deans Mill, no body sides were fitted, although each carriage appears to have had a simple flat dash plate at one end only (the outer end of each when coupled together).

The train then returned to Redlands, where a third loco (to be known as YVETTE) was under construction but not completed when Mr Younger died in 1947. The sudden availability on the market of both YVONNE and her carriages enabled Raymond Dunn of Bishop Auckland to secure them for use on an exciting new 15-inch-gauge line he had just opened at Saltburn.

A home at Saltburn

The Dunn family promoted a number of 15-inch-gauge lines, most of relatively short duration, along the Durham coast in such places as Seaton Carew and Crimdon Dene. Their most extensive – and long-lived – venture was the creation of the Saltburn Miniature Railway, which was opened for business in 1947.

Initially it was only an end-to-end line about 300 yards long, and operations commenced with three passenger carriages resembling four-wheeled coal wagons and 'No 7', a steam-outline 2-4-0 tender petrol loco (with the engine in the tender), previously at the Southend and Great Yarmouth miniature railways of Nigel Parkinson. At this time the line was still a short end-to-end push-pull shuttle without pointwork; the stock was originally stored when not in use in an above-ground 'tunnel' about midway along the line.

The fortuitous availability of the Redlands Railway equipment brought another steam-outline locomotive to the railway, and this steam-outline internal-combustion tradition has remained a steadfast feature of this line. The 'new' loco was YVONNE, still named thus and in full 'Redlands Railway No 2' guise, which arrived for the 1949 season; the two rebodied Blakesley bogie carriages also accompanied it to Saltburn. It is probable that the stock had all spent a brief intermediate period at Dunn's Seaton Carew line. The 2-4-0 and its passenger trucks left Saltburn at the same time.

Towards the end of 1948 work commenced on extending the line at both ends ready for the 1949 season, including the provision of a 'balloon loop' at its southern end and a turntable, with run-round loop, for YVONNE at its northern end adjacent to the new Cat Nab station. The balloon loop was of remarkably tight radius for this loco with its known dislike for sharp curves – of barely 100-foot radius – and the curves would have taxed to the limit the side play of the bogies.

Stories abound of the speed at which this loop was taken on each journey to avoid 'sticking', bearing in mind that YVONNE now had its higher-speed engine (nominally some 50 per cent higher than the 32mph NAG unit). A service frequency of about eight journeys per hour was

YVONNE, still in full Redlands Railway livery, hauls the two ex-Blakesley ex-Redlands carriages away from Cat Nab station, Saltburn, on 18 April 1949. The carburettor poking out of the right-hand side of the 'firebox' shows that the Austin 8 engine is now fitted, but the lack of a smokebox door reveals the original tubular annular radiator. *H. D. Bowtell, courtesy of Manchester Locomotive Society*

apparently often achieved. Once again, the arrival of BLACOLVESLEY at a new location heralded a longer railway, giving a further hint that this may have been rail from Blakesley.

It has been claimed that the re-engining mentioned above took place while at Saltburn. However, a photograph taken of it there by Harold Bowtell in early 1949 clearly shows the carburettor for the Austin 8 engine projecting from the 'firebox'. It might just be that Dunn did undertake the re-engining, rather than Younger, during the 1947-48 winter period, in preparation for its use on the new line at Saltburn.

Had this been the case it seems inconceivable that Dunn would not have changed its livery at the same time, but the Bowtell photograph shows that this did not happen until later. It is also clear from the new bodies on the ex-Blakesley carriages while at Exhibition Park that these had already been extensively rebuilt by Younger, thereby supporting a rebuilding of the loco by him at the same time.

About 1950 the line was purchased by Councillor J. C. (Cyril) Pickering, a notable local figure and businessman, who also owned Saltburn Motor Services, the local bus company. He invested substantially in the line and had a new extension built, including a bridge over the beck, to a new southern terminus at 'Smugglers Cove' (later to be known as 'Forest Halt'); a turntable and run-round loop were also provided here.

Both of these non-original layouts allowed the former BLACOLVESLEY to operate forwards at all times. She was repainted in a deep red livery around 1951, with a simpler and more conventional style of lining, losing her name and number but receiving 'SMR' in script lettering on the tank sides. This was followed shortly afterwards by a rather dramatic cosmetic change to her appearance, allied with changes to her now inadequate cooling system.

Although the streamlined era on the railways had been in the 1930s, the Saltburn line managed, around 1952, vaguely to 'streamline' the former BLACOLVESLEY through the application of curved side panelling ahead of the tanks; these received the same lined livery as the existing loco panelling. These additional panels fortuitously concealed the front lower sections of the 'boiler', which had now been partially cut away in connection with a new supporting framework for a replacement water tank.

It would seem likely that the original tubular radiator was also replaced at this time by a fairly home-spun one of conventional honeycomb pattern. A circular wire-mesh cover had already replaced the long-missing smokebox door. These changes are confirmed as happening around this

YVONNE soon lost her name, being painted in a lined, deep-red livery with 'SMR' in script lettering on the tank sides; a grill has filled in for the missing smokebox door. Her two ex-Blakesley carriages sport a four-wheeled brake-van between them. *Frith postcard, Tony Harden collection*

A nomadic period for *BLACOLVESLEY*

Above Around 1952 the tank sides were extended forward in a vaguely streamlined shape, largely to conceal the removal of large sections of 'boiler' plate, consequent upon the fitting of a new radiator and repositioned water tank. The script lined-red livery was retained. *Tony Harden collection*

Below A truly startling 'Coronation' livery for 1953, with a new name ELIZABETH. Freshly painted and on her turntable at Cat Nab station, Saltburn, the side panels, cab and bunker were in gold, bordered in silver and lined in red, white and blue! Holidaymakers relax in the commonplace flat caps, overcoats and dangling cigarettes of the time. *Dewi Williams*

The Blakesley Hall Miniature Railway

Above Seen at Cat Nab station on 29 March 1953, fresh carriages were provided for *ELIZABETH*, liveried to match the loco; although their bogies resembled those from Blakesley, they were from another source. *Dewi Williams*

Below These carriages were very soon rebuilt with much squarer flat-panelled bodies, with another variation on the 'Coronation' livery to match the loco. *Tony Harden collection*

time by a broadside-view postcard of around 1951 showing the locomotive in 'script SMR' livery (but without the streamlining); the chimney is there still in its original position, later being moved forward to accommodate the new radiator.

The early 1950s were a time of national celebration after the years of wartime austerity, including the Festival of Britain in 1951 and a new Queen in 1952. Her Coronation in 1953 saw these celebrations reach an unprecedented peak, and the then unnamed BLACOLVESLEY was not left out. A further, and rather startling, change therefore occurred within a few months of her gaining her new shape. She received a new and apposite name – ELIZABETH – and a truly distinctive and remarkable gold and silver paint scheme, with white lining picked out in red and blue, while the boiler was capped by a red dome, safety valve bonnet and chimney! The name and 'SMR' were also in red.

As already noted, the two Blakesley coaches that had accompanied her via Wombwell and Woolsington (and had been considerably rebuilt at the latter to 'toast rack' form) came with her to Saltburn. Soon a four-wheeled covered brake-van was acquired or built and coupled between the two carriages to provide some much-needed braking power. For some unknown reason, this brake-van was dispensed with around 1952.

In 1953 the carriages were finally retired. Apart from a few components, they were scrapped and replaced by other carriages, possibly from Seaburn. Shortly after, entirely new flat-panelled bodies were constructed for these; their bogies bore close resemblance to the old Blakesley ones (for which they have often been mistaken).

Three compartments, each with pairs of facing seats, were provided in each carriage, with passenger access through openings to each 'compartment' on one side – the west side – of the vehicle only (the other side having a continuous end-to-end panel). A new, almost 'Art Deco', livery was carried, in colours to harmonise with the current amazing loco livery.

Also in Coronation year, the Saltburn line acquired one of the remarkable and formidable TVO/petrol-electric 'streamlined' steam-outline locos built by Barlow, together with some new coaches. (Their oft-perceived resemblance to the LNER 'A4' 'Pacifics' was nearly as tenuous as that of the Cagney 4-4-0s to No 999 more than half a century earlier – or the Deans Mill petrol loco to the Sentinel steam railcar!) The new locomotive arrived as PRINCE CHARLES, initially still liveried and lettered for the Lakeside Miniature Railway at Southport.

BLACOLVESLEY certainly seems to have lived a charmed life throughout its existence. After a few seasons as spare loco to the Barlow, now renamed PRINCE OF WALES (though later reverting to PRINCE CHARLES again), ELIZABETH was felt to be no longer needed at Saltburn in view of the Barlow's rugged simplicity and reliability.

The loco was stored unused, but in search of a good home, for some considerable time in the bus garage of Saltburn Motor Services. Tony Stanhope was offered it for preservation for £150, but was unable to raise the sum sought. It was also offered

A less common view of ELIZABETH slumbering, awaiting salvation, in the Saltburn Motor Services bus garage.
Robin Butterell

by Councillor Pickering to the then Saltburn & Marske County Modern School but, as they had nowhere to house it, the offer had to be declined. Reg Blacklock, long-time Chairman of the later Saltburn Miniature Railway Association, was on the school's staff at the time and was consulted about the offer.

It was perhaps fortunate that the school refused the offer as it probably would not have survived as a piece of playground equipment for more than a few years. But once again a guardian angel, in this case Councillor Pickering, had nevertheless ensured its survival against all odds; having become disused, it was able to move on yet again.

Scotland – a near miss!

Kerr's Miniature Railway, a 10¼-inch-gauge line at Arbroath in Scotland, featured several historic steam and steam-outline locomotives. Its promoter and owner, Matthew Kerr, was quite keen around this time to acquire *ELIZABETH* as appropriate accompaniment to his recent purchase of the historic original *LITTLE GIANT* (at that time posing as *ROBIN HOOD*) from Mr J. Noble, at South Shields, in 1963. His intention was to re-gauge his own line to 15 inches and preserve – and operate – these historic locomotives thereon.

However, possibly as a result of the then appalling condition of *LITTLE GIANT*, this idea failed to come to fruition and Mr Kerr sold it on to Mr Tom Tate, while it was still lying derelict at South Shields. Matthew Kerr therefore did not acquire *ELIZABETH*, and, although he long held his dream of running these two historic 15-inch locos at Arbroath, this was not to be. Thus the 10¼-inch line at Arbroath continues to thrive today, with much historic steam and steam-outline stock, in the ownership of his family.

Rescue, disintegration and survival

Fortunately *ELIZABETH* was seen in the bus garage in due course by Mr Tate, who decided to buy it in 1968 to accompany his now-restored *LITTLE GIANT*. Tate was building a new 15-inch-gauge line, known as the North Eastern Railway, in his grounds at Haswell Lodge, County Durham. *ELIZABETH* left Saltburn for Haswell on Thursday 12 December 1968.

Before we leave, for the moment, Saltburn and Saltburn Motor Services, we should touch again on the remnants of the very much rebuilt Blakesley carriages. They seem to have all but vanished in 1953 when *ELIZABETH* appeared in its Coronation livery with fresh coaches; although now thoroughly worn out, one bogie did find further use in the bus workshops, until their closure, for moving equipment around.

Although the present course of the SMR is in no part on the same alignments as those of 1947-48, a short section towards its southern end (just north of the present Forest Halt station site) does survive more or less on the course of the railway of the early 1950s, and thus along which *BLACOLVESLEY* would have operated with its (rebuilt) original carriages, perhaps once even riding on ex-Blakesley rail.

Upon arrival at Haswell, *ELIZABETH* was immediately taken in hand by the experienced engineer there, Ernie Cheeseman. It was completely stripped down both cosmetically and mechanically, and a most thorough overhaul undertaken. The story of this work featured in an amusing article in *The Model Engineer* for 18 December 1970.

Other than the overhaul itself, the principal modification made was to try to curb the limited high-speed range and resultant poor low-speed pulling power of the Austin 8 engine by inserting an intermediate layshaft between the engine clutch and the Greenly reversing dog-box; this shaft was chain-driven at each end, thereby allowing relatively easy adjustment of the step-down ratio by changing the drive sprockets.

This has proved highly effective in controlling the speed problems, and enhancing its nominal pulling power, but it has introduced the significant and intrusive noise of rattling chains and sprockets (into an otherwise near-silent machine) when the engine is running, and its clutch engaged. To accommodate the new layshaft and associated cooling fan the cooling water tank in the 'boiler' had to be shortened by around 6 inches and the radiator had to be moved forward a couple of inches, requiring the dome to be moved back an inch or so and the chimney to be moved forward a similar distance, thereby spoiling slightly the balance of the original design.

The culmination of this restoration was the refitting of a proper smokebox door in place of the grill (or the opening) with which the loco had operated since the installation of the Austin 8 engine. It was hoped that the small new fan attached to the additional drive layshaft would provide sufficient extra cooling to get over the overheating problem, but this did not prove to be the case and the grill was refitted, although the door reappeared whenever the loco was 'on show' somewhere.

When received at Haswell the loco still retained its later-pattern Blakesley 'jaw'-style front coupling, which had survived through all its subsequent moves; unfortunately the historic and original nature of this was not recognised during the restoration, and it was scrapped and replaced by a Stephensonian-type draw-hook of a somewhat excessive size and weight compared to Bassett-Lowke practice.

It was also time for another change of identity. The half-hearted streamlining was removed, together with the garish livery, and it was painted all-over black, un-named and un-numbered but with the words 'NORTH EASTERN' on the tank sides.

During the very thorough preparation for this repainting, virtually all evidence of earlier liveries was destroyed through total removal of all earlier paint, making future cosmetic restoration more difficult and losing yet more valuable historical data. The black was later changed to a green livery, with the same branding. Contrary to various published reports, it never regained its original name while at Haswell.

Thus the Haswell refurbishment, while ensuring its continued existence, lost some original and authentic features of the locomotive, destroying significant archaeological information in the process. Following the restoration it was briefly loaned to the Ocean Park Railroad in Seaburn, Sunderland, from March to May 1971 to cover a locomotive crisis there, but then returned to Haswell.

In 1975 the anonymous BLACOLVESLEY was an operating exhibit during the 150th anniversary celebrations for the Stockton & Darlington Railway. Although the main events were centred around Shildon, there were also displays at Darlington and the loco was on outdoor show there at the Magnet Bowl centre on East Street, in company with a working scale steam crane and brake-van (which had been built by Ernie Cheeseman). At this time it was in all-over unlined black livery, with 'NER' on the tank sides.

It made its first visit to Ravenglass for the centenary celebrations of the Ravenglass & Eskdale Railway (the 'Ratty') in 1976. Although not operable at that time, it was on static display in Ravenglass station. Tragically, during the time it was there its original whistle, which had survived throughout the various traumatic changes in its long life, was stolen.

Yet another railway that never was!

An exciting project that emerged in 1977 was for a major 15-inch-gauge line, the Medina Valley Railway, on the Isle of Wight. This was proposed to run along the trackbed of the former standard-gauge line in the Medina Valley from Cowes to Newport; a single line of some 3 miles in length was envisaged with an intermediate passing loop at Pinkmead.

A Light Railway Order was actually secured for this line and, to provide some initial motive power and rolling stock, much of the equipment at Haswell was promised for it in anticipation. The 'Royal Scot' under restoration at Haswell was intended for the line, and the prototype LITTLE GIANT was transferred in the middle of 1977. BLACOLVESLEY followed later that year; some servicing, including of its Austin 8 engine, was undertaken in a warehouse on the island. They were joined by the two Barlow steam-outline 'Pacifics' from the Battersea Park line, which reunited BLACOLVESLEY with this loco design. It had been envisaged that the petrol loco would have been ideal for 'setting up' the railway each morning prior to passenger operations commencing.

Sadly this spectacular project did not go ahead, and the two Bassett-Lowke locos were, fortunately, eventually returned to North East England. Tragically the Barlows were scrapped but, yet again, BLACOLVESLEY providentially escaped such a fate.

Theme park display

In 1980 the developing theme park at Lightwater Valley in North Yorkshire received some of the Haswell locomotive collection, including LITTLE GIANT and BLACOLVESLEY from the abortive Medina Valley Railway. A splendid brick-built engine shed in the style of grand estate railways (such as that at Eaton Hall) had been constructed for the opening of this line, an irregular circuit around a lake, in 1979.

The Blakesley Hall Miniature Railway

Recognition at last! Still liveried as LNER No 1326, the disguised *BLACOLVESLEY* is on display in the National Railway Museum in 1982 for its Heywood Centenary exhibition. The original Class 10 *LITTLE GIANT* is in the background, with a Heywood brake-van from Eaton. *National Railway Museum/SSPL*

Initial operation there was by a steam-outline Severn-Lamb 2-8-0, but joining *BLACOLVESLEY* were a couple of its former colleagues from various stages of its nomadic career – the Carland 'Royal Scot' 4-6-0 from Seaburn and a 4-4-0 tender loco named *YVETTE*, which had come from the Redlands Railway of E. Younger at Ponteland, although this latter had not been completed when *YVONNE/BLACOLVESLEY* had left there.

Never operable at Lightwater, *BLACOLVESLEY* was placed on display in the new loco shed and exhibition area. It changed its identity yet again, this time being repainted into a black scheme with thin single red lining as used by the LNER on some of its secondary passenger engines. It also received fictitious 'LNER' lettering with the number '1326' on its tank sides, and was fitted with dummy vacuum brake pipes on each bufferbeam.

Although LNER No 1326 had indeed been a 4-4-4T locomotive, this was actually a three-cylinder machine of Class 'H1' (NER Class 'D') built at Darlington in March 1922, and in no way other than in its wheel arrangement did it resemble *BLACOLVESLEY*. There were 45 examples in the class, built between 1913 and 1922 (and thus they post-dated *BLACOLVESLEY*), although all were rebuilt to be 4-6-2Ts of Class 'A8' between 1931 and 1936. No 1326 was so converted in 1935, becoming No 69892 in BR days, finally being withdrawn in November 1958. One of the class's main spheres of activity was the Darlington-Saltburn line – so there was a Saltburn connection!

In October 1981 the historic importance of *BLACOLVESLEY* was perhaps finally appreciated, at least in some quarters, at national level when it joined an exhibition at the National Railway Museum at York to mark the Centenary of Minimum Gauge Railways in Britain. This exhibition ran until March 1982 and also included *LITTLE GIANT* and *RIVER IRT* (as rebuilt from the original Heywood loco *MURIEL*) from the 'Ratty', as well as some historic Heywood rolling stock.

15 Preservation at last

New ownership

By 1994 Lightwater Valley had decided to concentrate more on 'adventure' and 'thrill' rides, with the 15-inch-gauge railway merely another entertainment activity; for this purpose the existing Severn-Lamb steam-outline 2-8-0 locomotive was deemed adequate for all services. Accordingly they decided to dispose of their historic collection of locomotives in a carefully controlled manner, and yet again another of the guardians of *BLACOLVESLEY* was on hand to ensure its future.

Robin Butterell was particularly concerned for the future of *BLACOLVESLEY* in view of its historical significance, and commenced negotiations with Lightwater Valley to save it. He mounted a publicity campaign, which came to the attention of the author during a Spring Bank Holiday Week gala on the Ravenglass & Eskdale Railway. The author took over the negotiations from Robin and was able to purchase the locomotive.

As a temporary measure, the R&ER agreed that it could join the *RIVER IRT* centenary exhibition, which was being held at Ravenglass throughout that summer season. Accordingly it was collected from Lightwater Valley by pick-up truck on 10 June 1994 and delivered to Ravenglass the same day. It became apparent all too quickly that its worn, fine-scale wheels were not happy on Ratty's more massive coarse-scale pointwork, but it was soon on static display in the exhibition, still in its pseudo LNER 1326 livery.

Operation and restoration

Following this period on display, the author, with the assistance of other Ratty staff and volunteers, decided on 24 August 1994 to see if it was indeed workable. With little knowledge at that time of its mechanism, and uncertainty even over the engine cylinder firing order (not helped by the engine being mounted backwards!), it presented quite a challenge. The participants were eventually rewarded, after some 5 hours of 'persuasion', by the engine firing and running, if somewhat unevenly. It managed to run a few yards and, following further efforts, managed to run the length of Ravenglass station, the first time it had moved under its own power for very many years.

The operation was repeated a few days later on 1 September, this time hauling Ratty bogie open carriage 4-69 between Ravenglass station turntable and the road overbridge. It was decided that it would be better initially to undertake the cosmetic external restoration as a priority to restore its historic appearance rather than pursue the many physical and mechanical works required.

LNER green was officially described in the company's 1924 'Pacific' painting specification as 'GN Standard light green'. Close comparison also of the preserved GNR 'Atlantic' No 251 and the LNER 'V2' *GREEN ARROW* side by side in Doncaster Plant yard confirmed that identical paint shades had then been used in their restoration. In 1994, therefore, the author purchased, for the loco's restoration, reproduction 'LNER Doncaster Green' enamel (reference 620) from Howes Models 'Railmatch', a 1990s equivalent of the Bassett-Lowke model enamels of 1909.

The bodywork was dismantled for painting; importantly, a small area of original green paint was found on one part of the cab roof (its initial livery being the only time the roof was so painted). This suggested that, whatever CW's and Greenly's intentions may have been, it did not appear to have been painted in GNR colours, but in a somewhat unusual and rather pleasing shade of deep green.

The Blakesley Hall Miniature Railway

Ready for the off! The author struggles to keep the engine running in Ravenglass station on 24 August 1994, after it was started for the first time in some 20 years. Peter Tebb

As a result of this discovery, quite different from that expected, the author rejected the reproduction LNER enamel paint purchased for the loco. A 'Dulux Definitions' gloss paint (5040-G 'Sportsday') was found to be a close match to the actual shade found on the cab roof. After thorough rubbing down and preparation, appropriate layers of primer, undercoat, gloss and varnish were applied to build up a smooth, high-quality finish.

The tank sides were tackled similarly, although it was not possible initially to apply crests and name banners as the exact form of these had not then been researched fully. The bunker sides and rear were similarly painted, though without being removed from the loco. The deeper 'border' green was chosen to complement the main body shade, as nothing remained of this on the loco to show the original, though this is now known to be much too light in shade ('Dulux Definitions' 6030-B90G 'Woodland' being used).

Black lining, picked out in white, was applied in accordance with the original layout as evidenced from contemporary photographs. The 'boiler' was also painted in the same style and the loco bodywork reassembled by early 1995. At this stage the lettering for the works plates was also uncertain and temporary plates were made from magnetic plastic! The chimney and dome castings required extensive repair and renovation to restore their original form.

Despite the paint matching achieved, research into the origin of the somewhat unexpected green shade continued. In 1997 the author had applied the 'rejected' 'Railmatch' LNER green enamel to his metal garage door at home in Wakefield! By 2007 this had weathered to a much deeper green, quite different from the original – but had become almost identical in shade and tone to that fragment found on the loco's cab roof during restoration, and as shown on the LPC postcard!

A number of contemporary models, in various scales, of GNR and LNER locos on display in the National Railway Museum at York not only show a difference between Stirling and Ivatt/Gresley eras, but also display the GNR greens as significantly deeper than that on the LNER models – and indeed closer in shade to that found on *BLACOLVESLEY* in 1994!

At about this time, the author found and purchased a Gauge O clockwork version of the Bassett-Lowke LNWR 'Precursor tank' factory-painted most unusually in full Great Northern Railway lined green and chocolate livery (save for the omission of the darker border green), presumably using the Bassett-Lowke enamel paint of the period; this example almost certainly dates from 1914, as the green cab-back (alone) had been over-painted in black and neatly hand-lettered 'BRITISH MADE' to disguise its German manufacture by Bing of Nuernberg.

The green on this model matches the Precision Paints Ivatt/Gresley green shade, suggesting that the apparently curious paint specimen found on BLACOLVESLEY in 1994 had been misleading, and what had been found then was merely the originally accurate Bassett-Lowke version of GNR green enamel weathered by 33 years of service at Blakesley, together with standing outdoors for the years 1942 to 1944 in the then grimy and polluted environs of Wombwell!

It is also likely that the exhaust design, whereby the petrol engine emissions exited vertically via the loco's chimney before descending onto the paintwork (and particularly the cab roof), contributed to such weathering at Blakesley. This was compounded by the whistle, immediately in front of the cab, being powered by exhaust gases!

It would therefore seem that Greenly was correct in 1909 regarding the locomotive being in the process of being painted in GNR livery (or at least Bassett-Lowke's enamel version thereof) – and the loco as restored today thus may, unintentionally, reflect its circa 1944 livery shade (if not, hopefully, its condition!) as weathered from its as-built enamel. In another of those strange twists of fate it seems that, 98 years later, a garage door in Wakefield was able to prove Greenly correct!

Following a request, BLACOLVESLEY made its first public appearance in its re-created livery during a 'Little Giants Steam Gala' at the Cleethorpes Coast Light Railway on 20 and 21 May 1995. It was not operational, but was pushed or hauled by the other 'Little Giant' locos at this event, which comprised the original No 10 LITTLE GIANT itself, the late-production large-boilered Class 10 No 18 GEORGE THE FIFTH, the somewhat rebuilt Class 20 No 22 KING GEORGE (originally PRINCE EDWARD OF WALES) and the first of the Class 30 type No 30 SYNOLDA, thereby bringing together for the first – and last – time ever all the basic four-coupled 'Little Giant' variants.

Some frustration was felt at this time that, in the various photographic line-ups undertaken,

The inner workings of BLACOLVESLEY are revealed with the bodywork removed during restoration in 1996. *Author*

BLACOLVESLEY was incomplete as regards name banners and crests on the tank sides – it was therefore somewhat comforting many years later to discover photographs of the loco at Blakesley in 1909 in exactly this condition, ie fully painted and lined but without the branding adornments!

With the loco now almost fully cosmetically restored, attention could be given to the mechanical parts while research continued into the tank-side adornments and works plate lettering. The securing of an 'Austin 8' handbook enabled the firing order and position to be determined accurately and set. With the aid of a borrowed magneto from Ratty's preserved ICL No 1 petrol loco, the engine was started and found to run both smoothly and quietly, a tribute to the mechanical restoration work carried out by Ernie Cheeseman in the 1960s.

However, the perennial problem of overheating continued. Eventually the water pump was stripped down and found to have most of the propellant vanes missing, as well as all the seals being perished! With this refurbished, the overheating problems were almost eliminated – something that could probably have been as easily cured 40 years earlier! Its own magneto was also refurbished and refitted.

With the particular assistance of Blakesley historian Phil Kingston, the information was now to hand to complete the painting of the crest and name banners on the tank sides, together with replica brass works plates carrying, inter alia, the number '1'. Over the next few years the missing vertical handrails and the front lamp brackets were also replicated.

The first public appearance of the loco with its restored propulsion and identity took place on the Ratty during the 1996 May Bank Holiday 'Spring Extravaganza' at Ravenglass, where it hauled a single preserved four-wheeled carriage on the 'Engineers' Siding' alongside the main BR line. To add interest, this was also the first time BLACOLVESLEY had encountered a genuine Bassett-Lowke four-wheeled open carriage, as CW had conspicuously failed to have any of these at Blakesley!

Apart from a brief appearance at the Flookburgh steam rally in July 1996, the loco remained at Ravenglass, occasionally on display (both static and trundling around the station). However, its scale wheels with their narrow treads and worn flanges were resulting in occasional derailments on Ratty's beefy coarse-scale pointwork; operation also brought out further mechanical weaknesses and some significant attention was clearly required.

BLACOLVESLEY's 90th birthday on Saturday 11 September 1999 was, however, celebrated in some style with limited operation around Ravenglass station, followed by a series of photographs taken to recreate those taken on Saturday 11 September 1909 at Blakesley (11 September was not, in 1999, a significant date otherwise!).

Accordingly the loco was removed, on 28 October 1999, to the premises of CSM Engineering (then at Broadgate) in Cumbria where the proprietor, Ian Page, carried out

The author and his wife produced a 'scale driver' for BLACOLVESLEY during 1997; at the age of around 10 weeks, younger son Matthew objects vigorously to being on its footplate at Ravenglass in near-freezing temperatures! *Author*

Recreating photo opportunities so strangely missed at Blakesley, this view at Ravenglass in May 2000 shows ex-LMS 8F 2-8-0 No 48151 passing BLACOLVESLEY. The author must express a particular fondness for this scene, as the best friend of his elder son Peter at junior school was Richard, the son of No 48151's owner, David Smith. Author

significant remedial work including repairing the cracked right-hand frame, extending the wheel treads by means of steel rings added to the outside faces of the 'tyres' (the wheels and tyres being in practice one-piece steel castings) and fettling the water and electrical systems. Great effort was made to ensure as much of this repair work as possible was reversible, should conservation so require it in the future, and the locomotive returned to Ravenglass on 30 May 2000.

It finally left Ravenglass station limits under its own power on the evening of 20 July 2000 when it ran light engine, with the author driving and Ratty's David Taylor as Pilotman, to beyond the first station at Muncaster Mill, before returning non-stop to Ravenglass, a run of some 1¼ miles each way. Despite its long and varied history of operating on many different 15-inch-gauge railways, this was the longest each-way journey it had ever achieved under its own power!

During the winter of 2001-02, lining on frames (red) and wheels (white) was completed. There remains some doubt as to whether the front frames and the running plate edges did ever carry this red lining; the Locomotive Publishing Company coloured postcard suggests so, but the monochrome photographs show no evidence of this. However, photographic emulsions of the period could not readily distinguish between red and black, leaving such lining, when provided, quite invisible anyway on contemporary photographs.

Survival of a Blakesley bogie

The one Blakesley-built carriage bogie, which found a use at the Saltburn Motor Services bus garage and workshops as an engineering trolley for moving around bus engines and the like during overhaul, survived until those workshops closed. One of the engineering staff acquired the bogie and took it to his home as the railway was then moribund; once again fate and a 'magpie' instinct had, against the odds, ensured the survival of a piece of Blakesley stock.

Eventually he presented the bogie to the reconstituted and reactivated SMR, and it returned to active service on the reopened Saltburn line for many years as a light engineering trolley. The wooden side frames, still joined together by the original 'stretcher' planking in pitch pine, and the Cagney axleboxes and hornways, display its true heritage as the last

The Blakesley Hall Miniature Railway

The surviving Blakesley carriage bogie, seen after removal of extraneous (modern) wooden sections, but as received with non-original wheel-sets. Author

surviving piece of Blakesley – and Blakesley-built – rolling stock.

It is tempting to remember that the bogies used in the building of the original *PETROLIA* were standard, interchangeable Blakesley carriage bogies, and it is thus possible (if unlikely) that this bogie was so used initially – making it a further remnant of that earliest of 15-inch-gauge internal-combustion locomotives!

Through the kindness of the Saltburn Miniature Railway Association and its members, the bogie was transferred in its centenary year to the author's custody to continue its conservation and to aid in the recreation (or, more accurately, in view of this bogie's survival, rebuilding) of one of the Blakesley bogie carriages; it left Saltburn on 20 March 2004. Thus, after 100 years of virtually continuous transport service in one guise or another, this bogie finally entered the realm of formal preservation!

This bogie was slightly incomplete as received, including original components (the disc wheel-sets therein were not the originals, nor – probably – were any of the assorted axle ball- and roller-bearing races for these). It was initially restored to completeness in 2005, deliberately retaining all original or vintage material and adding new components identifiably different from the original lost ones. It was reunited with *BLACOLVESLEY* for a short trip at Ravenglass, prior to restoration, on 14 April 2004.

During conservation and restoration of this bogie in 2005, it was found possible to match the surviving fragments of original deep red paintwork with modern shades; a near-perfect match was found in Dulux 'Vibrant' colour 'Ruby Fountain 1' – Ref 00YR 08/40.

Thanks to the efforts of American Cagney enthusiast and collector Carey Williams, a complete set of original 1903 Cagney 15-inch bogie carriage hornways, ball-bearing axleboxes and ball-thrust-bearing wheel-sets was located and subsequently obtained through him from David Dollar of Oklahoma City, sufficient to re-wheel the original bogie and provide enough authentic equipment for a second. Once used at Elk City, Oklahoma, with a 1903 Class D loco, these arrived in England on 16 November 2006.

Other than a slightly smaller vertical hornway range, these were virtually identical to those of 1902 used at Blakesley. All axleboxes retained at least parts of the outer sections of their original ball-bearing races. Some of the wheels even retained traces of original Cagney red paint, fortuitously showing that the bogie colour that had been identified and adopted in the initial bogie refurbishment was a reasonable match to the original Cagney colour.

Some suitable rails, of the appropriate unusual cross-section, were traced (thanks to members of The Heywood Society) to the 15-inch Sherwood Forest Railway, which kindly transferred a virtually unworn, perfectly straight pair of them to the author for a token £1 on 11 November 2006 to provide the necessary longitudinal carriage underframe members.

Some early four-wheeled 12⅜-inch-gauge Cagney carriages in Carey Williams's collection have enabled the dimensions, together with the constructional details and materials, of 15-inch regular-style cars to be derived, allowing the fabrication of the three four-wheeler bodies, and the wooden framework for the new bogie, required to rebuild the Blakesley carriage.

Preserving integrity

Restoration must today be handled with care in view of the large percentage of original components remaining in this historic material. Although operable, starting the engine and running *BLACOLVESLEY* inevitably results in further wear and tear; conversely, leaving it in static 'preservation' may well cause even more deterioration in mechanical parts if, for example, oil does not circulate to otherwise unprotected and inaccessible parts.

Its operation has thus been limited to a few occasions each year when the engine is started and run gently until everything is reasonably warm and the oil freely circulating. Movement is invariably 'light engine' to avoid as much wear on the clutches as possible, and also restricted to a few yards.

In simple terms, the loco's condition is mechanically largely that following Ernie Cheeseman's work between 1968 and 1970, while cosmetically it is as near to that of 1909 as can be achieved using modern paints (albeit to a 'weathered' shade); otherwise modern components are restricted to those that are considered by their application to benefit overall conservation more than would be achieved by retention of older parts to allow this limited operability to continue.

However, where the historic value of more recent replacement components is perceived to be low (such as the relatively modern – post-1950 – but inefficient conventional-pattern radiator), efforts will be made to recreate replicas of original parts instead. Any such removed components are nevertheless retained in store.

In similar vein, the carriage rebuilding, though only truly 'genuine' in regard to the – undisturbed – major part of one bogie, is otherwise using accurate, identical or near-identical contemporary components where possible; only where no such parts exist are appropriate modern materials used to replicate those missing.

The believed surviving remnants of *PETROLIA* (excluding, possibly, the 'carriage' bogie), though not in the author's possession, are well cared for and, thanks to the recent research, their probable historical significance is now appreciated and their survival ensured.

Reunion

Despite the importance of safeguarding the loco's integrity by 'gentle' conservation, the 60th Anniversary celebrations of the Saltburn Miniature Railway in August 2007 could not be allowed to pass without a 'return visit' by *BLACOLVESLEY* to the railway on which it was the sole motive power from 1948 to 1953, and then shared power for many more years; the course of much of the line has changed significantly in recent years.

The Saltburn Miniature Railway Association extended an invitation and, accordingly, the loco was transported to Saltburn for the weekend of 11 and 12 August. It did not work any service trains or haul carriages, in view of its fragility, but it did pose with its one-time SMR companion, the Barlow 4-6-2 *PRINCE CHARLES* (now fitted with a diesel engine), it operated around the depot area, and the author was also able to coax it into an evening run light-engine to Forest Halt (to reach which it was able to run again on the surviving section of actual alignment and track it had last used some half-century earlier), and also along the full length of the line's present alignment to Cat Nab terminus.

Their place in history

BLACOLVESLEY was the world's first steam-outline petrol locomotive and, while it is not the oldest petrol-engined railway vehicle in the world, it is, so far as is known, the oldest internal-combustion-engined railway locomotive of any gauge or type that was built as such. (To be truly pedantic one could argue that the real *LOCOMOTION No 1* was the oldest steam-outline loco in the world when its tender was fitted with a petrol engine so that it could operate during the Railway Centenary celebrations in 1925!) Its importance lies not only in those factors, but also in the originality of the majority of its components.

In some ways this is all the more remarkable given its history from the late 1940s, when it effectively became simply a transient and nomadic workhorse for a number of commercial and showground-type operators of 'public entertainment' railways. Here historic

The course of the Saltburn Miniature Railway has changed many times over the years. Here, on 11 August 2007, BLACOLVESLEY runs, at the venerable age of exactly 97 years 11 months, from the 21st-century northern alignment onto the original south end route, itself opened in 1950 by this locomotive. *Author*

conservation would be expected to take a back seat to cost and convenience – however, this seems not to have been the case and BLACOLVESLEY's charmed life in the face of adversity continued unabated.

The petrol engine now fitted is, of course, not the original, but has been in the loco for more than half its working life. Similarly the radiator – and probably the water tank in the 'boiler' – are replacements, themselves of considerable, if imprecise, vintage. However, the structure and bodywork, the gearboxes and drive equipment, the wheels, frames, bogies, controls and their operating mechanisms are all the originals of 1909.

The work undertaken by Ernie Cheeseman in the 1960s in inserting a chain-driven reducing layshaft left the original gearboxes and their ratios unaffected, although certain surviving small original components were unfortunately discarded at that time.

The author has striven, since buying the loco in 1994, to conserve the physical components and, in the few cases where this has proved impossible for safety or other reasons, to archive them safely. The work in 1999-2000 to widen the wheel treads, for example, was deliberately carried out in such a way that it left the intrinsic structure of the original wheels intact, and they can be returned to their earlier condition very simply.

BLACOLVESLEY can therefore justify its claim for archaeological significance, not only as the oldest surviving petrol locomotive, but also as a near-original example of internal-combustion miniature railway locomotive design and construction, fully representative of small-scale engineering facilities of the Edwardian era, and thus worthy of conservation.

Combined with the probable remarkable and long-unappreciated surviving parts of PETROLIA, it is truly amazing to realise that this tiny private estate railway deep in the Northamptonshire countryside, with but three 'home' locomotives (and one visitor), three bogie carriages and seven wagons – and a 'main line' less than half a mile long at its maximum – can claim not one but probably two significant surviving historical artefacts of the pioneering days of internal-combustion rail power – with both of them preceding any other surviving locomotives, of any gauge, with such propulsion!

Nor must we forget the surviving Blakesley-built carriage bogie with Cagney running gear! There also remains the distinct chance that the Rothesay/Strumpshaw Cagney was the visitor to the Blakesley line in 1904 or 1905. The long tradition of 15-inch-gauge equipment surviving against all odds is truly upheld by this little line.

16 Full circle Blakesley?

Rising from the foundations?

Having slumbered peacefully for around half a century following the sale of the estate in 1949 and the demolition of Blakesley Hall in 1957, who could have expected that a development proposal might be forthcoming to create a new Blakesley Hall sited precisely on the foundations of the old, and retaining the estate virtually as it was all those years ago?

The impetus came from an unexpected source. Concerned about the drastic changes nationally in rural lifestyle, the Government in the late 20th century introduced 'Planning Policy Guidance Note 7'. This was the so-called 'Gummer's Law', which was specifically intended to encourage the re-establishment of the rural community structure, including such measures as permitting the building in rural areas of large new country houses of 'exceptional architectural merit'.

The then owner of the Blakesley estate, local farmer and businessman Philip Burt, proposed that a new Hall be built on the original site as his family home. The Roger Coy Partnership, in collaboration with Ian Lyne & Associates, prepared the design and was able to secure the necessary Town & Country Planning Consent from South Northamptonshire Council under the principles of that Guidance Note; only about 20 properties throughout the country were granted planning consent under PPG7.

Philip recorded:

'All my life I have had this great desire to see the Hall back where it belongs. I felt it was my duty. There had been a house of one sort or another on the site since Norman times and I decided … that it was of sufficient importance to try and keep the history alive.'

The new Hall would be a country house of some 7,800 square feet with full facilities including nine bedrooms, six bathrooms, etc, and though of pleasing and mature appearance (and of similar scale), would not simply be a replica of the old one. Increasing commitments led Mr Burt during 2004 to place the whole estate on the market, complete with the given planning permission for the Hall, initially at a guide price of £1.75 million.

The property consultants handling the sale were FPDSavills of Banbury, and their full-colour brochure featured a splendid view on the rear cover showing the site of one of the miniature railway bridges (in practice a much later replacement for bridge B1 on the same site) and the gateway G3 through the wall, which allowed the line up to the back of the Hall.

In addition also to views of the 'Pulhamite' waterfalls, the original brochure showed a close-up view of the surviving old cast-iron notice at the foot of the mulberry tree planted in the grounds on the Coronation Day of King Edward VII, 9 August 1902 '…by the Blakesley Horticultural & Agricultural Society, C. W. Bartholomew Esq, President…'.

Thus, 85 years after his death, his estate at Blakesley, largely untouched save by the ravages of time and the demolition of the Hall itself, could still proclaim the name 'C. W. Bartholomew' in cast-iron letters as a benefactor to the neighbourhood – and a sales 'asset'! It could even be that the course of the 1902 'garden' line – if it existed! – passed near this tree, or rather that the tree was planted in an accessible position close to the course of this possible line (the date fits perfectly), as it is otherwise rather remote from any other feature in the immediate grounds!

From 2005 further efforts were made to progress the creation of the new Hall, through new agents Howkins & Harrison. These pointed out that, if it does proceed, the new Blakesley Hall will almost

The Blakesley Hall Miniature Railway

Blakesley Hall, 2004: the photographer is standing on the course of the line to the rear of the Hall (it having passed through the gateway – G3 – seen to the right of the pole). At the left-hand end of the wall are the remains of another gateway (G4) through which passed the line to the engine shed. *Author*

certainly be the last property ever to be built under PPG7.

Apart from some surviving low earthworks of the long cutting near the station, the best evidence of the old railway then was two simple, narrow earth strips, 15 inches apart and about a foot in length, in the (somewhat broken) concrete raft across the old gateway G3 (uniquely still replete with its fine pair of wrought-iron gates) in the long north wall to the Hall gardens, by which the little trains had once passed directly to and from the Hall.

It is unlikely that a 15-inch-gauge railway will ever grace that gateway again, but Philip Burt, a life-long Blakesley villager and the guardian and conservator of the Blakesley estate through into a new century and a new millennium, should perhaps have the final word in this fascinating and complex story:

'The Hall site is just a little gem laying dormant, waiting to spring into life. There is so much history here and I decided I would personally make sure of its continuation.'

References

Much inspection has taken place of primary (and often private or unpublished) sources in the research for this book. The list below is *not* simply a Bibliography, but a listing of the relevant printed references and secondary sources that have been consulted during the research; all inferences drawn from them are, however, entirely those of the present author.

Abell, P. H. *Transport & Industry in South Yorkshire* (Author, 1977, ISBN 0 901182 02 8)

Ahrons, E. L. *The British Steam Railway Locomotive 1825-1925* (Locomotive Publishing Co, 1927)

Bartholomew, C. *The Life and Doctrine of our Blessed Lord and Saviour Jesus Christ* (Clowes, 2nd Edition, 1880)

Bartholomew, C. W. *Account of the Parish of Blakesley, Northamptonshire* (E. Hunt, 3rd Edition, 1910)

Bassett-Lowke, J. *Wenman Joseph Bassett-Lowke* (Rail Romances, 1999, ISBN 1 900622 01 7)

Bassett-Lowke, W. J. *The Model Railway Handbook* (Bassett-Lowke Ltd, 5th and 10th Editions)

Bennett, A. R. *The Chronicles of Boulton's Siding* (Locomotive Publishing Co, 1927)

Blagrove, D. *Northamptonshire's Lost Railways* (Stenlake, 2003, ISBN 1 84033 251 4)
The Railways of Northamptonshire (Wharfside, 2005, ISBN 1 8719 1820 0)

Buck, S. E. W. *Twining: Model Maker Artist & Engineer* (Landmark, 2004, ISBN 1 84306 143 0)

Butler, P. *A History of the Railways of Northamptonshire* (Silver Link Publishing, 2006, ISBN 1 85794 281 7)

Butterell, R. & Milner, J. *The Little Giant Story* (Rail Romances, 2003, ISBN 1 900622 07 6)

Cagney's Locomotive Works (reprint of 1901 Cagney catalogue) (Plateway, 1998, ISBN 1 871980 37 2)

Cagney's Locomotive Works (1902-3 catalogue) (Miniature Railroad Company [sic])

Cheeseman, E. *Stockton & Darlington Railway; 'Miniature Railways' & The Breakdown Train* (Author, 1975)

Christie's *Fine Historical Steam Engine Models and Ship Models*, Auction catalogue for 5 October 1966

Clarke, M. *The Aire & Calder Navigation* (Tempus, 1999, ISBN 0 7524 1715 0)

Clayton, H. *The Duffield Bank & Eaton Railways* (Oakwood, 1968)

Clayton, H., Butterell, R. & Jacot, M. *Miniature Railways, Volume 1: 15 Inch Gauge* (Oakwood, undated) (Note that Volume 2 was never produced)

Cooke, R. A. *Track Layout Diagrams of the Great Western Railway and BR Western Region: Section 29: Stratford-upon-Avon and Midland Jcn Rly* (Author, 1994, ISBN 1 871674 20 4)

Cormack, I. L. *The Rothesay Tramways Company 1879-1949* (Scottish Tramway & Transport Society, 1986, ISBN 0 900648 23 6)

Cossens, N. (Ed) *Perspectives on Railway History & Interpretation* (National Railway Museum, 1992, ISBN 1 872826 01 6)

Crabtree, H. (Clarke, M., Ed) *Railway on the Water: Tom Puddings & The Yorkshire Coal Industry* (The Sobriety Project, 1993, ISBN 0 9822592 0 6)

Croft, D. J. *A Survey of Seaside Miniature Railways* (Oakwood, 1992, ISBN 0 85361 418 0)

Crowhurst, A. R. W. & Scarth, R. N. *Locomotives of the Romney Hythe & Dymchurch Railway* (Workshop, 2004, no ISBN)

Crowther, G. L. *National Series of Waterway, Tramway & Railway Atlases: Volume 3k: Barnsley, Rotherham & Doncaster* (Author, 2000, ISBN 1 85615 304 5)

Dent, A. (Ed) *Bernard Shaw and Mrs Patrick*

Campbell: Their Correspondence (Gollancz, 1952)

Domesday Book: A Complete Translation (Penguin Classics, 2003, ISBN 0 141 43994 7)

Dow, G. Great Central: Volume 1: The Progenitors, 1813-1863 (Locomotive Publishing Co, 1959)

Dunn, J. M. The Stratford-upon-Avon & Midland Junction Railway (Oakwood, various editions)

Elliott, B. (Ed) Aspects of Barnsley 7 (Wharncliffe, 2002, ISBN 1 903425 24 7)

Elliott, B. Darfield & Wombwell Main: A Second Selection (Sutton, 2003, ISBN 0 7509 3039 X)

Franks, D. L. South Yorkshire Railway (Turntable, 1971, SBN 902844 04 0)

Fuller, R. The Bassett-Lowke Story (New Cavendish, 1984, ISBN 0 904568 34 2)

Glister, R. The Forgotten Canals of Yorkshire: Wakefield to Swinton via Barnsley: The Barnsley and Dearne & Dove Canals (Wharncliffe, 2004, ISBN 1 903425 38 7)

Goodchild, J. South Yorkshire Collieries (Tempus, 2001, ISBN 0 7524 2148 4)

Gorbert, M. Fifty Years On: 1931-1981: Scarborough's North Bay Miniature Railway Golden Jubilee, 1981 (Scarborough Borough Council)

The Great Central Railway Journal, Vol VII (GCR, July 1911-June 1912, and other volumes)

Greenly, H. The Model Locomotive: its Design and Construction (Percival Marshall, 1904)

Hadfield, C. The Canals of Yorkshire & North East England, Vols 1 and 2 (David & Charles, 1972 & 1973, ISBN 0 7153 5719 0 & 0 7153 5975 4)

Hartley, K. E. The Sand Hutton Light Railway (Narrow Gauge Railway Society, 1982, ISBN 0 9507169 1 X)

Henderson, A. Bernard Shaw: Playboy & Prophet (Appleton, 1932)

Hennessey, R. A. S. Atlantic: The Well Beloved Engine (Tempus, 2002, ISBN 0 7524 2143 3)

Heywood, Sir A. P. H., Bart, MA Minimum Gauge Railways: Their Application, Construction & Working (Author, 3rd Edition, 1898)

Heywood, I. M. Reminiscences, Letters and Journals of Thomas Percival Heywood, Baronet, arranged by his eldest daughter (Fargie, 1899)

The Heywood Society Journal (The Heywood Society, various issues, particularly No 47, Autumn 2000)

Hitching, C. The Pulham Legacy (www.pulham.org.uk)

Household, H. Narrow Gauge Railways: England & the Fifteen Inch (Alan Sutton, 1989)

Jenkins, S. C. The Northampton & Banbury Junction Railway (Oakwood, 1990, ISBN 0 85361 390 7)

Jenkinson, D. & Lane, B. C. British Railcars 1900 to 1950 (Atlantic, 1996, ISBN 0 906899 64 8)

'J. H.', Antiquarian Notices of Lupset, The Heath, Sharlston and Ackton in the County of York (Author, 1851)

Jones, M. (Ed) Aspects of Rotherham (Wharncliffe, 1995, ISBN 1 071047 27 4)

Jordan, A. The Stratford-upon-Avon & Midland Junction Railway (OPC, 1982, SBN 86093 131 5)

Kingston, P. B. Blakesley Hall & its Miniature Railway (Author, 1981; reprinted as a Centenary Edition, 2003)

Blakesley Then & Now: an Account of the Ecclesiastical Parish of Blakesley cum Woodend (Author, 1983)

Blakesley Then & Now Volume II (Author, c1984)

Koppel, A. Industrie- och Lokaljernvagar (1899; reprint, Museiforeningen, Stockholm-Roslagens, Uppsala, 1979)

Leleux, S. A. Brotherhoods, Engineers (David & Charles, 1965)

The Locomotive Magazine, 15 May 1906

Middlemass, T. Steam Locomotive Nicknames (Silver Link Publishing, 1991, ISBN 0 947971 70 X

The Model Engineer & Amateur Electrician (The Model Engineer & Electrician), various issues from 1902

Model Railway News, September 1965 issue

Model Railways & Locomotives (Models, Railways & Locomotives), various issues from January 1909

Mosley, D. & van Zeller, P. Fifteen Inch Gauge Railways: their History, Equipment & Operation (David & Charles, 1986, ISBN 0 7153 8694 8)

NAG Puck: Kleiner Viercylinder=Wagen (NAG, Berlin, 1908; facsimile reprint by Archiv Verlag, 1993)

Narrow Gauge News, various issues (Narrow Gauge Railway Society)

Nock, O. S. Classic Locomotives: The Great Northern 4-4-2 'Atlantics' (Patrick Stephens, 1984, ISBN 0 85059 683 1)

The North Midland Railway Guide 1842 (Turntable (reprint), 1973, ISBN 0 902844 13 X)

Parkinson, R. J. Ruston Proctor & Hornsby Akroyd Oil-engined Locomotives (Moseley Railway Trust, 2003, ISBN 0 9540878 5 2)

Pearson, H. Bernard Shaw (St James's, 1950; originally published 1942)

References

Railway Modeller, March and July 1968 issues

RCTS *Locomotives of the LNER*, various parts (RCTS, various dates)

Richards, E. V. *LMS Diesel Locomotives and Railcars* (RCTS, 1996, ISBN 0 901115 76 2)

Riley, R. C. & Simpson, B. *A History of the Stratford-upon-Avon & Midland Junction Railway* (Lamplight, 1999, ISBN 1 899246 04 5)

St John, C. (Ed) *Ellen Terry & Bernard Shaw: a Correspondence* (Putnam, 1932)

Saltburn Miniature Railway (SMR Association, 2nd Edition, Spring 1999)

Saltburn Miniature Railway. The Big Transformation: September 2000-April 2003 (SMR Association, 2003)

Scott, P. *A History of the Wicksteed Park Railway* (Author, 2002, ISBN 1 902368 15 0)

Sharp, C. & P. *Old Wombwell (and Hemingfield)* (CCS Enterprises, 1994, ISBN 1 872074 46 4)

Shaw, F. *Little Railways of the World* (Howell-North, 1958)

The South Yorkshire Times (incorporating The Mexborough & Swinton Times), various issues, 1938 to 1944

Spooner, C. E. *Narrow Gauge Railways* (Spon, 1871)

Steel, E. A. & Steel, E. H. *The Miniature World of Henry Greenly* (Model & Allied Publications, 1973, ISBN 0 85242 306 3)

Strauss, Ing Dr W. *Liliputbahnen* (Kichler, 1938)

Liliputbahnen (English Edition) (Robin Butterell, 1988, ISBN 0 9514796 1 X)

Taylor, K. (Ed) *Worthies of Wakefield* (Wakefield Historical Publications, 2004, ISBN 0 901869 46 5)

Taylor, M. *The Canal & River Sections of the Aire & Calder Navigation* (Wharncliffe, 2003, ISBN 1 903425 37 9)

The Sheffield & South Yorkshire Navigation (Tempus, 2001, ISBN 0 7524 2128 X)

Taylor, W. *South Yorkshire Pits* (Wharncliffe, 2001, ISBN 1 871647 84 3)

Thorold, P. *The Motoring Age: The Automobile and Britain 1896-1939* (Profile, 2003, ISBN 1 86197 378 0)

Threlkeld, J. *Pits: A Pictorial History of Mining* (Wharncliffe, 2003, ISBN 1 903425 50 6)

Tidmarsh, J. G. *The Sutton Coldfield Fifteen Inch Gauge Railway* (Plateway Press, 1990, ISBN 1 871980 05 4)

Walsh, B. D. J. *The Railway Club 1899 to 1999* (The Railway Club, 1999)

Walton, C. *The Changing Face of Doncaster* (Doncaster MBC, 1980, ISBN 0 906976 01 4)

Webb, B. *The British Internal Combustion Locomotive 1894-1940* (David & Charles, 1973, ISBN 0 7153 6115 5)

Williams, C. *Driving the Clay Cross Tunnel* (Scarthin Books, 1984, ISBN 0 907758 07 X)

Woodcock, G. *Miniature Steam Locomotives* (David & Charles, 1964)

A unique train headed (for the first and last time ever) by every variety of four-coupled 'Little Giant' loco, at Cleethorpes in May 1995. From front to back: BLACOLVESLEY, prototype No 10 LITTLE GIANT, No 18 GEORGE THE FIFTH, No 22 KING GEORGE and No 30 SYNOLDA.
Neville Knight

Acknowledgements

My first thanks must go to the 'Grand Vizier' of miniature railways, Robin Butterell. Although I had admired *BLACOLVESLEY* in photographs, and even seen it during a visit to Lightwater Valley in 1982 for the benefit of our then-young elder son Peter, it was barely 30 minutes after my first meeting with Robin that I found myself actively involved in seeking its purchase! Robin made freely available his knowledge and collection of material relating in any way to Blakesley and its locomotives.

The Blakesley village historian P. B. (Phil) Kingston published several booklets about the village, Hall and railway and I have drawn extensively on these for information and as a

Robin Butterell, arch-enthusiast and historian for and of miniature railways, poses in the cab of *BLACOLVESLEY* at Cleethorpes in 1995. The loco is in 1909 Blakesley Show livery, without name banners or crests. *Author*

starting point for further research. His son Robert has since been of great help; his agreement in 2003 to my republishing one of his father's booklets to mark the centenary of the opening of the Blakesley Miniature Railway was the impetus needed to commence work on this present volume.

My special thanks must go to miniature railway friends such as Simon Townsend, the 'Mr Cagney' of UK miniature railways; his own efforts have been most ably and thoroughly complemented by those of Keith Taylor of Maine, Don Micheletti of California, and Carey Williams of Illinois. Their researches and restoration work have shown that most previously published accounts of Cagney evolution are, quite simply, wrong, and their advice has enabled a far more accurate story to be presented here.

Carey has also been of inestimable help to me in securing genuine Cagney carriage running gear for use in rebuilding a Blakesley bogie carriage, a project impossible without the initial help and generosity of the Saltburn Miniature Railway Association members.

One of CW's grandchildren, Doreen Birks, has been most willing to share her vivid memories of long school holidays at Blakesley in the early 1930s, and her excellent knowledge of family history has enabled many parts of this story to be placed in their proper context.

Special mention must be made too of the considerable help given by John Goodchild, whose independent Local History Study Centre for the central West Riding, based in Wakefield, is a modern-day 'mine' – but of information rather than coal!

Joan Robinson and the infectious enthusiasm of her colleagues in the Wombwell Heritage Group have provided many useful and indeed invaluable leads. I give particular praise also to Chris Sharp of 'Old Barnsley', who has collected early photographs of the Barnsley area, and made good-quality 'proper' photographic copies freely available at reasonable cost – would that more would follow his example.

Richard Casserley has not only generously provided copies of the photographs that he and his father (H. C. Casserley) took of Blakesley station in the early 1950s, but has, with the aid of his colleague John Alsop, traced many illustrations of the railway, including several unique 'angles' on otherwise well-known scenes. Neville Knight has come to my rescue on several occasions tracing old and recent views.

Sir Peter Heywood, the present baronet, most generously and enthusiastically made available copies of the complex family tree and other private papers outlining the various relationships within the Heywood family, which enabled the links with the Bartholomews to be developed.

I offer special thanks to Sir William McAlpine Bt for his help in allowing access to the Charles Simpson material in his possession. Peter van Zeller, 'Ratty' engine driver, archivist, historian of miniature railways, and supplier of endless cups of coffee (thanks, Kate) has provided support in innumerable ways, physical, historical and in questioning some of my theories, quickly sorting out 'possibles' from 'no-hopers'.

Many of the Ratty's other staff members and volunteer helpers have also given huge support – so many that individual recording will almost certainly be invidious by inadvertently leaving out people. Nevertheless I must try, by mentioning such as the late Doug Ferreira and his General Manager successors Steve Wood and Trevor Stockton, Chief Engineers Ian Smith and Paul Turnill (long-suffering hearers of 'Can I borrow a …?'), Controller Graham Withers, David Clay, Martin Willey, Ron Clarke, Mike Jenkins, Neal Glover, Andrew Graham, Keith Rogers, and Arnold Staples.

Ann and John Weekley of Blakesley Hall Lodge have, with other local inhabitants, worked hard to preserve artefacts and memories of the Blakesley area. Their unbounded enthusiasm helped me to study the Blakesley area at first hand. Similarly, Philip Burt showed himself truly mindful of the estate's historic pedigree.

Ann's enthusiasm produced, inter alia, a very unexpected result – that I had actually known an only-slightly-distant relative of CW for a decade or more, and moreover one who lived less than a mile from where I live and normally keep *BLACOLVESLEY*; this was Peter Frost-Pennington of Muncaster Castle. Noel Barrett, whose mother still resides at Lowdale Hall, provided the previously unknown connections thereto. Finally, and certainly not least, Dick Bodily has traced and interviewed eyewitnesses back to CW's time – no mean achievement!

Other individuals (several sadly no longer with us) whose help has been invaluable include: Jane Adams (Howkins & Harrison), Bob Aran, Diane Backhouse (The Waterways Trust), David Barker (West Riding Small Locomotive Society), George Barlow, Barnsley Library Local History Section, Reg Blacklock (Saltburn Miniature Railway),

Terry Bracher (Northampton Central Library), Tracy Bradley (National Coal Mining Museum for England), Dr Arnold Browne (Trinity College Chapel), Stan Buck (Sian Project Group), John Bull (Markeaton Park Railway), Dave Colley and family (Sherwood Forest Railway), Michael Crofts (Perrygrove Railway), Tony Crowhurst, Graham Deacon (National Monuments Record), Sue Donnelly (LSE Library), Trevor Dunmore (Royal Automobile Club), Cressida Finch (Library & Museum of the Order of St John), Peter Flaskamp, Simon Fountain (L&NWR Society), Ian Gardner, Brian Gent, Tony Harden, Michael Hardy, Adam Harris, Joe Hedley, Loveday Herridge (Waterways Museum, Goole), Claude Hitching, Dave Holroyde, David Humphreys, John Knowles (The Railway Club), Jane Mason (University of Sheffield Library), Manchester Locomotive Society, Carol Morgan (The Institution of Civil Engineers Library), Austin Moss, Andrew Neale, Tony Peart, Rev Neil Redeyoff, Ron Redman, Frank Roberts, Steve Scott (Saltburn Miniature Railway), Phillip Sheppy (Royal Agricultural Society), Jim & Helen Shackell (Evesham Vale Railway), Mary Sinfield, Chris Smith (Northamptonshire Record Office), Jonathan Smith (Library of Trinity College, Cambridge), Sheffield Archives, Greville Sockett, Gordon Stephenson (Reckitt Benckiser), Mike Taylor (of Dronfield), Dr Mike Taylor (of Kidderminster), Andy Thompson, John Tidmarsh, Wakefield Library Local History Section, Tom Vine (National Railway Museum/Science and Society Picture Library), Geoff Warnes, James Waterfield, Terry Watford (owner of 'Two Trees'), Steve West (Reckitt Benckiser), Julie Williamson (St John Ambulance (Northamptonshire)), and Giles Wright (Fabian Society).

I will have missed people out. To all of you individually I proffer my abject apologies as well as my thanks – I trust that you find your contribution somewhere in this book and at least have satisfaction from that!

Index

Aire & Calder Navigation 18ff, 50
Alexandra Palace miniature railway 56, 97, 98
Aspdin, Joseph 20, 21

Bailey, George 58
Bain, Richard 41
Barnsley Canal 20, 22

Bartholomew family
Charles 13, 16-17, 82; marries Sarah Watson Linley 17, 82; marries Louisa May Hutton 17-18; death of 18
Charles William ('CW') 6, 13, 23, 81, 83, 120, 127, 139; early life and education 26, 48; marries Lucy Ussher 27; role in Blakesley 31ff, 35-36; failure of marriage 33, 36, 45; and Sarah Ann Floyd (qv) 33, 34; as motoring pioneer 37-38, 59, 101; and 15-inch-gauge railways 51, 56, 59ff, 93ff, 98, 101; and development of BLACOLVESLEY 107-108; death of 41, 140
Ivy 7, 33, 60, 127-129, 130, 142; marriage 39; family 43, 142
James 7, 10, 33, 41, 56, 59, 60, 66, 80, 99, 120, 127-128, 130, 138; education 39; marriage 39, 142; 21st birthday 39-40, 153; family 43
Sarah Ann (formerly Floyd) 33-35, 41, 45, 128, 140, 142; as model for Eliza Doolittle? 40-41
Thomas Hamond 16, 18, 21, 25
William Hamond 19, 21, 49, 50
coat of arms 1, 13, 25, 27
family tree 42

Bassett-Lowke, Wenman 'Whynne' Joseph 6, 40, 89, 90, 92, 119, 120, 138, 139
Bassett-Lowke, W. J. & Co/Ltd 8, 34, 62, 87, 89ff, 125, 132, 137, 139; and 15-inch-gauge railways 89; 'Little Giant' locomotives 91ff, 94, 101, 111, 116, 121, 133, 137; builds BLACOLVESLEY 107ff, 117ff see also Miniature Railways of Great Britain Ltd

Birks, (Cyril) Douglas 39, 43, 138, 142
Birks, Ivy see Bartholomew, Ivy
Blakesley & District Horticultural Society, Annual Show 32, 36, 41, 59, 108, 119, 121, 122, 132, 133-134, 138, 141
Blakesley Hall 11ff, 35-36, 70, 85, 88, 142; purchased by Bartholomews 27; used as hospital during WWI 32, 33, 133, 138; electric lighting installed 35; park and gardens 36-37; clockwork model railway 56-58, 59; after CW's death 41; sale of 43 demolition of 13; possible replacement 88, 175-176

Blakesley Miniature Railway
Bridges 71-73, 84
Carriages, bogie 66, 79-80, 84, 96, 158, 163, 164, 171-172; four-wheeled 78
Disuse and disposal 150
Engine shed 73, 125
Goods/coal trains 93, 94, 98ff, 133
Goods wagons 93ff; tip wagons 93-95; 'trolley' 93
Gradients 117-118
Layout: 62ff; 1906 layout 66ff; 1909 extension 117-118; 1910 extension 8, 118-119, 141, 130; as connection to E&WJR station 62, 64; descriptions of 64-66; station at E&WJR 66-68, 124, 131; latter days 141
Locomotives, usage of 129ff
Cagney 2-3, 7, 61, 66, 72, 73, 76ff, 81, 96, 98, 119, 123, 125, 126, 129, 131, 132, 137, 140; 'visiting' Cagney 95-98, 99, 141, 143, 174; loaned to Sutton Miniature Railway 107-108, 123, 125; fate of 142-145
BLACOLVESLEY 2-3, 6, 8, 10, 84, 85, 87, 88, 119, 126, 129, 131, 141, 146, 150, 180; built by Bassett-Lowke 107ff; LNWR 'Precursor' tank as inspiration 109ff, 121; NAG engine 113-114, 126; throttle 114; gearbox 114-115; bogies 115; brakes 115, 132; cooling system 115-116, 160, 170, 174; couplings 130; lamps 133; arrives at Blakesley 119-121; development of livery 121-123; acquired by Dorothy Elliott 151, 154, 155; to Redlands Railway 157; re-engined 157-158, 160, 174; becomes YVONNE 157-158; to Saltburn 159ff; 'streamlined' 87, 160-161; becomes ELIZABETH 161-163; stored 163-164;overhaul by Ernie Cheeseman 164-165; to Lightwater Valley 165-166; to R&ER 167; acquired by Bob Tebb 167; restoration 167ff, 173; 90th birthday 170; place in history 173-174
PETROLIA 67, 108, 109, 121, 123, 126, 129, 130, 131, 133, 137, 140, 172, 173; building of 103-106; rebuilding of 123-124, 125, 136, 150; subsequent fate of 145, 146ff, 174
Operation of 131ff
Signalling 64, 75, 119, 133
Tickets 84, 133-134
Track, rail and sleepers 65, 74-75; formation 73-74; pointwork 75
Turntable 73
Visiting parties 126ff

Blakesley village, history of 11; Bartholomews' involvement with 31; St Mary's Church 31, 83, 141
Boyton, Capt Paul 56, 76, 97
Broxholme House, Doncaster 17, 26, 28
Burt, Philip 36, 64, 175-176
Butterell, Robin 167, 180
Byfield 33, 45

Cagney Brothers 51-55 see also Miniature Railway Co
Cagney locomotives 52ff, 78, 97; bogie carriages 96; four-wheeled carriages 54-55, 78, 79
Cagney railways in the UK 56
Cheeseman, Ernie 164, 165, 170, 173, 174
Cortonwood Colliery 15, 30, 31

Darfield, All Saints Church 25, 29, 30, 86

183

Deans Mill Railway 144, 145-146, 147, 148, 149, 150, 158
Dearne & Dove Canal 15, 20, 22
Dreamland Miniature Railway, Margate 148, 149
Dunn family 158, 159ff

Earls Court miniature railway 56, 76, 97
East & West Junction Railway 33, 44ff, 64, 65, 67-68, 79, 97, 131, 134
Eaton Railway (Eaton Hall) 62, 92, 99, 101, 131, 135, 136, 138, 139
Edmunds & Swaithe Main Colliery 15, 29, 30
Elliott, Charles 39, 40, 41, 152
Elliott, Dorothy 41, 86, 151, 152ff; 'Two Trees' scandal 151, 152ff

Fairbourne Railway 138
15-inch gauge railways, development of 47ff; 'freelance' locos 48
Floyd, James and Mary Ann 33
Floyd, Sarah Ann see Bartholomew, Sarah Ann
Frost, Anne 10
Fuller, Roland 90

Glasgow Exhibition miniature railway 56
Goole 18-19
Great Central Railway 32, 45; ambulance competitions 32, 126, 127-129, 138
Green, Fred 6, 120, 122
Greenly, Henry 6, 56, 62, 64, 89, 91, 98, 107, 108, 109, 117-118, 120, 123, 132, 138, 139, 140, 149; and 15-inch-gauge railways 100-102, 134-136; and BLACOLVESLEY 107ff, 113ff, 121; animosity with Bartholomews 106, 136
Groom, Mark 7, 105

Haswell, 'North Eastern Railway' 87, 164
Heywood, Sir Arthur Percival 23, 26, 102, 130, 136, 138, 139; family of 23-25, 49; and 15-inch-gauge railways 48ff, 59, 99; and 'minimum gauge' 49, 101; rolling stock 49; at Dove Leys 48, 49, 50, 62, 100, 138; at Duffield Bank 49, 50, 60, 62, 99, 119, 131, 133, 138; conservatism 50, 93-94; succeeds to baronetcy 50
Heywood, John-Pemberton 23, 25
Higham Railway 8
Howey, J. E. P. 138, 139

Internal-combustion engines, development of 103

Kerr's Miniature Railway 164
Kingston, Philip 61, 64, 65, 170
Lehigh Valley Railroad 51
Lightwater Valley 165, 167

Locomotives
BERTWHYNNE (HUNGARIA) 137
BLACOLVESLEY see Blakesley Miniature Railway
Cagney see Blakesley Miniature Railway and Cagney
COUNT LOUIS 8
EFFIE 10, 100, 101
ELLA 102
ENTENTE CORDIALE 106, 108, 112
GEORGE THE FIFTH 139
JOHN ANTHONY (COLOSSUS) 138, 139
KATIE 99, 101, 139
LITTLE GIANT (LITTLE ELEPHANT/ROBIN HOOD) 91, 92, 112, 164, 165, 166
MIGHTY ATOM 91, 106, 108, 112, 121, 123, 125
NIPPER 101
PEARL 48
PETROLIA see Blakesley Miniature Railway
PRINCE CHARLES 163, 173
SHELAGH (URSULA) 99, 135, 136, 138
SHELAGH OF ESKDALE 102
SYNOLDA 8, 136, 137, 139
TRIXIE 146
VILLE DE NANCY 106

Lowdale Hall, Sleights 18, 28

McGarigle Brothers 51 see also Miniature Railway Co
Manchester, Sheffield & Lincolnshire Railway 15, 18
Medina Valley Railway 165
Milnes and Busch/Milnes Voss 94
Miniature Railway Company 51ff, 77; produces complete railway 54
Miniature Railways of Great Britain Ltd 90, 92, 106, 107 see also Bassett-Lowke

Narrow Gauge Railways Ltd 138
New York Central & Hudson River RR, record-breaking 4-4-0 No 999 52-53
North Midland Railway 16, 20

Page, Ian 170
Payne, E. W. 59-60, 61, 76
Pitmaston Moor Green Railway 59-60, 61

Pulham, James & Son (and 'Pulhamite') 36, 37, 175

Railway Club, The 2-3, 119, 126, 134, 138, 144
Ravenglass & Eskdale Railway 50, 87, 99, 102, 136, 137, 138, 165, 167, 168, 170, 172
Redlands Railway 157, 159, 166
River Don Navigation 14, 17, 20, 22
Roberts family 15, 82, 152
Romney, Hythe & Dymchurch Railway 138
Rotherham 16
Royal Automobile Club 37, 39, 114, 130

Salomons, Sir David 37, 50
Saltburn Miniature Railway 87, 88, 159ff, 172, 173
Sand Hutton Railway 8, 136, 138
Shaw, George Bernard 39-41, 126
Sheffield & South Yorkshire Navigation 15, 23
Simpson, Charles 35, 94, 98, 123, 133
South Yorkshire Railway 14-16, 18, 22
Stanley Ferry 21, 23, 49, 50
Stephenson, George 20, 36
Stratford-upon-Avon & Midland Junction Railway 45ff, 135, 144; Blakesley station 47, 66, 131, 151; 'Road-Railer' on 46-47, 141 see also East & West Junction Railway
Sutton Miniature Railway 106-108, 125, 136-137, 140

Tate, Tom 164
'Tom Pudding' compartment boats 21, 22, 23, 31, 49, 50
Trinity College, Cambridge 25, 26-27, 30, 39, 43, 48, 137
Twining, Ernest W. 126, 136, 138, 139, 141

Vaughan, William 117

Wakefield 20, 21, 23
Walker, Sir Robert 136-137, 138, 139
White City miniature railway 97, 108
Wicksteed, Charles 114-115
Williams, Carey 172
Wombwell 28-29, 39, 151, 156; St Mary's Church 29, 30, 39, 86
Wombwell Main Colliery 14, 15, 18, 28, 29, 30, 36, 39, 41, 45, 82, 85, 141, 152, 155
Wyatt, Alec, estate engineer 6, 8, 35, 129, 130, 132
Wyatt, Percy 7, 35, 80, 99, 130, 132